Ian Heads joined the (Sydney) *Daily Telegraph* Sports desk in early 1964 and began writing on the sport of rugby league that year. He was chief rugby league writer for the *Daily* and *Sunday* Telegraphs from 1969–1980 before leaving to become Managing Editor of *Rugby League Week* magazine. On numerous tours overseas and in the recording of the domestic premiership competition he covered the careers of many of the game's most famous players and was there for many of league's most famous days.

Leaving *RLW* in 1987 he continued to write about sport for various publications, including the *Sydney Morning Herald, Sun-Herald* and *Sunday Telegraph*. In the last 18 years Heads has authored or co-authored 35 books – many of them involving rugby league. These include a history of the Kangaroo tours, the seminal work *True Blue*; the story of the *NSW Rugby League*, histories of South Sydney and St George clubs, four books with the great coach Jack Gibson and autobiographies with the likes of Frank Hyde, Noel Kelly, Wayne Pearce, Peter Sterling, Benny Elias, Ken Arthurson, Malcolm Reilly, George Piggins and Arthur Beetson.

Warhorse

LIFE, FOOTBALL AND OTHER BATTLES

SHANE WEBCKE

with Ian Heads

MACMILLAN
Pan Macmillan Australia

First published 2006 in Macmillan by Pan Macmillan Australia Pty Ltd
1 Market Street, Sydney

Reprinted 2006 (four times), 2007

National Library of Australia
Cataloguing-in-Publication data

Webcke, Shane.
Warhorse : life, football and other battles.

ISBN 9781405037525 (pbk).

I. Heads, Ian. II. Title.

A 823.4

Set in 12/16 pt Janson by Midland Typesetters, Australia
Printed in Australia by McPherson's Printing Group

For Mum and Dad
Dad, your gift to me was one of strength, work ethic and decency.
Mum, yours was the courage and resolve to see it through.
My life to date as laid out in these pages is a testament to your
sacrifice and love, and is my gift to you both.

CONTENTS

FOREWORD
BY WAYNE BENNETT

Back in 1991 I took a phone call from an old mate, Graham Tucker, who I had played with at Toowoomba and in the Queensland side. 'I'm a garbo up here in Toowoomba these days,' he told me, 'and I'm doing some coaching with the 18s. We're in the grand final on Sunday and there's a bloke I want you to come and have a look at. His name is Stephen Price.' The Bronco year was over. We had been knocked out of the finals, so off I went. And as it turned out, I fell in love with a guy from the opposing team . . . a guy named Shane Webcke. He was out of control that day – just manic. He played in spurts, but he absolutely terrorised them. He was smashing guys just by putting his body on the line, and when he carried the ball he would hit as many of them as he could. Webcke was inspirational that afternoon and his team won the game against all the odds. I drove back to Brisbane, and told the club: 'We've got to get this guy.' Canterbury were showing a fair bit of interest in Stephen (Price) and I knew we'd be in a bidding war if we went that way. I wanted Webcke for the Broncos. And that was how it began . . .

There was pure rawness and enthusiasm about the way he played that afternoon. He gave his all, to the extent that he'd have to stop and walk for five minutes because he had nothing else to give. Once he had his breath back, he'd rip into it again.

We put him on a scholarship, and then a contract, and we placed him with Brothers Club for a year. I didn't get to see him that season until right at the end – in the under 19s grand final – when they played Redcliffe. Brothers had a small pack and Redcliffe had a huge one, and in the end were too good and won the game. But again he just ripped and tore into everybody. He was fighting them and bashing them and running over and through them. Again, he'd play until he was exhausted, then he'd be back into it again. I knew now we had something a bit special. That 'something' was that the guy just played flat-out. Shane was full-on tough – but he could play too. And in those early days he didn't want to just tackle, he wanted to *smash* whoever had the ball. He wasn't selective with his tackles at that stage – he learned that later, as his career developed. Back then he just wanted to inflict pain . . .

We started him training with us (the Broncos) the next season, 1994, and when we first hit the Gap (our training spot) he weighed in at around 125 kg. He nearly passed out on that first run!

When his dad died in mid-1994, I told him to take as much time off as he needed to sort himself out. I didn't know how he would handle the situation – but he handled it really well and all of a sudden he started to grow up. He realised he now had some responsibility for his mother, and accepted it. He thinks the world of his mum, Vicki, and he wanted to make her life as good as it could be. At that point in his own life he matured very quickly. I never met his dad, Tom, but I came to understand that he was a dominant type of bloke, someone whom Shane feared to an extent and who he was happy to see as the 'boss'. But when his dad suddenly wasn't there, he realised he had to pick up the slack.

At the Broncos we gave him time to find his feet, find his balance and find his direction. He was a prop from day one, and right from the start he didn't remind me of any other player. He was pretty much unique. In terms of the way he came to play the game and the way he trained, he became a standard-setter. There was no one like him.

One of the real joys I have had from Webcke's career, apart from watching his football, has been the great feedback I have had about him from so many areas over the years – on how he conducts himself and presents himself and how people seem to have a great admiration for him. He is extremely impressive – a very articulate, very disciplined guy who is very focused and very honest, with himself and with anyone he deals with. He is also extremely modest, although there is real strength of character in him. There was a brief period some years ago when he felt he was developing something of a problem with the drink. He was quite distraught about that, but with typical honesty he addressed the issue – and then intelligently carried through his plan to make sure it was no longer a problem. Being ethical and honest is the underpinning of his life. The thing that is most important of all to him is his reputation. It means he will not tell you a lie, he will not do a dud deal with you, he will not do the wrong thing by you, and if he is at fault he'll say, 'Mate, I was in the wrong . . . it was my fault.'

The nature of Shane Webcke is to challenge himself. Football has challenged him – but he is also challenged by how he can be successful away from football. He is challenged too by the way he presents himself, so he is continually looking within himself all the time, to find ways to improve.

I believe his career is a unique model for any player in the game. But to be honest, I doubt if my young blokes (at the

Broncos) have fully appreciated that. I doubt they realised what a man they were working with. There have been times when I wanted to shake them and say, 'Listen, do you realise how good this guy is? Do you realise who is sitting beside you in the change-room? Do you realise how committed he is and how much you can learn from him?' Shane's approach to training was always a strong part of that message. He trained the way he played, and his attitude on the 2004 Tri-nations tour in the UK was a perfect example. We'd head to training on the bus on those freezing-cold English days, with everyone rugged up and an attitude among some of the players that they didn't really want to be there because it wasn't what they were used to. Webcke would sit up front, dressed in shorts and a T-shirt. As soon as the bus stopped he would be out the door and onto the field running. This was the mind-set: 'I've got to do this. I don't want to be here – but I've got to do it – and so I'm going to do it as well as I can. And that's what he did, session after session. He'd hit the ground running, and be into it. It was his way – to train as he played. He was always unsparing on himself. He would always beat himself up at training. Never was there any thought of going easy 'because he had to play on Sunday'. And if I (as coach) told him, 'do this' – he would do it to the utmost limits of his ability. And he'd keep doing it until he had nothing left.

Throughout his career Shane defied the odds medically so many times you couldn't possibly count them. Peter Myers, the orthopaedic specialist, said to me that he had never treated a tougher guy. The events that are the standouts in my mind concern the broken arm he carried into the 2000 grand final and the piece of bone he had removed from his knee before we played the Cowboys in the 2004 finals. Shane had the operation on a Sunday, the day after he had played against Melbourne, in the hope that he could be ready to face the Cowboys the following Saturday – he tells the full story of the experience in the pages of this book.

Unless you are a medical person, you don't know all the issues that go into an operation – how muscles in the specific area of the operation stop functioning, giving you the message to take it easy. Shane had just six days to get his leg functioning. He worked day and night that week, and in the process beat up our physio something terrible. The physio had tried to tackle him a few times as part of the testing process and Shane had beaten the hell out of him. On the Saturday morning of the game he was limping on his first couple of runs, but got better as he warmed up. Within half an hour he said, 'I'm going to play' – and he did that night, and was outstanding. I still find it hard to believe that he did it. We got beaten by the Cowboys, and he never got the recognition he deserved. What he did was one of the most courageous and toughest things I have ever seen in football – to have had an operation and then six days later go out and play a high-pressure game of rugby league at the standard and intensity he played at. It wasn't a case of him just going through the motions. He played better than most of the guys who were fully fit. But he makes no fuss about things like that, and I don't either. If you lose the game there are no heroes in your team – all the heroes are on the other side. That has always been one of the tragedies of sport.

During the Tri-nations tour that followed the 2004 season, his leg became sore again. Before the tour the doctor had said to him, 'When you get home we'll take one of these spurs out of your knee . . . they will probably grow while you are away.' The week before the Final against Great Britain we played a Test in France. Shane was due to play but his leg had tightened up and was really sore – mainly because he had gone on a 6 km run by himself. A fanatic about fitness, he was always doing extra work. I pulled him out of the French match to give him the chance of being right for the Tri-nations Final, and backed him off training – although by the end of the week he was running well. There seemed to be no problems. And then . . .

At breakfast on the morning of the final, he went to stand up – and just collapsed. His leg had given away. A piece of bone in the knee had broken off and was caught – preventing him from flexing the leg and meaning that he had no strength, no power, no nothing. It was 10 am when I found out about it. The physio immediately began a day-long process of 'working' the knee, trying to dislodge the chipped-off bone from the spot where it was locking the knee. I remember going to see him at about 2 o'clock to ask him how he was going. 'Mate, this is really fucking with my head,' he said. 'I don't know whether I can play, or whether I can't.' I knew I had to give him good advice at that point. Shane is a great listener, but you can't give him grey . . . you've got to give him black or white to focus on. 'We're going to take you to the game,' I said, 'and we're going to put everything in place and warm you up – and if you're not right, we'll pull you out. If you get through the warm-up, we'll play you – and I don't care if you go for 10 or 15 minutes, or whatever.' That gave him something to focus on, and I knew he would be right. We rang the English League (RFL) and told them the situation – that we had a player with a real problem and would need a bloke on standby. 'We're not playing games here, we're not trying to pull a shonky,' we told them.

Anyway, he went out and warmed up, and when he came back in he said to me, 'It's better running than walking. I'm right.'

'Mate, away you go,' I said. And he went out and had a magnificent 40 minutes in what has been called by some the greatest half of football ever played by an Australian team. Early in the second half he was hobbling – his knee was gone – and I took him off and he didn't play again on tour. That was an unbelievable day.

Back in 2000 I didn't believe we could win the grand final unless Webcke was out there. He had broken his arm five weeks before the preliminary final against Parramatta and only begun training with us again in the week before that match; at the session there was a terrible crack and everyone thought: 'Jesus, he's broken it again.' Thankfully, he hadn't. I recall a conversation we had on the Thursday or Friday before the game. In the course of a long talk he said to me: 'I don't know whether I can do this.'

And I told him, 'We need you – and the worst-case scenario is that if you break it again you've got the off-season to get over it.' The doctors were all saying he couldn't play, that the healing time had not been long enough. But he played . . . and played a great game and we won the match 16–10 and went on to win the grand final with Webcke in the side. The bottom line is that the bloke has true grit; he's the strongest person you're ever likely to meet.

In late 2005 he did a ligament in his knee and the medical advice was that he'd be out for four to six matches. He missed one game and was back the next week.

Webcke the footballer was the bloke who turned up every week ready to play. I could ring him today and say, 'Mate, I need you to play in half an hour', and he'd be full-on ready. To win the Paul Morgan Medal at the Broncos in 2005 (Player of the Year) was a great moment for him, the moment when he realised that he really *was* special. He has never regarded himself that way. That is a bloody hard award to win – there have always been so many good players at the Broncos. But he won it twice.

When he came to us he couldn't pass. But every time he trained he worked harder than everybody else, improving his passing skills. He picked it up through sheer repetition, and his passing and decision-making ability improved enormously throughout the years. I think he worked every day of the week on the skills needed to play the game. Inevitably he would be out there after training, trying to find ways to do it better. Blokes like Alfie (Allan Langer) and Kevvie (Kevin Walters) were great for him. In the early days he was very intense and worried himself out of playing well. Because he didn't want to let anybody down, he worried like hell. And if it wasn't for the advice that our sports psychologist Phil Jauncey gave him (which you will read about) and the input of Alfie and Kevvie, laughing and joking in the dressing room, anxiety would have beaten him every time. The carry-on by Alf and Kevvie made him laugh a little, just helped relax him.

Glenn Lazarus, who was at the Broncos in Shane's first three years there, was a magnificent footballer. Shane Webcke took over his mantle in the game. There was no better prop in the game than Lazzo. He turned up every week . . . and put in every week. The handover to Webcke was seamless.

Shane was never a football watcher, but it never worried me because I knew no one was more committed to the game and to excellence than him. We might go into a team meeting and suggest, 'We'd better keep an eye out for John Skandalis (Wests Tigers prop) today' and he'd say, 'Who's John Skandalis?' He didn't watch footy because he was not interested in watching it. His interest was in *playing* the game. When that was done, weekly, he would walk away to other things.

It has been an experience to watch him grow. He can see some grey in the sky now and he's not as judgemental as he was in earlier days. If he'd stayed in the bush he would have been as big a redneck as you'd find. He would have been a prick by now! There would have been no grey. I'd like to think my influence has helped with that. I believe that to lead successfully you can't have a black-and-white mentality. There are always grey areas. Shane lives his life his way but has come to understand that other people live differently, see things differently, and he has come to be very tolerant of that difference. Shane's tolerance today is learned tolerance. He has learned to understand or at least to try to understand why another guy mightn't think like him, or behave like him. I think the change began when he got out of the farm environment and came to Brisbane, bringing with him a narrow view on a whole lot of issues. Straight away I think the change started to happen – his gradual acceptance that there were other ways and other very different opinions. And that was the path he continued down. And that is the growth in him.

At the Broncos we encouraged him to assume a leadership role, and it was easy. If he has to speak on an issue, he always seems to articulate it beautifully. And he learned within our organisation that it was never about mouthing off or talking trash; that's not his nature and it's not his style.

In 2005 he made a strong and very difficult decision to pull out of Origin football and therefore to end his Australian career, something that would have cut deep, because he loved the inter-national stuff. I know that we missed him (Queensland and Australia). Shane Webcke brings an attitude. In 2004 I put (St George prop) Jason Ryles in as his roommate in the Australian team and Jason said to me later: 'I have never met a better guy. I learned so much just being his roommate.' Any team would miss a player like him because of the influence he had on all the other players.

The terrorist thing in 2001 was another great example of how solid Shane Webcke is. He stood tall above everyone else in that. After 9/11 the players had all pulled out of the Australian tour to England, said they weren't going to go, and then there was the backflip by the ARL and everyone was on the plane. But Webcke didn't flinch. 'I said publicly I wasn't going, and I'm not going,' he told them. He stood against the odds and against the majority. That's strong stuff. He rang me at that time.

'If I was you I'd be doing exactly the same thing,' I told him.

There have been many occasions over the years when he has come to me for advice on issues. But most of the time I have found he has got it absolutely right and I am there just for re-inforcement. When it's settled he goes away and does whatever it is . . . and invariably does it bloody well.

We've certainly had our run-ins. He gets the shits really easily – and he'll carry on and sulk, although that's nowhere near as much a part of him as it used to be. But when it's over, he'll walk up and say, 'Mate, I was out of order; I did the wrong thing there . . . I carried on like a sook.' And life goes on.

The question of Shane and money is an interesting one, and something that is misunderstood. There is a perception in the game that he's a bit of a tightwad, that he wouldn't lend you a dollar. It isn't true. What Shane Webcke is is *conscious* of money. He was brought up in virtual poverty in struggling circumstances and it's always been his way that he's not going to waste money. In fact he is an extremely generous man who does a good deal for charities. And he has given a lot of money to junior rugby league in the bush from successful business ventures he has been involved with. He has done successful deals and said, 'I'll take this much out of it and whatever is left over I'll give to junior league.' I'm talking many thousands of dollars. There are not too many in the game who do that.

Just like me, Shane understands very well what the game has done for him and appreciates it enormously. The Broncos gave him something that he would never have had in his life – and he will never forget it. With him and the club there was no quibble over money, although there were occasional questions. I remember when he came home from the World Cup tour of 2000 and called in to see me. Lots of things get talked about on tours, including, this time, who was getting what at the Broncos. He had heard of players not as good as himself getting more money than he was. 'I'm okay, I'm fine,' he said to me. 'I signed the deal here and I'm happy with that – and that is the way it's going to stay. But, Wayne . . . I've just got to talk it out. Those guys are getting all this money?'

And I said to him: 'Well, Shane, that's the way it is. You knew when you signed that there were blokes getting more than you.'

'Yeah, I knew that,' he said. So we talked the process through. At the end of it he said, 'Well, bugger them. I've signed the deal and that's it . . . I'm playing. I just needed to get the shit out of my head.' That was it . . . and off he went. It was never mentioned again.

Shane has always looked after his own business. But in negotiation he is better than any manager. He knows what he wants, he knows how to ask for it, he knows how to handle himself and he knows what a fair deal is. He is not about ripping you off and he is not about coming in short for himself. He is about commonsense. And that's Webcke. He doesn't need any manager. He would buy and sell them all ten times over.

It's been a pleasure to coach him. I was there, as coach for his first first-grade club game, his first Origin match and his first Test for Australia. The Origin and Test experiences were special moments. I had seen him as a kid, brought him to the club, brought him into first grade. Now he had gone to the top. We have had a pretty unique shared experience and it has been based (I believe) on respect from him to me and certainly on respect from me to him. From that solid base a friendship developed.

And the future for Shane Webcke? Well, he thinks he'll go home to the farm and be a farmer, but he has no chance of that. People are going to seek him out. Through being a footballer and through the stands he has taken on issues and the way he has conducted himself he is already experiencing the demand which will follow him when football is finished. And that's good. He'll be looking for the wider experience himself, even though he loves the farm and the place he came from. Without football there will be some challenges missing – and he needs to be challenged. The farm won't challenge him enough. He has the realisation now that he carries with him some influence and commands respect, and he'll find it very difficult to sit on his hands when he sees something that needs to be done.

Shane can have anything he wants in his life ahead. I can see him being the premier of the state if he decides to go into politics. If he chose that path he would be absolutely refreshing. He is a strong-willed, strong-disciplined, bloody great thought-process person – but he can also be a great team player too, and that's one of his real strengths.

In football administration he could go as high as he wanted to. He would bring great qualities to the leadership of the game. He's got balance. He's a bright bloke who gained a high TE score at high school, and has remained a prolific reader. And whether he's digging a hole to put a post in, or training for football, or playing a game of footy, he has a great work ethic. Give your best . . . do your best – that was his dad's upbringing and that was the way Shane was brought up too. The Webckes worked from dawn to dusk and he wasn't allowed to negotiate on that. He is extra-ordinarily single-minded. When he eats, he doesn't eat to enjoy the food, but more to refuel so he can go back out to the task at hand. Within the football framework at the Broncos we had this extremely strong, single-minded bloke and yet a real team person who brought along everything that was required within that context.

The closest thing to him of all is his upbringing, that spiritual bloody thing that the bush gives you. That has never left him. But he's been to the city now and seen other sides of life, and he has gained balance. And that's what he'll take back to his community – a perspective and a position that most of them have never explored. He will bring change because of that.

Rugby league will miss Shane Webcke. He has been one of the very special ones and I am delighted he is telling his story in this book. It's an important story of what a sporting career can do for someone who applies himself, opens his mind to the possibil-ities, learns from them and grows along the way. And it is a story of what a special player can do for a sport, too. There are great messages here for any young boy or girl who wants to make a success of their life. In its own way it's a 'textbook' for any young player. At 32, Shane has done both his sport and himself proud.

Now, after a brilliant career, one door in his life has closed. Outside, the world awaits . . .

Wayne Bennett, 2006

ACKNOWLEDGEMENTS

The compiling of a book such as this is always the sum of the efforts of a great many people, some of whom contributed directly and others who simply are part of the fabric of my life. I will attempt to mention everyone that I should, but if I have missed anyone it is merely to do with a mind that is jumbled with many things. I apologise if I have been remiss.

My thanks to Tony Durkin for his introduction to Ian Heads, who worked with me on the project and in the process became a lifelong friend. Ian, you are one of the most gentlemanly blokes I have ever met and I am privileged to have had you assist me with this book. You are part of the reason our game is great.

To everyone at Pan Macmillan and particularly Tom Gilliatt, Siobhán Cantrill and Tracey Cheetham – your help and friendship through this whole process has been tremendously professional.

To the Broncos and Wayne Bennett, who are the reason this book can be written at all, I am forever indebted.

And to all the people who in one way or another contributed material and resources and effort I offer my lasting gratitude.

To all my mates, particularly Shaun Rauchle and David Joppich, my closest and oldest friends, thank you for your friendship and support to date . . . for what is life without friends?

And to everyone who has ever given me a leg up, a helping hand or simply offered a sympathetic ear, you are too numerous to mention on these pages but nonetheless are pivotal in my life.

To the players I played with at all levels, I am fortunate to have had the privilege to take the field with you all. To the game of rugby league – what a life you have afforded me! In my view you will always be 'the greatest game of all'. To the supporters of the game, your kindness to me through all the ups and downs that a professional sporting career inevitably involves leaves me feeling humbled.

To the people who have supported me in my endeavours away from the field, thank you for your caring tutelage.

To my brother Dallas – only you and I know the wonderful cherished secrets and treasures of our shared childhood. I loved it all and am fortunate to have you as my brother.

To my darling Nan, you taught me what it is to live life with dignity and courage in the face of enormous adversity. I'll never stop missing you.

To Mum, words don't do justice to your contribution to all that is me. I love and cherish you. To Dad, my heart aches that you never got to witness much of the story told here, but you live on in my soul and are my ultimate inspiration, for so many reasons.

And to my darlings, Ally, Erin bear, Haydie boy and Gracie Girl, what else is there if I don't have you? You are my everything and my life. Thank you for you.

Chapter 1

THE BEGINNING OF THE END

One day in the off-season of 2005–06, during a brief break from Brisbane and football training, I was out at the country-place of my beginning, Leyburn, wandering around a small paddock I own close to town. There, something amazing happened. For a few moments I was transported back 20 years. The field in question is beautiful – tree-lined and running down to a creek. It is one of several bits and pieces of land I now have around that town on the edge of the Darling Downs where I was born and grew up. I have no idea of exactly what triggered the experience I had that day – was it a smell? . . . a sound? . . . a flash of memory? . . . but in an instant I was back in earlier days, as if I had ridden a time machine into the past. Suddenly I was experiencing clear images of what it was like when I was a kid, reliving forgotten feelings, the way I used to think about things back then.

It was just on dark, on a still country afternoon. The fleeting experience was both sad and uplifting . . . and quite profound.

1

Adjoining the paddock where I stood is one that my dad Tom used to lease; on top of a hill there stands an old and very familiar set of sheepyards. It may have been the angle, or the late afternoon light, but on glancing across, immediately I was back at the yards with my dad (who died in 1994), chucking sheep around. It was almost real enough to touch, a moment that was very emotional for me.

Later, I thought about what I had experienced and thought some more too about those growing-up days out west and the contrast with where I was in my life now. I had long been a professional rugby league player with a great club, the Brisbane Broncos, and was currently getting ready for my 13th season, nearing the end of what most people would perhaps rate a worthwhile career. Whenever I undertake that exercise of reflecting on the great leap from those early Leyburn days to the present, I am astounded. The time that came back to me so clearly that afternoon was one of struggle and some sadness – and especially the memory of the death of my dad in a shocking work accident at nearby Warwick when I was 19. But the memories are of tremendously happy times, too, in a solid family that provided the grounding for what I have been able to make of my life. My great stroke of fortune was to have such a foundation for my life laid down out there at Leyburn. Lives can be built on proper, solid foundations, or on straw; I always felt that mine was built on granite – and that what was nurtured and grew within the family of Tom and Vicki Webcke gave me a wonderful chance for whatever lay ahead. I hold onto that thought – and especially on such rare days as I have written of here.

As I stood in the paddock that afternoon, I felt a warm glow. Knowing that the sort of memories and feelings that had just flashed by would never leave filled me with a great happiness. That it happens occasionally out there at Leyburn – triggered, I suspect, by a combination of many things: the air, the remembered country, the ghosts of my growing-up years, the memories, and a true and deep sense of 'home' – is a very special and reassuring thing in the life I have today.

First thing next morning I was in my car, heading back to a harder reality: the big city and the toughest pre-season training program I had ever experienced. Changes in the ranks at the Broncos after our premiership fadeout in 2005 had seen old hands like Kevvie Walters and Gary Belcher depart from the team administration, amidst much controversy, and a new deal put in place. At the helm now, charged with the duty of producing a leaner, fitter, meaner Broncos outfit, was a Victorian named Dean Benton, who had sparked some resentment in me at the start (for which I subsequently apologised). He proved to be a tough taskmaster who never veered one centimetre from his goal of turning us into a lighter, fitter football team. The fitness program he had set us was as hard and challenging as anything I had faced. Eventually, at 109 kilos, I was lighter than I had ever been at that start of a season and my skinfold measure was at its lowest reading ever after I had achieved a target that had been bloody hard to reach.

Fast forward to Sunday, March 12, 2006, a sweltering Brisbane afternoon worthy of mid-summer. It's 1.30 and in the Broncos dressing room, deep in the bowels of Suncorp Stadium, I'm stretched out on a bench and in a twilight zone, almost asleep. Kickoff in the first match of what I already know will be my last season of football is in half an hour. And I'm feeling like dog-shit. In the days before I had picked up a heavy bout of 'flu, maybe brought home by one of the kids from playschool or kindy. The fact that I'm lying down is a tell-tale sign. Usually I'm fairly bouncy in the sheds before a game. And over the seasons I've been very good at stuff like that – good at getting through the days when I was crook. If I'd had a special strength in this game, it had been on the mental side of the equation. On a match-day like March 12, 2006 I would usually have said to myself: 'Well, I'm sick. Big deal. Just go out and do this for 80 minutes and then you can walk away from it and go home.' But on this first premiership afternoon of the year I gave into it a bit. I felt crook and I lay down. In the years before, I wouldn't have done that. It was a small sign of the change in me, an acceptance deep down that after all those years and all those matches I was already looking towards the end.

Before 46,000 fans that afternoon we got flogged by the Cowboys, 36–4. On a day when none of us played well, I wasn't the worst on the field. But there was a time when I would have been better than I was. The problem for the Broncos was that via all the changes at the club – the arrival of the new fitness bloke, a significant change in our training – a certain perception and expectation had been built up by the media. I think people were expecting to see us hit the season at a million miles per hour. We, the players, were not necessarily thinking that way. Yes we *were* a lot fitter, but the benefits were never going to be there instant-aneously on day 1. In fact we were a fairly tired footy side, because we had worked extremely hard so that we might have something in the tank for later down the track. Maybe our build-up to the season got mistimed a bit, or maybe all the hype bit into us mentally. Whatever the reason, we didn't perform anywhere near close to our potential, and we got our tails kicked on our home ground. Yet it wasn't such a bad thing, to be honest. We have started seasons doing exactly what the Cowboys did that afternoon and fallen away very seriously – the early success masking deeper deficiencies that emerged later in the year when the pressure was on and when it was too late to do anything about it. I remember thinking in the days after the match that history might well prove that first game a better thing than it seemed to any of us at the time.

So, this beginning to the story of my life and times in football has some strangeness about it: first, the rather mystical incident at Leyburn, then the image of an old front-rower dozing on a dressing-room bench just before one of the biggest season's kickoff matches in years. Strangeness was in the air. But this of course was no normal year in my life in football. I can tell the story now: I knew quite clearly by the end of pre-season training that the season would be my last as a rugby league player. I realised that for quite a time I had longed to be free of it, not so much free of the playing of the game, something I still enjoyed, but free of the pressure.

I remember very well the day in November 2005 when I went home cranky from our first pre-season training session. We trained on a Friday and the deal was that the blokes whose skinfold readings weren't right would be back for extra training the following day. I was confident it wouldn't involve me; in recent years I had always been given a bit of grace. But as I walked out the door with my bag, Dean Benton called to me, 'Webby, we'll see you in the morning.'

'What? . . . What for?' I responded. Inside, I was real cranky. And he told me that my skinfold had to be 'X' and in fact it was 'Y'. For me it was the first peek through a little window where I hadn't been before.

When I think about that moment now, I realise that I wanted to be a bit soft on myself – that as an older player I anticipated being given some leeway. But Dean's message right there was that this was going to be a year of no shortcuts. Everyone would have to toe the line and there would be no favours given. I drove home cranky that Friday and was still cranky when I did the 'extras' the next morning. At the Broncos I had always been big on being the same, doing the same as everyone else. Now some resentment had crept in.

A week later, in a discussion with Dean and our coach Wayne Bennett, I apologised to our new fitness man. I told him I knew

that things were going to change at the club – but on that first day
I hadn't been as ready to accept that change as I could have been
and I was sorry about that. Inside was a feeling that maybe I was
getting a bit sick and tired of all this. By the end of the pre-season
training, weeks later, with my crook knee giving me some curry,
I knew for sure that while I would be fine and 100 per cent
committed for 2006 . . . I deadset didn't want to go on after that.
The grind of pre-seasons can be like that, though, and I knew
that I had to play some footy and give it a chance.

Dean Benton is a very precise, regimented sort of bloke.
Everything is measured and recorded and players have to live up
to the standards set. I struggled with Benton's way more than a
little – probably more than most. Dean has no rugby league background at all. He comes from a completely different culture, and
in some ways he didn't fit in with the way we were at the Broncos.
But he's a good fella who knows his stuff and he set the bar high
in physical preparation and brought a real freshness to the place.
I had the growing feeling though that he and I would one day
learn to be enemies. Not because of anything specific about him –
he was just doing his job and being tough about it. But I knew for
sure that eventually I wouldn't want to cop it.

No one at the Broncos panicked after the loss to the Cowboys,
even though a firestorm involving media and disappointed fans
raged around us. In the eyes of some we were too old, plus a light
of earlier days in rugby league, Lockey (Darren Lockyer) was
'gone' . . . and generally, the end of the world was nigh. At the
club we were totally untouched by it. That's one thing you
quickly learn as a professional footballer, but that the media never
really grasp: in any given week in football all sorts of weird and
wonderful things can happen, and sometimes they amount to you
winning and sometimes they don't. The basic message for all

professional footballers is: learn what you can from the game you've just won or lost . . . and move on. I discovered long ago that there was no point reading the Sunday or Monday papers. Very rarely did the match reports hit the mark. Instead, we would close ranks, analyse as a team and a club and listen to the coach.

At the Broncos it's what we've always done. And in the week that followed, it's what we did.

The next weekend, on a huge and emotional night for the Sharks as they remembered the late and great Steve 'Sludge' Rogers, we toughed out a 16–12 win over them at Toyota Park. It was our first win since July 29, 2005; we had been beaten in our last seven games of that season. My 'flu was hanging on, and a couple of nights before the game I managed only three hours' sleep. But we grafted back from 12–0 to win and I scored a try along the way, hitting a gap from a Darren Lockyer pass. Boy, that felt good. There has always been a thing with me when it comes to tries. I like to get one a year. And to do it that early (Game 2!) was like the weight of the world coming off my shoulders. Well, I don't have to worry about *that* any more, I thought. The try came off a short charge to the line – obviously, as the years go by, that distance covered will dramatically increase. By 2050 it will be over 70 metres at least in the telling, and maybe with a chip kick and a dummy thrown in.

Suddenly, after beating the Sharks, we were heroes again. Everyone was singing our praises. We had turned things around, shouted the media. The truth, of course, was that we hadn't turned anything around – the only thing was that we had won the football match. We hadn't miraculously become the side we wanted to be overnight. We went out there with some grit and determination and we won. No less, no more.

Reaction to the match was pretty much a snapshot of the modern media. The previous week there had been veiled speculation that the great Darren Lockyer was 'finished'. The fact was that Lockey had come into that first game seriously underdone – off an injury and with little training under his belt – and hadn't shown his best hand against the Cowboys. That beginning followed a 2005 season which wasn't his greatest – but a season that 95 per cent of the players in the competition would have been pleased to call their own. Suddenly, against the Sharks, when he recaptured some form, he was 'back', and I was happy to go in to bat for him in the media. I was just bemused by it all – this was a wonderful player who had played a brand of football which we had not seen before and may not see again. And yet there was a rush for people to write him off.

Home in Brisbane with two premiership points from windy Toyota Park, we were off the mark and on the move. From here a season of some promise began to take shape . . .

For me, this was a fascinating season, a real trip into the unknown. After years of ultimate disappointment in which we had fallen short at finals time, we were trying to be a different football club, one that wasn't plagued by the past. Our training program was different from anything we had tackled before; in fact, just about everything we were doing was different. Wayne had said something wise to us early on – setting the standard. 'If you can win three out of every four-or-so games . . . that's enough,' he told us. In a competition in which teams have drawn so close together in ability, thanks largely to the salary cap, it was a slice of typical Bennett wisdom. You don't need to win them all. Of course you always go *out* to win – but it doesn't always happen. Consistency is the thing . . . an even-keeled approach . . . winning your share . . . losing on a highly competitive basis when that happens. Get that formula right and you're going to get a shot at the finals. When you win a string of games in succession, every one of them builds pressure, brings you closer to the (certain) defeat that awaits. Often when that happens to a team and a match is finally lost, it can be such a comedown that it can trigger a losing streak.

As the warm autumn rolled on, my determination to lock in 2006 as my last season grew. I remember a conversation I had with Wayne at training (and I had a few of those in the opening weeks) when I said to him: 'I'm starting to feel like I want to do something else. I'm not coming here every day thinking that I want to be here.' I had decided and declared that I would wait until halfway through the season before making my decision about the future – but in every interview I did, I was asked the question.

We beat the Eels (30–10), a club which had controversially pulled the plug on coach Brian Smith for 2007 before a ball had been kicked in season '06, and the next week headed to Wollongong to play the Dragons. It was there, in Wayne Bennett's hotel room on the day before the game, that I told the coach of my decision to retire at the end of the season. 'I've thought long and hard about it – and I respect your advice about playing half a season before I decide,' I told him. 'But I know now I don't need half a season. I've had enough. I'm ready to go.' When I think about it now I can't believe how hard it was to say the words. The coach, who was stretched out on the bed, watching TV, simply answered: 'That's good.' I was a little taken aback by the brevity of the response . . . and then I wasn't. Wayne knew me well enough to know how much thought I would have put into what I had just said – and he knew I hadn't come to hear him say no. The hard part out of the way, we talked, and I told him how when I came to training these days I'd be thinking of other things and that when we played away (like this match) I'd be thinking that I'd rather be home with the kids and there for the weekend and doing something *normal*. And I told him I just didn't want to face another pre-season – not only because of the physical tiredness, but because of the whole mental routine. I was past it.

We had a long chat and when I left the room I felt much better.

We lost that football match (30–12), and in the days that followed a reaction set in, the sudden realisation that come the end of the year there would be no more of this. What would my life look like then? For a short time it was really quite frightening – the idea that I would have to construct a whole new life, even though I reckoned I had all the pieces in the jigsaw ready and I knew a lot of blokes didn't at the end of football lives. My head was full of it; for all my adult life I had led this regimented football existence, where everything was laid out and I knew what I was doing at all times, because I had been told. Now I would have to find my own way. At the end of 2006 my life would be a blank canvas.

Wayne suggested we get the news out into the public arena straight away, and I agreed with that. I just wanted to get it done so I could head on with finishing the season. 'It's a good thing to do,' he said '. . . from now on a lot of the grounds you'll be going to, you'll be playing there for the last time.' It was a sobering thought.

Monday, April 24 was the day, with a press conference scheduled after training. I had insisted to Wayne that I wanted all the boys to know first, so after training he moved around spreading the word, and blokes were coming up and shaking my hand . . . and I started to feel the emotion welling up.

There had been one bout of tears already that day . . .

I have always reckoned that when you first open your eyes in the morning it's the most honest time of the day, and that right then you're going to think the most honest thought you've got in your head. That particular Monday morning it was this: 'After today, you can't go back.' I got ready for training as ever, said goodbye to the kids and gave my wife Ally a kiss and a cuddle in the kitchen, as I always did. 'Good luck today,' she said. 'I'm really proud of you.' I put on a brave face, but I was struggling.

'I'll be right,' I said as I jumped in the car. But on the way to training I started crying . . . the tears were just rolling down my cheeks. I was thinking about footy and all the things I loved about it and that a huge part of my life was ending. I was laughing and crying at the same time and thinking, You bloody idiot!

I'm so glad it happened, because my little self-absorbed moment took away some of the emotion from the rest of the day.

The press conference at which I shared my secret with the world was both big and enormously humbling. I was dumb-founded and flattered at some of the things that Wayne and Locky and Bruno (Cullen, Broncos managing director) said. Because of the occasion, they said things they would probably never say . . . well, not to me, anyway. The media guys, some of them good mates, asked intelligent questions, which took me further into what it all meant to me. I couldn't have hoped for it to go any better. I had a Diet Coke with Bruno and Wayne afterwards and we yarned for a bit, and then as the afternoon unfolded, I did (what seemed) a million interviews. Next day the story was everywhere and I rode an emotional roller-coaster.

Ergon Energy Broncos warhorse Shane Webcke has today announced his retirement from rugby league. Webcke made his announcement in the Broncos boardroom this afternoon, surrounded by managing director Bruno Cullen, chairman Darryl Somerville, coach Wayne Bennett and captain Darren Lockyer. His retirement becomes effective from the end of season 2006. Webcke said the decision to retire had been a relatively easy one.

Beginning of the official Broncos press release that
took the news to the rugby league world

I had played 243 first-grade games for the Broncos, 21 State of Origin games and 20 Tests.

In the wake of that day a phenomenal number of offers started coming in – for guest appearances and endorsements and guest speaking jobs. And with retirement in mind and the thought of building relationships, I got swept up in it all, overtaken by it – and briefly lost my direction as a footballer. I became deeply engrossed in all this stuff outside football.

After we lost to the Knights at Newcastle – 32–30 after a desperately see-sawing game – I was totally pissed off with myself and really embarrassed. I didn't really have a crook game and there was no lack of effort, but I just didn't do anything of great quality. And I had an unhappy day, giving away some penalties. Also, I didn't do much for the team – and that had always been a fundamental concern in my career, how my performance had affected the team on a given day. As I sat in the dressing room after the match I was filthy with myself. I didn't feel I'd cost us the game . . . but I hadn't done much to help either.

It was to be another one of those small 'turning points' in this most extraordinary of seasons. I made a conscious decision after that match that for the rest of the year I would go back to the things that had made me the footballer I was. 'Bugger everything else . . . it can wait until the end of the season,' I decided. And if I missed out on some commercial opportunity, well, bad luck. I was still a footballer, still loved the game – and I was not going to start down a path where other things were more important. Not yet.

So I did something very straightforward: I went back exactly to the routine that had served me well throughout my career. Right through, I'd always kept our last day off (two days before match-day) as my day, and family day. It was a day when I'd always walk right away from football and do something with Ally and the kids or go to the farm. That day had been 'mine' for years – but in recent times I had let the tradition go in the interests of the future. So I returned to what had worked for me – and as soon as I made the decision, I was instantly 'back'. I went to Wayne and said, 'I've been a dickhead . . . I have let things get out of control. That was the final straw on the weekend (v Newcastle), and I just wanted to tell you I have fixed it. I am now back, focused entirely on football.'

And the coach just chuckled. 'What are you laughing at?' I said. And he told me how Darren Lockyer had come to him after the (Newcastle) match and quietly expressed some concerns about me – that I was cranky and didn't seem myself. And Wayne had agreed with him and had said to Locky, 'I'll speak to him if you want me to, but I reckon he will have got to me before I get to him. I'll guarantee he'll come to me next week and tell me he's fixed it.' By a single decision, I had set myself free. I have never been a footballer who needed Sunday to Monday doing nothing but getting ready for the match. But I did need that one day. The decision I made restored the balance.

In the lead-up to the next match against Manly I had not felt better before a game of footy in a long time. I knew I was going to play well, because all the old stuff was in place. I felt like a teenager again. But footy being footy and fate being fate, I mistimed a tackle very early in the game in trying to wrestle one of their big blokes to the ground and there was a bit of a snap, crackle and pop and I was on my way to the dressing sheds. I had 'done' my ribs, and it was very, very painful. There was no break, but there was a rib cartilage tear – and it was bloody sore.

It meant a couple of weeks' recuperation, and that was a shame. But I was clear in my head now. I was going to be able to enjoy this last season. The fear of dropping away form-wise troubled me a little, but I was thoroughly determined not to let that happen. I wanted to go out on the best note I possibly could. I wasn't thinking of fairytales at the end (although such an ending would be nice!). It wasn't needed – I had had so much out of football already. To go out strongly and to be remembered as a consistent player right to the end . . . that would be enough.

I looked forward to the last match 'at home' – at Suncorp – and knew that would be a massive day. And then that final day of all as a footballer . . . the day when my ship would sail. I was thinking there would be some emotion around that day! And I knew that that one simply *couldn't* be a bad day, whatever happened.

And so I headed on, in good spirits, into this 'new' Broncos season which was building such a nice head of steam. It was a funny feeling – almost of being in a state of limbo . . . poised on the dividing line between two lives, and wrestling with an ending and a beginning at the same time.

Around me the 99th premiership season of rugby league in Australia ebbed and flowed colourfully, as seasons always did. A Test match (Australia v New Zealand) came and went, followed by the annual Origin carnival, which produced a fabulous Maroons fightback to take the series – built on the old 'Queenslander' passion. Bulldog fans misbehaved badly at a match, found themselves on the front pages (again!) – and then lifted their game. An old teammate, Wendell Sailor, tested positive for a recreational drug, drawing the most painful headlines of an eventful career, and probably ended his footballing days – his dilemma brought into sharp focus a major problem facing all professional sports, rugby league included (and you'll read more of that later). I was even painted in oils (even though I'm no oil painting!) – the Broncos paid $10,000 for the picture and will hang it in the club-house, which I regard as a huge honour. And all the while the weekly battle for the NRL Telstra Cup – for me the last one – rolled on . . . including one memorable Sunday in July on which I captained the team in my 251st game for the Broncos and on which we defied the odds to beat Cronulla (26–12) despite being without 11 topline players. I even scored a try!

So this story of a life in and around rugby league sort of begins at the end, or close to it, although I much prefer to view it as a new beginning. My journey so far is one that's not even anywhere near half-made. And I am excited about what lies ahead.

This story of my life is told straight. I didn't want it to be a bullshit book, just a real and honest account of the way it was for me. And if I have had to say some things that aren't particularly good for me, or are a bit blunt about others, well, I've said them. I didn't want the book to be seen as generic footy rubbish. There have been more than enough league books over the years that said a lot without saying anything. When I decided to tell my story I was determined that if people were going to get anything of value from it, the telling had to be real. And I knew that if I was ever going to give a copy of this book to someone, I wanted to be able to do that with some pride. In outlining my strong reservations about some things in and around the game in the pages ahead I never intended in any way to paint a picture of myself as being self-righteous, or without fault (I'll always readily admit I have some of those!).

So, it's Webcke, warts 'n all – and I will begin at the place of my heart . . . out there on the edge of the Downs.

Chapter 2
THE PLACE OF MY HEART

It was because the game of rugby league became both my vocation and my life that I came to terms with the necessity of living in a big city. But my heart has always dwelt somewhere else, at a place two hours west of Brisbane, which nudges against the black soil plains of Queensland's Darling Downs. Ever since I became a Bronco in 1994, the Downs country has been my escape – somewhere I can refresh, rebuild and revitalise my whole being. To point the car due west and cruise through the sprawling suburbs flanking the city and out into the countryside beyond lifts my spirits. Every time.

I came from out that way, you see. My dad, Tom, grew up in and around Ipswich, but he and Mum eventually moved further west, to Highfields, a lovely place on the edge of the range outside Toowoomba, and eventually to Leyburn (population 150) – the town and surrounds I think of today as my past, my present and my future all wrapped in one. My background is German/Scottish/Swedish. Dad's family way back were German, and I guess you could say I am part of something of a football tradition. I am aware of names from around there of the more distant past – the legendary Toowoomba prop Herb Steinohrt and the Heidkes, Bill and Les and Eric Frauenfelder, Harry Liebke and Lou Meibusch, whose backgrounds were Germanic, and who played rugby league. There is still a heavy German influence around Ipswich today – especially at Calbart, where many German people settled in earlier years. The Scottish and Swedish input to the Webcke family came via my mum Vicki (née Yule). So for a bloke playing what has become one of the most Australian of games since it took root here early last century, I'm a bit of a mixture.

The German influence on rugby league in south-east Queensland was considerable. In the late 1880s a large number of Germans migrated to that area and took up farming near Ipswich (Fassifern Valley) – and some migrated to the Darling Downs. From the 1920s onwards league was the main game in the region, and the size and power of German descendants made them naturals at our game. Herb Steinohrt was one of them . . . he farmed on the Downs. I knew Herb well – he was a Queensland and Australian selector in the Ron McAuliffe era. He was also an early mentor of Wayne Bennett, whom he coached at All Whites in Toowoomba. I never saw Herb play . . . but from what McAuliffe told me Webcke would be in the same mould – tough, uncompromising, but scrupulously fair and wholly decent.

Jeff Wall – rugby league historian and chief RL writer
for crikey.com.au

People have always had trouble spelling my name, as probably they did with someone like Herb Steinohrt. They would have had even more trouble in its original form: Woebcke. Dad's family changed the spelling during World War II to try to remove some of the Germanness from the name. It didn't work too well, and Mum tells me that my grandfather on

17

that side copped a really hard time during the war. He was a teacher, but because of the distrust that surrounded people with Germanic backgrounds, he missed promotions that should rightly have come his way. My name is still often spelt wrongly – usually Webke. I don't even correct it most of the time. But it's not that difficult, and it's almost a hurtful thing to see your named spelt incorrectly.

My dad was a good rugby union player, who went to Christian Brothers College, Ipswich and, as the family story goes, was 'encouraged', when his working life began, to join the navy, having got into a spot of bother . . . as young blokes can. He was a navy man, a Petty Officer stationed in Sydney, at Garden Island, when he and Mum met – at a famous venue, the Texas Tavern, King's Cross. Mum grew up in Sydney, living at Newtown and Marrickville, and finally at North Ryde. She was working then for the Health Department in downtown Sydney. It was at an office dinner party at the Texas Tavern that a mutual friend introduced her to Tom. She reckoned they hit it off from the start. Both of them loved sport and at various times my mum played netball, vigoro, basketball and went ice-skating.

> *I had a wonderful family life. I was ever grateful to my family because they gave me a beautiful life and I grew up with good values, knowing how good family life could be. I also knew there were times when it wasn't that way.*
>
> *Vicki Webcke*

The courtship was a short one ('We instinctively knew that this was it,' said Mum of her meeting with Tom) – and Vicki Yule and Tom Webcke were duly married in a simple ceremony at the Registry Office, Queen's Square. They lived in Sydney for a time after that, at Manly, then Lilyfield. My older brother Dallas was born at Bethesda Hospital in 1972 – 'nine months and three days after the wedding', as Mum tells it.

Dad was in the navy for 15 years, and from all reports was a rugby player of talent who represented Australia at Combined Services level. And whatever his reasons for going to sea, he sure did see the world. He went to Vietnam twice during the war and at different times was stationed in Borneo and on the Malay Peninsula.

I suspect that what I have felt deeply during my Bronco years in Brisbane parallels what my father wrestled with in his time in the navy. His grandparents had a little farm and I think that Dad's one true dream was to be a farmer – to get back onto the land and work with his hands.

Tom had a great love of the land and I thought, 'I can't keep him from this.' I am pretty adaptable, and the thought of a move (to Queensland) didn't worry me all that much.

Vicki Webcke

When Dallas was two the family moved to a small property, 'Ulalah', two or four hectares at Highfield, north of Toowoomba. Although edging closer to his dream by then, Dad stayed in the navy for a time and commuted from the little farm to his various assignments. It was there, in Toowoomba Base Hospital, that I was born, on 28 September 1974. I weighed seven pounds 14 ounces and am reliably informed that on arrival in the world I was 'long and lanky'. I was christened Shane Patrick Webcke. An entry in a scrapbook kept by my mother notes: 'Shane – God's gracious gift (Hebrew)'. Hmmm. Of my christening at St Patrick's Cathedral, Toowoomba, it is reported that I screamed the place down throughout, moving the officiating priest to remark that I was the most upset baby he had ever dealt with.

When he got to three months, something happened. He just blew up into this huge child. He really changed. Shane grew into a very affectionate child . . . an easy child who was very loving.

Vicki Webcke

19

There came a day sometime in those early years when Dad caught a cab from Brisbane to Toowoomba after being away, and on arrival at home declared to Mum – much to her shock – that he was no longer in the navy. I think the fact that he was away from his kids and his family all the time eventually just wore him down.

Dad had been an engine driver through those navy years, and subsequently landed a job working with the steam boilers at the local hospital. We had two years at Highfield – a period of my life too early to be in my memories – before Mum and Dad bought a property outside Leyburn, an hour south-west of Toowoomba, heading towards Goondiwindi. Dallas was asthmatic, and the Toowoomba damp was doing him no good. Leyburn, warmer and drier, is a funny little place – a slice of Queensland where you've got genuine rich Darling Downs black soil plains which gradually become harder land – sheep country mainly, back then. It was there, on the tougher, wooded country, sandy country, that Tom and Vicki Webcke bought their couple of hundred acres, 2 or 3 kilometres out of town . . . and it was there that for us the really hard times began.

Because Leyburn is so much a part of me and my story I'll try to draw a picture of it for you. You certainly wouldn't class the country there as typical Darling Downs (i.e. rich and productive); I have always reckoned there were two distinct ways of looking at it. It is prone to drought (and, occasionally, bushfire) and you would reasonably call it 'poor' country if you were looking at growing something there – but it is very good country for sheep and, in places, for cattle. It is very good timber country, too, with its big parcels of state forest. But generally a farmer would need huge tracts of it to make it viable.

At its best the country around Leyburn is very pretty – and back in 1976, the Webckes struck it in its prime when they made their move. It had been a rainy year, and the country out there responds quickly and is truly beautiful when the rains arrive.

When it doesn't rain, it's bloody terrible. It gets dry and dusty very quickly and has built a bad reputation through people who have struck it like that, particularly in winter if there has been a bit of frost around. Then it can look pretty dastardly. But come springtime and a bit of rain and it is just absolutely beautiful; I think of it that way. I am not a fan of the black soil plains, productive as they are. I am a man who much prefers to be surrounded by the trees and Australian bush.

The small town of Leyburn itself is described in the tourist brochures as 'bursting with history', and includes the Royal Hotel, Queensland's oldest continually licensed establishment. The town itself has various claims to fame. Many years ago it was a stopping-off place for the bullock trains that travelled between Queensland and NSW. It stands at the centre of an old gold-mining area, which once drew many Chinese to the district, and there are still remnants of those days, sites of old diggings. In earlier times Leyburn had as many as 11 hotels – and if the railway hadn't by-passed the town and gone instead to Clifton, and on to Goodiwindi, who knows how much different it would be today? During World War II, there was a Liberator bomber base at Leyburn – and it was there, on the triangular runway system at the airstrip, that the first Australian motor racing grand prix was held, in 1949. These days the Historic Motor Sprint through the town's main streets attracts big crowds each August. Old buildings are dotted here and there, including the school I attended (built circa 1862). All these years on, the town is really thriving, with a lot more local industry than there was back then, including some big olive plantations and the beginnings of a wine industry. But it remains a quiet little hamlet and has found its niche in the scheme of things – especially among retirees who like a bit of country living without being too far from the city. I love the place.

Our move to Leyburn came at both the best of times and the worst of times. While the season of that big step was good and the land was in fine shape, there were other forces at work. It was the time in Australia when interest rates were gradually climbing up towards 19 and 20 per cent, a time when the price of fuel rose steeply . . . a time when it seemed that everything was changing. Once, a hard worker like my father would have made a fair living on his 200 or 300 acres. But all of a sudden, not any more. For the Webcke family, everything went a bit pear-shaped.

My overriding memory of my childhood years is of seeing my parents struggle – the whole time. It was never easy. My dad had had instilled in him a tremendous work ethic; he would work the socks off anyone I have ever known. But without being harsh, the truth was that he had no idea about money or financial planning or such things. Financially, he was a failure, and all the hard work, year after year, never really got him anywhere. He also experienced quite a bit of bad luck and too many dry seasons – and when you put the two things together, it added up to a never-ending struggle. I don't think Mum, a city girl, loved the life out there at first – although I think she *grew* to love it because it was our family home. When I think about Mum today, I know she appreciates the good things about country life, but back then she lived through too many hard times and bad experiences to have had any great affection for it. I can picture her now, on one of those freezing-cold winter nights at Leyburn, sitting in front of the old wood stove, reading a book. We had an old Crown Number 5 stove, which I remember produced beautiful roasts. On cold, wintry nights we'd get it to glow red and we'd sit up close and make toasted 'sangers' and just talk. Those memories are very happy ones.

It was a hard life – but for my children it created an awareness that life isn't easy and that you can't expect to get everything you want. The boys missed out on a fair bit when it came to the material things, but they understood. They had good lives there; they were free and could ride their bikes and roam wherever they liked. But as time progressed, things got harder – and when their dad had to go away to work it became a real struggle . . . really bad. The boys were very different, and it's interesting how they have gone completely different ways in their lives – and been successful. The way it used to be in those early days was if they were out doing something difficult, like carrying bags of oats, Dallas would get on the back end and Shane would be at the front . . . and Dallas would have one finger on it, and Shane would be doing all the work. Or Dallas would say, 'I'm just going to get a cup of tea' . . . or 'I'm just going to the toilet' and he would disappear . . . leaving Shane to do the work.

Vicki Webcke

In the midst of the struggle I remember good seasons at Leyburn, too, years when the rain came and Dad would grow hay and we'd have thousands of bales stacked up. The sheep and cattle would be fat and we'd make some money and everyone would feel good and look to the future with hope. But there just weren't enough of those years back to back. Yet I still think of life on the land as the most wonderful life you can lead. I love it now and I know I'll love it until the day I die – but the way things have got to today, it's just become too hard and too dangerous to think that living out a single dream, like working the sort of property that ours was, can be your livelihood.

We started out with cattle and progressed into sheep and some cultivation. But the going was hard, bloody hard, and for all the effort my parents put in, the farm was never really a viable business, especially when interest rates soared to unbelievable levels. It eventually got to the point where my father made the tough decision – that he had to go away and work to support his family. And that's what he did, taking on jobs that were some-times good and sometimes not-so-good – and being away for as long as two years at one stretch when I was just at the end of primary school years, between the ages of 10 and 12. But even that sacrifice – of him being away – got us nowhere. I remember Mum telling me later that in those two years they didn't get any further in front. Hardship was their life, a life that was essentially about survival. All these years later I still have issues about all of that, about the struggle and about my dad being away from home so much. He died young, and in some ways I don't feel I ever knew him, don't feel I ever knew his real story. I live with the certainty that I'll always carry an empty space in me because I never really got to know my father as a man.

I can picture him now – a man of about my own height, but considerably lighter than my 110 kilograms. He was a tough man and very, very strong, and that strength passed down to Dallas and me. I can remember Dad retrieving bogged cars and trucks with sheer strength. He was a man who was black and white in his opinions – with Tom Webcke there was no middle ground. He was outgoing and opinionated, and always happy to share his views.

Dad's hardness rubbed off on us boys, I suppose. There is a story told about me when I was a nine-year-old . . . of a day I drove a garden fork right through my foot, and was ready to keep on working. Dad was away at the time and I thought I'd do the right thing and go and dig the vegie garden, which I did – in bare feet. I was digging away industriously when suddenly the fork was stuck on something and I had trouble getting it out. What it was stuck on was my foot.

I couldn't get the fork out, so I called my mum, who in turn called the local policeman, Des Ehlers, who happened to be very good mates with the father of the girl who was years later to become my wife, Allison Knapp. So it was that Ally heard the story about the kid with the garden fork through his foot long before we ever met. The funny thing was, I wasn't feeling any

24

pain. It quickly progressed to a real country crisis, with the local schoolteacher arriving and then a nurse who lived in the town. Everyone rallied around, with me sitting there, and it never occurring to me that I needed to worry too much. Eventually a couple of them held my leg while someone else pulled the fork out. I went inside and washed my foot and the water was pouring straight through the hole. And everyone afterwards talked about how I hadn't cried and how brave I had been. Well, I can reveal that the only reason I hadn't cried was that it hadn't hurt. Trust me, there would have been tears if it had! There were no heroics.

Aspects of Shane's character that developed then are still with him today. He was a real workaholic – he just loved work – whether it was outside work or something to do with school. He was fastidious, and a real achiever. The two boys were just totally different characters. With Dallas it would be: 'It'll be right . . . I'll do it tomorrow.' But Shane could get overbearing at times because everything had to be right and in place and done correctly. Even as a youngster he had a lot of ambition. I always felt that he would be successful at whatever it was he took on. He had amazing drive in him. Always. From when he was very little he used to say: 'I am going to be a millionaire by the time I'm 30.'

Vicki Webcke

I know for sure that my dad left me a special legacy in the day-to-day example of the work ethic that underpinned his life. Of the things I learned from my dad and his life this was it – a message that has been such an important one, at the very foundation of my life. And I know that my brother Dallas has built his own successful career in the finance industry on the same quality; Dallas doesn't have to literally 'sweat' at that – but he'll 'put in', work 12 or 14 hours a day.

Mum and Dad were continuing their struggle to make a go of it at Leyburn at that time. Dad would work most of the day at the property, have three or four hours' sleep, and then drive off and work the night shift at the Warwick Woollen Mills.

There was a period in those hard, early days when Dad left us and went and worked on Nauru, the place that came into the public consciousness in Australia in more recent times when the federal government built a detention centre there. He worked with a phosphate company up there, training local people in running the powerhouse and other aspects of the operation. A family holiday we had on Nauru remains as a wonderful memory of my childhood. To get on a plane and fly off into the tropics was an amazing experience for a couple of primary school kids from the bush. It was a brief, happy respite as Mum and Dallas and I worked to hold things together on the farm.

Apart from that single trip to Nauru, holidays were never really part of our lives. There just wasn't the money. All I remember is one other year when we went over to the coast. Des Ehlers, the local policeman, had a holiday house at Coolum. He and his wife knew our situation and she offered to take us there for a break.

When Dad finally came home from Nauru, he brought back with him a drinking problem. My memories of the time that followed are really, really bad. I understand now that Dad had arrived at a critical point, a point at which he realised that the life he had was not amounting to much. Normally a happy man who would get up in the morning singing, he descended into some dark space and was at the pub almost every night. He looked the same – but he wasn't. He wasn't a very good drinker: he'd get very cranky, although never violent, and the way he was must have worn down my mum. That was a hard time for all of us. When I started to play footy I can remember going to games worried about the fact that Dad was coming along – just hoping he wouldn't drink too much that day and become loud and obnoxious and embarrass us. I remember those times too vividly, and because of them I have a real thing about my own drinking (and I'm a bloke who enjoys a beer). I don't ever want my kids to feel the way I did on some of those days. The worst thing of all about such days was that blokes would look at my dad, and you knew they were thinking he was a real prick. And he wasn't. He was a really, really good bloke and a wonderful father in so many ways. But he had a chink in his armour.

I suppose you could say there were other lessons I learned from my father in that time. It certainly became clear to me that the grog could be a dangerous and difficult thing, for one. And I think the experience of seeing my dad like that, and observing people's reaction to him, gave me a pretty good grounding and taught me not to be judgemental about people. Tom Webcke became the way he was in that period because of the hardship of a life that was such a struggle and which seemed to have no ray of sunshine at its ending. He had worked so bloody hard for so long . . . and got nowhere.

During the difficult times I quite often got away on my own, and walked for miles and miles. On Sundays when Mum and Dad went to the football, I'd sometimes stay behind, grab something to eat and a bottle of water – then head off. I loved being out-doors and I'd just walk along stock routes, across other people's properties . . . just tramping along, looking at the things around me and thinking. I wasn't walking to get anywhere . . . I was just walking. I loved it, and I still do today. It's wonderful therapy. Some days I would walk 15 or 20 kilometres. I suppose it was an escape. For a single afternoon I didn't have to worry about Dad and his problems, or worry about what he might do. I was alone with my own company, and I enjoyed that, enjoyed that it was just me.

Even today I wrestle with a bit of a hangover from that time. Whenever I have to go to a function I get this nervous anticipa-tion beforehand. And if I happen to take someone somewhere and they get start getting drunk, I can't be around that . . . can't deal with it. It takes me back to bad days and nights – and I promised myself I would never feel like that again.

Two excerpts from a scrapbook my mum prepared for my 21st birthday probably give some useful insights into the sort of kid I was and the things that interested me:

You loved books, country music, Wal and Cooch from Footrot Flats, *mowing,* Blake 7, Dr Who, *bread and butter pudding, the old song* Going to the Races Stealing Chicken, *which you boys would sing as you followed me around the kitchen trying to steal food, bananas, hard work, tractors, chopping wood, cattle, the farm, your pushbike, school, Mum and Dad sometimes.*

You were loving, happy, loyal, obsessed with being the best, neat, tidy, clean, talkative, couldn't keep a secret, bad-tempered, friendly, outgoing, a workaholic, active, athletic, opinionated, quick-witted, healthy, helpful, very strong, wilful, willing to learn.

Vicki Webcke

The good thing was that the bad times did not last forever, and my dad came through. As the fortunes of Australia started to pick up, so too, gradually, did those of my mum and dad. They were never going to be millionaires, but at least they came out of that period when it seemed there was never going to be any hope. Dad stopped drinking as much, and things were getting better.

Even when times were at their worst I always had a tremendous affection and admiration for my father. I never hated him, although at times probably I thought I did, for what he was doing. He had his failings and weak points, sure. But we've all got those. And when his life was cut short, I know it left a huge hole in my own, and many regrets. My mum remembers me from my days as a tiny kid as my dad's 'shadow' – wherever he went, I would follow.

I think it's sad that modern life doesn't always reward great effort. I doubt that the foot soldiers of the world – like my dad was – are valued as they should be. We need all sorts of people in society, from the dynamic ones who are leaders down to the workers. But the gap between them has widened. In my years as a footballer, I had the chance to live on both sides of the street, to mix with both ends of the spectrum. Today the rewards are much more likely to go to the smooth-talking dealmaker than to the worker doing his honest toil. Yet I think there is a certain decency, thoroughness and good-heartedness about being a hard worker; I treasure what I inherited and will be forever grateful to my parents for instilling it in me.

Dallas and I very quickly learned the value of a dollar – because we never had many of them. While we were struggling, people around us seemed to be doing tremendously well. But being poor teaches you to appreciate money, and be creative in doing what you can to get some. My brother and I would collect metal and cans and bottles, and whenever we went to town we'd cash that in, and that would be our little bit of spending money. Dad was a bit of a bottle collector from way back, and some days we used to hitch the trailer up behind the car and head out for the whole day, picking up bottles and any scrap metal we could find. It was probably my earliest introduction to the world of business – as a bottle-o and scrap-o, driving all over the bloody country-side picking up things.

On any day in town I would always feel for my mum. She'd go to the bank and inevitably spend a lot of time there. I'd wonder what she was doing . . . and know deep down that she was juggling credit cards and accounts and trying to come up with enough money just to buy groceries and the basic stuff. Through all of it Mum was the rock that kept us all together and kept us going. She was amazing.

But for all the ongoing struggle, life was a great adventure for a young bloke growing up in Leyburn. Unlike some kids, I loved my schooldays – to me they were absolutely wonderful. I used to ride to school on my bike from the farm, and along the way I'd pick up my best mate, Shaun Rauchle, and we'd gradually make our way to Leyburn State School. Progressively, we left earlier and earlier in the mornings. It was only a ten-minute ride to school, but it got to the stage where we'd take an hour and a half, having some wonderful adventures on our way there. A special favourite was to go via the town sawmill and ride through the part where they used to dump all the offcuts, and where it was *really* dusty. Boys being boys, we liked nothing better than to see the dust kicking up behind the bikes, and by the time we got to school, we'd be black. Getting home after school could be a slow process too, especially when the weather got warmer – much to the displeasure of my dad some days. There might be a hit of cricket on or Shaun and I might just head off on our 'pushies' and get lost in a balmy country afternoon. By the time I got home I'd be in strife, with Dad waiting and chores to be done. Dad milked the cows at the end of the day and it was Dallas's and my job to find them. They used to piss off all over the place, especially if they had been turned out onto the road for a feed, and sometimes it would take hours to round them up. I was like all kids . . . I got into strife now and then. At times Dallas and I fought like cats and dogs. My mother remembers me having a favourite saying, which I used whenever there had been a spot of bother: 'I was there, but I didn't do it!' Even today she reminds me of that now and again.

There are notes that remain of my primary school years . . . of me peeing in the sandpit (not exactly the done thing, I suspect), of Dallas and me having a fight in the school library one day and knocking over a row of shelves. Somewhere the fact is recorded that my name is the last to appear in the Leyburn State School Punishment Book of the time. An old school report remains. On Shane Patrick Webcke it records: Physical skills: 'Good catching and throwing skills'.

For all the ups and downs and the ongoing struggle, which are definitely part of my story, I had a wonderful childhood. Bad things happened and there were troublesome days – but the good things far outweighed them. We never had much, but when I think back on it, I know we had all the important stuff. Yes, there were little bits and pieces that I wish weren't there. But for the most part I have wonderful memories.

In the family collection is a poem I wrote when I was at Leyburn State School. I think it provides an insight or two:

I wake up on a crispy, sunny Spring
The screen door creaks open
I walk out onto the verandah
To experience the beauty and wonder of it
Inhaling the sweet, fresh odours of Spring

Now it is approaching lunchtime
Sun shining fresh Spring flowers
A delightful fragrance of flowering green peas
Swaying gently in the wispy breeze

Sunset is now upon me
Sensational brilliance of luminous ray
Shining across the sparkling water
What will the sunny Spring days bring me in the future?

Anyone surprised at the thought of Webcke the poet might be interested to know that as a young fella I also won a prize for floral arrangement at the Leyburn CWA Flower Show.

I especially loved my primary school years – although I have to say the enjoyment was mainly about the fun I had, not so much about the schoolwork. I was lucky enough to have some really good teachers, at a great little school. A teacher named Mark Henderson, who I met again years later in Brisbane, had a fairly big influence on me. He was a bit of a radical, but a positive bloke

– and I felt encouraged by him to be as good as I could be. He had the knack of making you feel you were worthy. He was a good teacher and I always felt I wanted to please him.

Probably what I remember more than anything from those early school years is the concerts we used to put on, and the plays. I loved them – and played the lead role in a couple of productions. I think I might have fancied myself as having a bit of a flair for the stage. I enjoyed any sort of role-playing. We would rumble down to the local CWA Hall to put on our show, and half the town would be there.

When I moved on to high school, it was a travelling life. If you were going to live in Leyburn (as we did) and go to high school in Clifton (as I did), it meant an hour and a half on the bus each way, each day. So for five years a lot of my life was spent on a bus, snaking its way between the two towns. I'd step onto the bus at 7.30 every morning and alight at 5 pm each afternoon. And the days started much earlier than 7.30 am for Dallas and me. Dad would have us up at 6 o'clock working, and we wouldn't get back into the house until about 10 past 7 – at which point there'd be a mad scramble to get ready for the bus. The culture that developed on the bus, the closeness, explains how that same group is today: the friendship and easy conversation flows even though we may not have seen each other for quite a time.

After school, especially in the summer months, we'd be back on 'duty' at the farm, rounding up the cows, milking them – and feeding the 25 or 30 poddies that we always had around the place. I can milk a cow as well as any man alive, I reckon . . . I had so much practice.

I have been all over the world playing footy, but the little town of Leyburn will always be my spiritual home. We buried my dad there, and I told my wife years ago that when my turn comes, that's where I want to be laid to rest too. The fondest memories of my life are out there. It is the place where it all began . . . the place where I truly feel at home.

High school years for me at Clifton were something of a mixture – enjoyable a lot of the time, but troubled to an extent too, and with an ongoing sense of discomfort. My father's problems with the drink extended into the early years I was at high school and I found it an uncomfortable time because of that ongoing worry. Apart from that, there was always something of a stigma attached to the kids from Leyburn . . . well, I felt that anyway, maybe more than others. Being poor represents some sort of stigma too, and the fact was, we Webckes were poor. Life didn't seem to be getting any better for the family – and I guess I just worried about what my own life might hold, having grown up with that year after year. Maybe all of it sounds a bit shallow now, but you don't know what being poor does to you until you have experienced it. Whatever the reasons, I felt somewhat inadequate throughout my high school years. The confidence I have now came later. Back then, amidst the enjoyment I took out of the friendships I had, there was an ongoing feeling of pressure and unease.

But I was lucky to go to a good school – one where I wanted to do well, and which gave me the opportunity to do well. Like most kids, I found out things about myself along the way – for instance, that I wasn't much good at maths and science. I was good at social subjects, like history and geography. And I loved English – absolutely loved it. Writing had never been a problem for me: from primary school days I could fill a page in an exercise book so fast that it wasn't even funny. When I started writing something it just jumped out of me, just flowed. At high school, I liked debating and public speaking and I tackled them with some relish.

But when I got to Years 11 and 12 there was pressure for me to push on with maths and science. So I battled with those subjects, and hated them, and my failure to grasp them undermined my overall confidence. Even though I got through – with a TE score of 885 or so – I know I could have done better.

He was a good student and up to a point he did his homework and the things he had to do. But he would drive us up the wall because everything had to be exactly right. And he was competitive in everything. I remember a day, earlier, in primary school years, when the teacher took them all down to the oval to do some exercises. The teacher stressed to the kids that it was in no way a competition – but Shane turned it into one anyway. And when it was all over he said, 'I beat everybody!' It was terrible.

Vicki Webcke

It was sometime during my last year at school, 1992, that the three paths of studies, work and the game of rugby league started to intersect.

Chapter 3

BAREFOOT, BAD-TEMPERED AND BRONCO-BOUND

The way my mum tells it, she first took me to the footy because I had an atrocious temper. She figured that if I played the game it might suck up a bit of my anger and energy. And out where I grew up, 'football' meant only one game – rugby league. I don't have a memory of my first match, but I'm told I was about seven when I first went along, on a day on which my brother Dallas, then nine, was playing. According to Mum I just trotted up and down the sidelines like a show pony on that morning and perhaps the next couple of Saturdays too, and didn't show much interest in playing. But one day in 1981, lost somewhere back in the mists of my mind, it started – at Clifton with the Allora–Clifton Bulldogs (later Wattles) JRLFC (Under 9s) in the Warwick District competition, which included teams from Warwick, Texas and Goondiwindi. We wore green and gold. And it all sort of just rolled on from that day . . .

I remember very well that very first Saturday morning. He just wasn't interested in playing. He put the jersey on and walked

35

around looking at himself. No way was he going to play . . . but he thought he looked pretty cute all the same. He liked the gear, but at the start he was pretty determined. It was a case of: 'I'm not going to play this game!'

Vicki Webcke

From that inauspicious beginning, and with kids from Leyburn making up a fair bulk of the teams, I went on to play season after season in the age group competitions. We didn't lose a premiership from the year I started to the year I finished (Under 16s). And in that final year, with a freakish group of foot-ballers, we won every game by 100 points or more, including the grand final by 102–2. Mum and Dad (when he was home) were great supporters. Mum was quiet . . . Dad wasn't. Apparently Dad was the biggest braggard around about his sons when the match was in progress. But when we came off the paddock it could be very different: 'How'd I play, Dad?'

'Oh, bloody terrible!' But as Mum said, he was very, very proud of us . . . he just didn't let us know.

He had a really hot little temper, Shane. He wouldn't harm anyone else, but he'd perhaps bang his head on the wall or punch the wall if he got frustrated with something . . . if it wasn't perfect. I sat him down one day and explained things: 'If you lose your temper on the field and do something silly, throw a punch or whatever and get sent off, you are going to let all your teammates down, and they are going to hate you.' Tom and I drummed into Shane the need for him to control himself on the field. I guess it's part of the reason that he developed into being so cool on the field. He learned control – and he learned it from an early age. I'm proud of him for that. Sometimes I've watched him playing football and he has seemed very cool when some 'incident' has happened – but I know what sort of a quiet boil is going on underneath the surface.

Vicki Webcke

We played most of our football on black soil ovals – and in the heart of a typical Darling Downs winter, through which it generally doesn't rain, they were bloody hard! And most Saturday mornings they were bloody cold too. As kids in the Under 9s and Under 10s we played early in the day, sometimes with frost still on the ground. It can get bitingly cold in that part of the world. Only last year we had a morning out there on which the thermometer registered –10. Oh, and back in those early footy days we played in bare feet.

He liked the front-row position from the start. And he played hard then, the way he has always done. One day when he was about nine and going through a little pious stage he said to me, 'Mum, I wonder what God thinks about me . . . because I go out and do terrible things to other players.' It floored me.

Vicki Webcke

I remember the things around my *early* football much more than I remember the games themselves. Playing football just happened to be what Dallas and I did in our winters, and to me all the things around the game itself were as much, or more, a part of the enjoyment. Leyburn to Clifton is about 30 kilometres, and we'd pile into cars after school and head off to training. The friendships I formed then are friendships for life. The blokes I played footy with out there – they will never not be part of my life. It goes back so far. There is tremendous comfort for me in that – that even though my life has moved in a different direction, I am still part of the community I grew up in. The memories that we shared together through rugby league – the parties we had, the car-pooling, the bus trips out to places like Gundy and Texas – they are priceless for me. Those are the things I remember so much more than the footy. The game was just part of the whole experience, and I never used to worry about it. I would just go out and play. I guess if it's fair to say that it happened that I turned out to be a pretty good footballer . . . well, I never intended to be. I was just happy to be involved. But that's not to say that once I did get into the game of rugby league I didn't want to be a winner. I have always been very competitive – with anything I took on. I think it's one of the main reasons why I enjoyed debating at high school, because it was a 'contest'. My mum remembers very clearly that even at primary school, if I was going to tackle something, I wanted to be the best at it. I wasn't always the best, but I wanted to be.

There were players in those junior days out there who were better than me. I think it's a common story – that it's not always the best players who get the opportunity to go on in sport . . . or who necessarily want to. And I have to say that in some ways I'm a bit envious of some of my mates from those days, all of whom have been reasonably successful and who lead these *other* lives, as chippies, and who are really happy. My own life is good too – but different. To the outsider looking in, the life of a professional rugby league player probably looks wonderful. And in many ways it is. I know that becoming a footballer has given me things in life that I never thought I would have. But it also robbed me of some of the things my mates experienced – the chance to grow up in an environment you love through the fun years of your late teens and into your 20s. Because I did it differently I had to bypass just about all of that, and when I reflect on it, I know I lost out a bit, lost something I can never recapture. I was there, of course, for bits and pieces of it – for the 21sts and special events. But I missed the Friday night gatherings at the pub and happy, regular occasions like that. But, of course, I had other things . . . the things I have here in Brisbane in my career as a footballer. And that's just life.

As a young rugby league player I was always a forward – even a hooker at one stage, I think. I was a goal-kicker too – a toe-poker – and it's amazing I didn't break my toes some days. You might imagine a very cold morning, and a hard cold football and a kid kicking with very cold bare feet . . .

Along with my best mate Shaun Rauchle, I was in the front row of all the teams through those years. We were big kids and I guess we built a pretty formidable pairing *because* we were bigger and were able to steamroll the kids we played against.

Rugby league was the game – always and exclusively. In summer there was a cricket team and a cricket comp, but I think the situation was that Mum and Dad couldn't afford for us to play both games (rugby league and cricket). And I don't think Dallas and I had all that much interest in cricket anyway. If we had been keen our parents would probably have found a way. I remember summer afternoons when Dad would be watching the Test match on TV – and all I wanted was to be outdoors, doing something. 'Dad, I don't want to watch the cricket – is there something I can do?' I'd ask. One such day he suggested I might go and start making some new gates for the farm. And that's how I became good at making wire gates. We had lots of little paddocks and eventually I replaced every gate. I would pile the gear on the old paddock-basher ute, put the radio on and head out and work. When it wasn't gates there was always something else to do. I didn't care how hot it was – that never worried me. Just to be 'out there' was what I loved.

I remember an afternoon when Shane's father was planning to watch the footy on the television, but Shane was much keener on the idea of getting out and doing some work around the farm. He was about 15. Tom had been wrestling with the problem of retrieving a huge tree stump, which he had decided to put in the garden. 'Watch this,' he said to me. 'I'm going to get him to take the truck and bring the stump home. That'll test his mettle!' A couple of hours later Shane was back with this huge, heavy tree stump on the back of the truck. Tom just looked at me and said: 'I haven't got a clue how he did that!' Even then Shane was as strong as an ox, and what he had done was nudge the stump up against a big tree and somehow gradually manouevre it onto the truck. And the thing was massive.

Vicki Webcke

For Dallas and me the league season stretched all the way through those hot summers too. Down in the front paddock we had a set of goalposts in place – and so the footy continued. If we weren't doing that we were either working (and Dad made us do plenty of that) or down at the dam swimming, and catching yabbies. But I loved my footy, and both Dallas and I were pretty good at it and couldn't wait for the season to come around.

Dallas was a better footballer than me – and that's not just me talking my brother up. Ask anyone out our way who saw us play, and they'd tell you that. He was a natural ball-playing sort of forward, taller and leaner than me. Geez he could play footy: he was one of those blokes who could do everything – kick the ball, make breaks, create play for the blokes around him. But in terms of 'sweating', he had no work ethic. He hated training, really despised it. And it's one thing I learned pretty early, that if you don't train, you can't succeed. He lacked (or chose not to have) the discipline you need to make it as a footballer. I believe my brother could have had the pick of wherever he wanted to play if he had decided to go on with it. But he hurt his knee, had to get a knee reconstruction and, being who he is, never really rehabilitated. Eventually he put on weight and that was the end of football. It was ironic; Dallas was one of those lucky blokes who could eat what he liked and do what he liked and always keep this beautiful lean build. In contrast, I always tended to get chubby if I ate the wrong sort of food. But one day it all sort of turned around. Dallas hurt his knee and put on a heap of weight. Meanwhile, I kept plugging away. He finished in football; I played on.

In those early days, before either of us toyed with the idea of going further in rugby league, it was just a game. The first time I remember thinking anything serious about it was when I went to the Under 12s Schoolboys Championships, in Cairns. But at the end of that tournament I didn't get picked for either the Possibles v Probables game or the Queensland side. It was from that time onwards that I had the belief firmly in my head that the absolute *pinnacle* of rugby league was to make a Queensland representative team. The way the system worked, the next opportunity to do that was in the Under 15s, and in the ensuing years I played on, with that thought at the back of my mind. When those years ticked over and the chance finally came, I had been playing some pretty decent football, and I thought, 'Righto . . . here's my shot.' But I missed out again, and when the Under 16s came around the next year and there was a Queensland representative club side to be picked, I didn't make that either, nor the Under 17s School-boys team the following year.

I have to say I was fairly shattered by then. A lot of my mates had been regularly making it into these teams and we were at the age when young blokes start getting it into their heads that maybe they are going to do something special as footballers. But through my own disappointment at not getting the call for even one of those teams, that was never, ever part of my thinking. I had no doubts; to go further in the game you had to be a Queensland rep player. It struck me that that was it – that Shane Webcke was going to play some football, for sure (because I enjoyed it), but not at any higher level. There was disappointment, yes . . . but acceptance too. I knew I could play the game – after all, I played first grade for Wattles out there at 15 or 16 – but it seemed to be the reality that I couldn't get to that next level. So I learnt to live with it. I had made my first-grade debut for Allora Clifton–Wattles against Oakey one day in the late 1980s. The opposition prop that day was a bloke named Darren Denman – and he deadset almost killed me.

My mind turned to other things. I was about to leave school and really my only concern was: I've got to go and get a job.

I always assumed that when Dallas and Shane left high school that would be the end of it as far as football was concerned. But they just kept going . . .

Vicki Webcke

I came to realise later that I was quite different from many of the blokes I ultimately did get to play football with. In talking to blokes like Gorden Tallis and Steve Price, I learned that football was *always* what they were going to do. There was never even a question mark in their heads about that. My thinking was not that way; the idea of playing 'serious' football never even entered my mind. It's probably what happens to many young blokes . . . you start to accept that you're not quite at the required level, and that's just the way it is. But I made local district sides – Toowoomba and South West – and came down to Brisbane a couple of times for annual state-wide carnivals and was happy to be part of that.

When I made a trip with the 17s to play at Lang Park, I think it was the first time that Cyril Connell, the longtime Broncos talent scout, got to see me play – and I can trace that occasion as some sort of 'beginning' to what was to follow in my life. It was directly afterwards that I was invited to go to a Broncos camp at Leslie Dam, just outside Warwick. That was the first time I met Wayne Bennett; I remember him pulling me aside and asking me a few things about myself. He had seen me play, I know, in the Under 18 Grand Final at Toowoomba – when Steve Price played for the other side. After the camp at Warwick, I got a call from the club and they told me they were awarding me a scholarship of $1500 to help towards my education, plus some Broncos gear – and I thought: 'What the hell is this?' I was still a minor, a Year 12 student, so Dad had to sign the agreement for me – and the document remains a treasured possession that I still have tucked away somewhere at home. The year was late 1993, and it remains the only thing in my football career which involved my dad. For that reason it is extra special to me.

There is a story that is not very well known about my career, that even before the establishment of that first link with the Broncos I had trialled with Eastern Suburbs (the Roosters) in Sydney at a time when Mark Murray was coaching. Mark spoke to my mum, but it came about originally through a bloke named Jack Evans, who lived in Leyburn and who happened to be connected to Easts. He made a phone call to someone at the club and arrangements were made for me to travel to Sydney for a trial, at Henson Park, along with my brother Dallas, Danny Nutley (later bound for Cronulla Sharks) and halfback Paul Green. As it turned out, I hurt my leg in the first five minutes of the game . . . and for me that was the end of that as far as the Roosters were concerned. Part of the experience of the week was to attend a camp at Narrabeen, on Sydney's north side, and it was there that I first met the legendary coach Jack Gibson, who I learned later had had a big influence on Wayne Bennett's career. I remember being very impressed with the man who by then was reputed to have totally revolutionised rugby league coaching – but for no greater reason than that Jack had a Landcruiser station wagon! When I was growing up I had a thing about Landcruisers . . . I thought they were just the most unattainable thing I could ever possibly set my sights on. When I saw Jack roll up to Narrabeen in his, I knew for sure: right here was an important man. These days I have a Landcruiser ute and a Landcruiser wagon. Funny how the world works.

My other memory of my brief experience with the Roosters was of fitness guru Ron Palmer, who is still with the club today, flogging the guts out of us at the Narrabeen Fitness Centre. I had my defeatist attitude well in place back then, so even though I was happy to be down there, I remember thinking: 'Nothing is going to come of this.' When it came to taking the next step in football, I had been to the well a few times already by then and never had the chance to drink. I wasn't going to get too excited about it. Anyway, the way the dice fell, I didn't become a Rooster. I came home and they rang me a few days later to say thanks for coming down . . . and that was the end of it.

Reflecting on that early show of interest from the Broncos and the Roosters I can reveal here that my team was . . . Balmain! My brother loved the footy and my dad liked to watch it too, but honestly, I wasn't that passionate about it. When there was a game on TV they'd be in the house watching and I'd generally be outside, doing something around the place. My interest in Balmain came about mainly through the Tigers' long-haired front rower Kerry Hemsley, a bloke who rode a Harley Davidson and was a bit of an offbeat character. I used to think he was a *great* player. He possibly wasn't that at all – but he was a wild bugger and I liked him.

As for the Broncos? Well . . . I had no emotional attachment to them at all.

They were formed in 1988, and until that time the kids up here used to wear Brisbane club jerseys. The Brisbane comp was strong then and Queensland kids used to identify with it ahead of the Sydney clubs. We Webckes never had enough money to buy jerseys, but I used to lust after the Wests and Norths (Brisbane) jumpers that some of my better-off mates had. When I think back, I didn't really follow any Sydney or Brisbane club, apart from that interest I took in Balmain, sparked by Hemsley. But I loved *playing* rugby league, and I thought then (as I do now) that it's a wonderful game. I was never much of a watcher, and I'm still that way today. Later, when football became my day-to-day occupation I didn't watch much either – because it was now 'work', and even watching a match I would get the feeling of apprehension and nervous tingling that happened when I was playing. I couldn't separate myself from that – so most of the time, I just didn't bother.

1991 was a funny time in my life. I now had my scholarship with the Broncos, but football had only ever really been in the equation as something I did (and enjoyed) at weekends. Confronting the future, you could say I was mixed up . . . caught somewhere in the middle of competing forces. I know in my heart now that all I ever wanted to do in my life was be a farmer. But if peer pressure ever played a major part in my life it was back at that time when I was finishing school. If you were trying to be a popular kid it sure wasn't cool to say you were going to head back to the farm, when everybody else was planning to get away and do other things. To be honest, all I had ever experienced of the farming life was how tough it could be. How could I expect to make a living out of that when my dad couldn't manage it? I asked myself. I convinced myself to accept that I wasn't going to do the one thing I really wanted to do . . .

Towards the end of 1991 I was wrestling with all of this. Not really having a clue where I was heading, I applied for – and was accepted into – a communications course that was a path towards journalism. I think it was the University of Queensland. But almost straight away the realisation hit me hard that I really didn't want to go to uni. By then I had had a gutful of school. I wasn't an indoors sort of bloke and the thought of another three or four years studying just didn't appeal to me. Two years before, Dallas had finished school and joined the ANZ Bank. Maybe that influenced me as I agonised over the question: 'What am I going to do now?' So the kid who really wanted to be a farmer and was also drawn towards journalism and writing went and applied for, and got, a job with the Westpac Bank in Clifton. To this day I don't really know why, except that Australia didn't seem to be quite the prosperous, stable place it is today, and to have a solid job, something sound to build your life on, seemed really important.

For the next two years of my life I woke up every morning thinking: What the hell am I doing working in a bank? They paid me about $200 a week, which was barely enough to scrape by on, especially as by now I had an old Valiant sedan, which ate up most of the money. I started out in data processing, worked my way up into handling vouchers and then became a teller. They were my two 'lost' years . . . how I hated that time.

The old Valiant was the joy of my life throughout, despite what it cost me in petrol and repairs as I trundled the 30 kilometres daily from Leyburn to Clifton and back. The car had belonged to my brother and he had painted it blue, but it eventually turned a shade of purple, with the paint falling off. So I'm loath to admit it, but for a short time I had a purple Valiant. It was an awful-looking thing, but I had a mate who did up cars and we got to work and dolled it up and painted it white. One day Dallas borrowed it and the white bonnet flew off and was damaged. Needing the car for work, I had no choice but to put the old blue/purple one back on. So for a time I'd chug to work each day in this white car with a crook bonnet – not a good look – and with the thing eating up most of the $200 per week that the bank paid me.

But I was playing footy and loving that, and it all changed for me on a particular day – or night, to be strictly accurate – as life can. A bank teller with a particularly crook-looking old Valiant went one Saturday night in Leyburn to the 21st birthday party of the brother of a great mate of mine. It was there that I met Allison Knapp, from Brisbane. I didn't realise it instantly, but my life was about to take a brand new direction.

Chapter 4

THE GIRL WHO LED ME TO BRISBANE

It was a story that lived within our family: sometime on the first evening Tom Webcke was introduced to Vicki Yule at the Texas Tavern he posed the question: 'So, when are we going to get married?' I can reveal that I put exactly the same question to Allison Knapp on the morning after we first met in 1992. Now I realise that in cold print that doesn't read too well. It sounds like we had spent the night together, but it wasn't that way at all. We just happened to have met up at one of those old-fashioned country parties in shearing sheds where people came from all over the place and the party went very deep into the night and the bulk of them stayed over. I admit that the setting for the question I posed to Allison wasn't all that flash. In fact, I was sitting on the bonnet of my car at the time, swinging my legs. And Ally's reaction? Well, she just laughed and joked about it . . . and we kept on talking. I was smitten from the moment I met her, and it remained that way . . .

For me the meeting was a life-changing event in many ways.

Not long afterwards I was transferred in my job to Brisbane; to anyone looking on it seemed like a straightforward work arrangement. But the secret was that Allison was living in Brisbane and I organised the transfer specifically so I could chase her! I kept that pretty quiet – so the emergence of the news now will probably come as some sort of revelation to my mates. Over the years it has been pretty much taken for granted that I moved to Brisbane because of football. Well, it wasn't the bloody footy, I can promise you that. If Ally hadn't been working there I wouldn't have gone and so wouldn't have got to play for Brothers. Maybe I would never have taken the path I did – to the Broncos. I came to Brisbane for her – no way would I have made the move willingly otherwise. I suppose it's a classic example of the sort of things that shape our lives.

By that time a few of the blokes from around Leyburn way had moved to Brisbane and were playing some footy with Brothers club. Graham Quinn, a renowned centre who had played for Brothers before starting a long career with St George in Sydney, and who had represented NSW, Queensland and Australia, was coaching the (Brothers) Under 19 side then – and I linked up with them.

I was still part of the Broncos' scholarship program, and when I made the decision to move to Brisbane I rang Cyril Connell and let him know of my plans and of the fact that I was going to have a game with Brothers. One afternoon not long afterwards, Cyril and Wayne Bennett came out to Lang Park to watch the Under 19s play. It was one of my early meetings with the coach and the man who was to have such an influence on my career and life.

I was living in Brisbane then, sharing a place with my mates – and in absolutely terrible shape. We got paid fortnightly, so in the first week we'd live on pizza and beer, and on the second, short on cash, we'd eat noodles and drink water. It was a boom and bust economy – every fortnight. As you might imagine, I was in really bad nick – and yet in my football, even then, I always used to do a bit more than just the organised training. I'd do some running on my own, some extra stuff. Even though I'd sunk fairly low in terms of expectations and being competitive – I was a slob, to be honest! – the old work ethic carried me through. I never missed training and the extra work I did helped get me through, despite the lifestyle and diet. But I was overweight, and a long way short of what I could have or should have been.

The day that Cyril and Wayne came down to the ground it must have been an interesting spectacle. Cyril used to like telling the story that someone would whack me in a tackle and for the next five minutes I'd go nuts and chase the bloke and try to get square – and then I'd be so buggered I'd do nothing for the next ten minutes. It was the boom-bust pattern again!

I played right through the year with Brothers and had a taste of all three grades (colts, reserves, firsts), and at the end of the year the Broncos called me in and virtually said, 'Well, do you want to have a go?' I wasn't expecting anything really, but I said, 'Yeah' . . . and they gave me a two-year deal. I remember going home and telling my mates: 'You're not going to believe what happened today.'

To sign the contract, I had to go into the Broncos' office at the old club at Red Hill, before the renovations. Wayne (Bennett) was there and Kelvin Giles (the conditioner) – and I was *shitting* myself. But Wayne is such a good bloke, as I was to discover, and he did his best to make me feel comfortable, asking me questions about the farm, and stuff like that. I was probably in a bit of a daze and I don't remember too much about that morning, although I do remember Kelvin Giles saying to me at one stage, 'Stand oop!' (he was a Pom), 'Turn around' and then, 'Geez you've got a fat arse . . . we'll get rid of that!' As I was to find out, Giles was a bloody hard taskmaster . . . one of those sergeant-major types.

To be honest, I didn't really know Wayne Bennett from a bar of soap in those brief early meetings, and he could have been feeding me any old crap that morning. But right from the start I felt a rapport with him, felt he was a man I could trust. I had no idea of the magnitude of his reputation either. I wasn't a young bloke who bought *Rugby League Week* magazine . . . mainly because I couldn't afford to. I was about as far removed from being a footy nut as anyone can be. It was around that same time that league journo Tony Durkin wrote about me for the first time in *Rugby League Week* after the 17s carnival, calling me a 'player of the future'. It's funny how the ball bounces; Durko has now been Media Manager at the Broncos for years, and we are good mates. The contract, I think, was for $2500 the first year and $5000 the second, and, oh boy, that was a nice little top-up for a rookie bank teller and the son of a struggling farm family.

Needless to say, my mates and I celebrated in the usual way – trekking down to the pub to buy some cartons and some rum, and then home for a drink. But even at that point, even after being given some recognition as a footballer, I still struggled . . . still had no expectation deep down of going any further. And when my first season with the Broncos began, 1994, I just couldn't get comfortable – because of this feeling that I shouldn't really be there – and that belief bloody well held me back . . . it really did. I'd look around the senior blokes, some of whom were or had been wonderful footballers, and I'd think: What the hell am I doing here in this company? I was constantly uncomfortable.

But even in the midst of all that uncertainty I came up with a plan: notwithstanding my doubts, I had been handed an opportunity and it was up to me to give it my best shot. Unfortunately, this just had the effect of heaping more pressure on me, and for those first six or seven rounds of the season I played terribly. My overriding thoughts were that I didn't want to make a fool of myself, and that I would try my guts out. And I did – tried so damned hard that I choked myself. And it just doesn't work when you're that uptight with desire to do well. Making it more difficult was that I still didn't really know what it took to be a footballer.

I was 19, going on 20, and arrived at the club a well-upholstered 123 kg (which they smashed off me pretty quickly!). I was a young country bloke without confidence. The additional ongoing problem I faced, of getting away from work at the bank at Milton to train, only added to the pressures I was feeling. Training started at 5 o'clock and work at the bank finished at 5, and it was quite difficult for them to let me get away. I remember a particular afternoon when I did manage to slip away early enough to make it on time for one of the team sessions, at The Gap – a notoriously tough training venue. The Gap is a reservoir that used to supply some of Brisbane's water, and around it there are running trails snaking through the state forest. This day I was scared to the point of being gutted. I wasn't scared of the training itself, I was just deadset scared of going there, and the thought developed in my head that if I arrived a bit later and they had started, at least I wouldn't have to stand around and worry about who I was going to talk to. That is the way I used to think back then. I could have easily been there at 5 o'clock that day – but I took it slow, so I didn't have to worry about who I was going to talk to! To some of the people who know me now this little story will sound unbelievable. But it's true – I just didn't feel like I belonged.

That day we did a bloody hard hill run, up a steep slope through the bush for about 1 kilometre – and onto the dam wall. And I couldn't do it; I had to stop and walk up. Later on, when I really got down to it, I could smash that run. But at that point in my career I had no idea about what it took to push yourself. My mind just told me I was buggered. And so I walked.

The whole experience of suddenly becoming part of a trail-blazing professional club like the Broncos came as a huge shock to me. The thing that saved me was the bit of extra training work I had regularly put in. I was pretty terrible to start with, but if I hadn't been doing that extra stuff I would have been *abysmal*. I think that the blokes who had always had it at the centre of their lives that they were going to be footballers would have had a pretty fair idea what to expect. I didn't have a bloody clue – had never given it a thought. I just rocked up there . . . and learned a hard lesson. I would have to say that at that early moment in my career I had a bad ethic about football almost because I was scared to have a good one.

I had no mates at the new club and the early weeks were very awkward for me. I am not by nature a shy bloke; I make friends fairly easily. But it seemed that for that first, short period with the Broncos, before the shocking event that was to separate the first part of my life from anything that would ever follow, I just froze. I had the nervousness of anyone starting a new job. But it went on far too long and I just couldn't get my head around what I had taken on.

It was when all of that was going on in my world that my dad was killed – in the early morning hours of the winter solstice of 1994. June 21.

I have two parts of my life. One ended with a phone call that morning . . . and the other began. In any assessment of my story you can draw a strong line in the sand – between the years before that date and the years since. It is always through the prism of that line that I see my life.

Chapter 5

THE WORST DAY OF MY LIFE

My father Tom was killed in a work accident a few hours after the third State of Origin match of the 1994 season. Ally and I were together by then – living in a little flat at Ascot, which we shared with my mate Shaun Rauchle's brother Dene. We had watched the game on television – Mal Meninga's last for Queensland – and seen NSW take the series with a 27–12 victory. At 4 o'clock the next morning the phone rang and I answered it.

It was my mum . . .

You just know that when the phone rings at that time, chances are it's going to be something terrible. It was. 'Your dad's been killed at work,' Mum said. When I put the phone down I was just howling. I think when you're young, as I was then, you don't really believe that people die . . . especially your father . . . it's just not part of your thinking. And my dad had died in a terrible way – crushed in a wool press at the place he was working then, the woollen mills at Warwick. It was a production line accident – a hydraulic line gave away and he was crushed. Thankfully, he died instantly.

For as long as I live, I'll never forget that night. We threw some things into the car in the pre-dawn and headed out of Brisbane. Allison drove – because I was in no shape to do anything. She cried, and I cried, all the way home, and the more so when we arrived and I saw my poor mum. What followed was the toughest and worst day of my life . . .

I had to go over to Warwick and begin the funeral arrangements, because my brother couldn't do it and Mum was certainly in no shape to. There was a funeral to be arranged and a casket to be selected and all of those things that I had never thought about. I was 19 years old, and it was just horrific. Making it even worse was the innuendo surrounding the circumstances of his death, issues that had to be dealt with concerning the way he died. There was speculation about safety factors at the plant and my dad's death, resulting from a work accident, automatically required a coroner's inquest.

Finding words to talk about it even now is very hard for me. There are feelings harboured down very deep inside me that I know will always be there. I will never forget that period in my life . . . the pain of that time will always remain.

The day Dad died is the day that separates the two distinct time periods of my life. There are the first 19 years . . . and then all that has followed. The day of his death was the day I grew up, became suddenly much older than I had been. All of a sudden things that had seemed important to me were no longer that way. I grew up, because I had to – because now there were people who needed me and depended on me, especially my mum.

We buried Dad in the cemetery at Leyburn, followed by a wake, and people came from all around to pay their respects. Wayne Bennett drove out from Brisbane to the funeral – a mark of the sort of bloke I already knew he was. He didn't have to do that – I was a nothing player at the club, after all. The first phone call I made after I got the news from my mum had been to him. 'Wayne, my dad's been killed; I have to go home and I don't know when I'll be back,' I told him.

'You just go,' he said.

The funeral in the little Catholic church at Leyburn was a massive event, with the building packed to the rafters. Through my tears I was so proud that day. I used to worry about what people thought of him because of the problems he had had. And perhaps there were those who thought badly of him. But even they had known him as a friendly man and a generous one. Through his life Dad had had nothing to give but himself, so he had done that. He was a really, really good man, but like most of us in life, he'd had issues which he'd struggled to deal with. On that day people came from everywhere. I have only one regret about the funeral: that I didn't speak, didn't at least try to share some of the things I was feeling about him. But I couldn't do it then and the three of us, Mum, Dallas and I, just sat there and cried. Today it would be different, I think. I have matured and today I can write the words that convey the way I was feeling. I would love to have done it then.

We buried Dad a kilometre out of town. Dallas and I lingered and were the last to leave . . . and then we walked back together. It was something important we shared. We were really close as brothers. Essentially, he was my best mate as a kid. Maybe I was his. I guess that day we just needed a bit of time together to mull it all over, so we walked slowly together into town and talked as cars carrying the mourners drove past. People later commented on that – on the pair of us on that walk. And they saw it as very sad. But for us it was therapeutic, the chance for two brothers to take stock of the reality of the present and the future. We took our time and yarned, and I remember it still as one of the really good moments in my life – something I treasure.

We went to the local, to the Royal, and had an almighty drink, which lasted long into the night. Someone put a hat on the bar and people just kept chucking money into it. All my mates were there and it was almost a celebration, and in part at least I reckon that's how a wake should be. I laughed and I cried and it was a beautiful way to nail it all down. People kept coming up to me with their own little stories about Dad – giving me a broader picture, which helped my own understanding. As sad a night as it was for us, there was happiness too in all those good things I heard about my father. Funerals are about saying goodbye and the stories people tell are the most important things, putting the life being remembered into perspective. It's funny about that day. It was a horrible one . . . but ultimately a happy occasion too, thanks to that very special night. At the end of it, I felt we had said goodbye to Dad in a way he would have approved of.

Ally eventually headed back to Brisbane, to work – and for five, maybe six, weeks after my father's death, I stayed on with Mum at the farm. There was work to be done, sheep and cattle to be looked after – and as if in some sort of daze, the pair of us, my mother and I, went about our daily duties. Then one morning she said to me: 'You've got to go back.'

'Mum, I don't want to . . . why should I go back?' I argued. 'I am not going anywhere with my footy.'

'You can't stay here,' she said. 'What is there here for you?'

'But what will you do if I go?' I asked her.

'Don't worry about me,' said my mum. 'I'll be all right. You must go back.'

This was a bad time for him. He really wanted to give it all up and come back to Leyburn. I had the devil's own time convincing him otherwise. 'Stay, by all means,' I told him at the start. 'Give yourself only six weeks or so but use that time to think about your life. The best thing you can do is to do your grieving and to think about things and to never forget – and then to get on with your life. You have to accept that sometimes things happen and you cannot change them.' He saw that I needed help – and I was struggling and did need some help for a time. But eventually I said to him: 'You must go and live your own life. You are not coming home here. Go . . . and don't worry about me; I'll be fine.' The club (the Broncos) was wonderful. They gave him the space and the time he needed.

Vicki Webcke

The shocking suddenness of it all was the worst thing. My dad was 47 when he died and I never even had the chance to say goodbye. The saddest coming to terms of all for me then was accepting that I would never get the chance to know him any better than I knew him at that moment. And the cruellest cut was that life at that time was just starting to look a bit better for Mum and Dad – with signs that they would keep on getting better.

In the aftermath of my father's death I used to have these little fantasies that had he lived and if it happened that my footy career kicked on, I would have been able to pay off some of his debts and get him a nice car. For me it would have been a wonderful thing to be able to do that for him. In my growing years I couldn't wait to get to the age at which I started earning money and could help Mum and Dad. I'm still dirty that I never got the chance to do it for him. Another thought that nags me is how happy I'm sure he would be if he could walk back into our lives now – and see how things are for the three of us, Mum, Dallas and me. It is a positive thing, that each one of us has got on so well with our lives . . . and I'm sure that knowledge would make him immensely proud.

Perhaps the best way I can put it is that at the time his father died, Shane lost his youth. He became a man. I think when death touches a young person like that it can be either make or break. With Shane, it made him, and in the period that followed, he developed a differ-ent outlook on life. In the years that have followed he has helped me

immensely – but there are also many kind and generous and bene-
volent things he has done for others that no one knows about . . . and
I am under strict instructions never to say anything about them. I
think he always had the ability and ambition in him to do what he
has done. But Tom's death was the profound turning point in his life.
Vicki Webcke

Mum was so adamant with her words urging me to head back
to Brisbane that I went . . . reluctantly, and with a feeling that
I was deserting her. Dallas had already returned to Brisbane
and his career, but my own return was with a heavy heart . . . and
dragging feet.

I was a different person, even physically. I hadn't eaten well in
the period since Dad's death and had lost heaps of weight. I went
back to training not really giving a rat's arse about footy. I just
didn't care about it. But the funny thing was that in being that
way, I relaxed and started playing really well in those late rounds
of the 1994 season. I had a sort of fatalistic approach to football
and life. My attitude was pretty much: 'What happens will happen
. . . nothing can possibly occur now that will hurt me any more
than what I have been through.'

There was a night when I hit rock bottom. I found during that
period that whenever I had a few drinks with the boys I started to
get cranky – something that had never happened to me before.
One evening a few of us went out to a club and in the course of
the drinking that was taking place I tipped a drink over Allison
when someone bumped into me. I turned around and saw what
I had done and saw that she was crying . . . and didn't do a thing.
She ran out of the place. And I didn't even follow her. I just stayed
there and drank and drank. I finally stumbled home at 5 o'clock
in the morning and I was buggered . . . just gone, physically and
emotionally. During the next day we just sat around and talked
and things gradually unfolded, and I think maybe the scales fell

from my eyes. I changed that day. There was a moment when I realised *something* had to change in me or I was going to lose her. It hit me hard. I knew that if I carried on with the sort of shit of the night before, she would be gone. Ally by then was tremendously important in my life. That day was a sort of a watershed for us – the day when I woke up – and as a result of it I knew I was going to be with her forever.

My mum had been right in herding me back to Brisbane. Those were tumultuous times for the Webckes – and in the months and years that followed we all changed, Mum, Dallas and me. And, I believe, for the better, somehow managing to take strength from the dreadful blow of Dad's death. What my mum has achieved from the day Dad died to now represents an enormous change. Her life had been one of sacrifice in so many ways, a tremendously difficult life of sadness and hardship. There are many stories around her: first, her father, her mother and her brother all died of cancer. And her life as the 'rock' of the Webckes was never less than hard, and she made all kinds of sacrifices to ensure that Dallas and I had the right education, and could play the footy we enjoyed so much. I have seen photos of my mum when she was a teenager, her face shining with the expectation of what, perhaps, lay ahead for her. Instead it turned out to be a life about as hard as you could possibly imagine and one with far too much tragedy. I think of those photos and then I think of the way it became – the sadnesses, the jobs she had, the things she had to do, the clothes she had to make do with. But it has been fantastic the way she has risen above all the things that have happened to her. The person who struggled through all that hardship has somehow come out the other side and built a new life for herself. I think her journey has been both amazing and inspirational.

The wonderful thing is that for all the hardship she endured, and all the difficult times, Mum does not in any way hold a grudge against my dad. She simply says, 'He was your father and what we went through we were in together.' Honestly, she stood by him through some horrible stuff. But from her today there is no hint of ill-feeling. She is a person of true grit and there's not enough of it in the world today. She lives out there still, in Leyburn, and loves it. She won't ever leave. She has friends there, she's comfortable there – and she takes comfort, I imagine, from the fact that I've kept that old home territory as a big part of my life and that we will be out there in future. My mother went through a terrible couple of years after Dad's death, then set about reshaping her life in a way I really admire. She did all sorts of things, including picking broccoli, and when she worked as a cleaner at three different schools, she learned that she really loved working with kids. They offered her a teacher's aide position, which she accepted – at which point she headed off to do a computer course and then to do the various levels of the teacher's aide training program. She was nominated for trainee of the year after completing a higher level in 2004. Mum found the thing in life that she was born to do and became a completely different person because of it. Working with kids, she says, keeps you in great shape and keeps your head going. She loves getting up each day and going to work.

Mum and I are close, and we have talked often about the way it was, and the way it is. Deep down I sometimes think, I wish Dad was here to see this, and then I wonder whether there would have been anything much left to see. And I have said to Mum, I don't want to sound horrible, but Dad dying was the catalyst for so much good that has happened in our lives. Maybe the things that have happened would have happened anyway. I don't know. All I do know is that Dad's death was a defining moment for us all – Dallas as much as Mum and me. My brother is enormously successful now. He wasn't back then. He struggled, he wasted money – and like me the successful building of his life didn't happen straight away. But for the three of us – separately and together – gradually our lives have strengthened and grown. Of the three of us, Mum is the one who has done the most. My success might be more public, but hers is bigger. It is quite amazing. And it is probably a bloody silly, romantic notion, but a nice thought – that in a way it is the legacy Dad left us.

Dad would feel his life was one of worth if he could see what he gave to me and my brother. Without doubt the work ethic that underpins my life comes from him. And he was a great reader (as is Mum), and I have inherited that love of books, and they are an important part of my life. My father would read a novel from cover to cover in a couple of days. The natural strength that I have and which helped my football career also came from him.

I would think of my dad before I play football. Over the seasons I have had this little ritual which involved Dad. I guess it waned a little bit as the years passed and I got on with my life, but he's still there in my mind. I grew up in a Catholic family and I am quite a spiritual person – although I have my reservations about organised religion. But I believe in the good things that religion is about. Before the Broncos played I would say a little prayer to God, asking that He keep us all safe. And I'd add a little bit more: 'Dad, if you can help . . . let me play well.' For a long time before the start of any big game I would look to the skies and think of my father. And I would wonder: 'Can he see me?'

Back then in the summer of '94, as my life underwent its big change, I gave up my job at the bank and began working for the QE2 Sports Club – the club that operated under QE2 Stadium, then the home of the Broncos.

When Shane told me he was going to leave the bank and play football . . . I suppose you could say that was pretty much a parent's 'Aaaagh!' But I was never going to stop him. 'Do what you think is right,' I told him. I knew by then that whatever he did, he would be all right. If he failed at football, he'd go and do something else and he'd be fine.

Vicki Webcke

I got myself into a nice little routine of looking after my job at QE2, training hard and finding enough time to go back home and help Mum on the farm. Something clicked in me during that hot Brisbane summer, and I decided I was really going to get into shape. I started to train harder than I ever had in my life. I knew where we were going to train as a team and I went out and ran the bastard every week, sometimes twice a week. By the time of the first session of the year I was really in shape.

The place was, of course, The Gap, which I mentioned before, and which, with its lung-busting hill, is a big part of the Broncos story. I suppose it became a sort of symbol for me back in those days. If I could conquer The Gap, well . . . I figured I could conquer first-grade rugby league. Journalist Mike Colman wrote in the *Sunday Mail* years later: 'Webcke, on his own, on his "days off", drove out to The Gap and ran (Wayne) Bennett's torture course. Day after day, week after week. He didn't tell anyone, just went out and did it.' And that's pretty much the way it was.

It is right there that my football career began. It stands as another one of those separation points in my life. Up until then I had played football. Now, I was ready to *become* a footballer. Now I knew what it took to be fit and to be part of it. They graded me in reserve grade for 1995 and that in itself was a big deal for me. Halfway through the year I made first grade. I was on my way . . .

Those 1994 memories of 'first contact' with the Broncos are pretty fractured, as you can imagine, considering the events of the year. I had joined a club full of star players – the likes of Allan Langer, Glenn Lazarus, the Walters brothers Kevin and Kerrod, Steve Renouf, Wendell Sailor – and yet in those days there was a separation between the elite players and the rest. Today we have the 'Top 30' – so there is regular interaction among the players. In '94 there was virtually none – and especially so for a bloke like me. I had waltzed into the place meaning nothing to them . . . and essentially they were nothing to me. The first time I ever had anything to do with the (first-grade) side was the day in '95 that Wayne told me I was in the team. That, I can tell you was a very harrowing experience.

It was almost a year from the day my father died that I first ran out on the field in a first-grade match with the Broncos. June 18, 1995 was the milestone date – and I can report that on that rather historic (for me) Sunday afternoon at ANZ Stadium I disappeared from the game very early indeed and Illawarra gave us a 34–18 caning. Great start! A couple of rounds earlier I had received a late call off the bench for the final ten minutes or so of the (first-grade) match against the North Sydney Bears at North Sydney Oval, providing my first, brief taste of the top grade. Just about the only thing I can remember of that experience is being back in the dressing room afterwards and thinking, What the heck's going on here? I got changed quickly and went straight to the reserve-grade bus. I was much more comfortable there.

But things had been going well. Ivan Henjak was our reserve-grade coach and my form had been good and I knew it. As I mentioned, I had accepted during the off-season, in what was almost a revelatory moment for me, the things you had to do to be a good footballer. The hard work I had put in through that off-season into the pre-season had set me up to play well and I had started the year with a bang. I remember one of Ivan's early team sheets carrying the note: 'You are playing to first-grade standard. You will get your chance.'

Yeah, good . . . whatever, I thought. Being the way I was, I still didn't hold great hopes – even though it seemed I was only an inch or two away from taking the next step.

But then, the day came . . .

I remember the moment so well that I can nominate the spot at our training ground where Wayne Bennett walked up to me. 'How are you going?' he asked me and we engaged in the blah, blah, blah of some small talk. And then he said to me – and he might deny it but this is deadset what he said – 'Well, you're in first grade this week – don't stuff it up.'

I was so nervous that the training run that followed was a nightmare. Back then Benny (Wayne Bennett) had a habit of peppering young blokes at the training sessions. 'If you're not going to talk you can go back to reserve grade' – just stuff like that, putting the pressure on. It's just his way (although he's mellowed a bit in more recent years) . . . and it works. Anyway, about halfway through the session I started feeling really sick. To this day I don't know whether it was nerves or whether I had something wrong – but I was really crook in the stomach and somewhat sheepishly I had to excuse myself from training and head for the toilet. 'Mate, I'm crook. I can't train . . . I'm going to have to go,' I said to trainer Kelvin Giles. And so it was that I left my first first-grade training run halfway through. I think I was overawed.

But I was tremendously excited too, and I couldn't wait to get home and tell Al (Allison) – and to ring my mum.

They named me in the second row, alongside Peter Ryan, in a team which read this way: O'Neill, Sailor, Hancock, Johns, Carne, Plath, Langer (C), Lazarus, Kerrod Walters, Gee, Ryan, Webcke, Smith. But I was never a second-rower, although I was listed in the program there a few times. I was always a front-row forward – reserve grade, first grade . . . forever.

The week was a long and nervous one, but by the time I got to the game on the Sunday I wasn't feeling too bad. I had come to terms with it in my head, telling myself that I was just going to the footy – and whatever was going to happen . . . well, it would just happen. The unfortunate thing was that the length of my debut that day wasn't very long at all, thanks to a high ankle sprain I suffered early in the match. Before that I had made a couple of good runs, in fact had started very, very strongly and was feeling good. I remember thinking, This isn't as hard as I thought it was going to be! I'm sure I was like every youngster playing his first top-level game . . . you go in thinking it's going to be something *colossal* and it's not. It's just footy.

Anyhow, about five or six minutes into the game at ANZ I tried to step out of a tackle and the bloke who had me hung on – and I wrenched the ligaments at the top of the ankle. And that was the end of me for the day. A question I can't answer is if the exact same thing happened to me now, would it stop me playing? In football, as you get older, you get tougher. When you're young I think you tend to panic a bit when something happens to your body and you're more likely to succumb to it. In the later years of my career I had a much greater understanding of what I could or couldn't do or whether something was just sore . . . or *dangerously* sore.

Toughness can be learned, I think. Anyone can teach themselves to be tougher. In football some blokes are born tough, but some learn it along the way and are just as effective. I would probably rate myself this way: that I was reasonably tough, but that I progressively learned to be much, much tougher with myself when it came to dealing with injuries. And to be mentally stronger, to the point of saying to myself when I was hurt: 'Okay, this is going to be bloody sore, but it is not going to do me any damage per se. I can play with it.'

When I check the scoreboard of that match, and the flogging we took, I'd like to think that things just fell apart when I left the field! Actually, it was a painful experience to have to sit there watching, with my leg in ice, taking no part. I was bitterly disappointed and I also felt quite embarrassed. Footballers are like that; you can't help getting hurt, but when it happens, you feel like you've let everyone down. It was such a let-down after the excitement of making first grade against all the expectations I had had over the years. But the coach was good about it. To a man of his experience it was just football, I suppose – the acceptance that things happen on every football afternoon and you deal with them.

I went hell for leather in the days that followed, desperate to try to get my ankle right. Wayne gave me the nod – if I was fit I'd be in the side. Holy Cow, that was a let-off. My immediate thought after the game had been, Well, there's a chance blown; I'll be back in 'Reggies' (reserve grade) for sure. As it turned out, the ankle needed a couple of weeks, at which point Wayne was still going to pick me in firsts. But around about then, my luck ran out. I fell ill and was diagnosed with glandular fever, thankfully the version of it which is a fairly quick hit. But it was bad enough to have me finish up in hospital for three days. I lost 5 kg or so very quickly and felt really bloody crook. My progress was good, though, and when I got out of hospital my thoughts were directed to getting straight back to football – although I knew it would be reserve grade, considering the setback I had had. Back in training, I needed a final clearance from our club doctor, Peter Friss, and he ordered a precautionary scan of my spleen, because glandular fever can affect the spleen. And the bloody test showed that my spleen was seemingly enlarged, swollen to abnormal size. 'You can't play,' said the doc. It was enormously frustrating, so much so that I sneaked a reserve-grade game (against Auckland) a few weeks down the track, much to the displeasure of Dr Friss. And that was it for me in season 1995. I had put a toe in the water of first-grade football and immediately been crash-tackled by something way beyond my control. The worst realisation of all came later in the year when I had a further test on my spleen. It was exactly the same size as in the first test, and the medicos reached the conclusion that it wasn't swollen at all . . . just naturally big!

It was a strange year, 1995. One of the biggest stories in rugby league history pretty much went straight through to the keeper with me along the way as I wrestled with my own footy career, and the problems that emerged in it. It was in '95, of course, that the 'Super League War' first broke out as the opposing forces of the ARL (backed by Kerry Packer) and Super League (backed by Rupert Murdoch) began their bitter fight for control of the game. The rugby league world was in turmoil, but for a 20-year-old prop from the bush trying to make a start, most of it passed straight by. I was just a reserve grader really, although graduating to be a 'fringe' first grader, and no one was heading my way waving one of the big cheques that were a feature of that season. And why would they? The decision made by the club to join (or it could be said, lead) the Super League bandwagon was made at the top level – and the reserve graders were just towed along in the wake. My thought was not much more than, Oh well, something new is happening. I didn't go to a single meeting connected with the Super League thing and it didn't affect me one bit, although I think even the reserve-graders got a bit more cash because of the bucketloads of it that were flying around. I was already on a contract with the Broncos and no one was going to seriously upgrade that just to be a good bloke. I was happy purely to be there. It was never about me thinking that I should be getting what the other blokes were getting.

After my illness, the season became a constant frustration, me sitting there week by week watching, busting to play but thwarted by a swollen spleen (that wasn't). It was the completion of my first two-year deal with the club, and as the football year ebbed away my thoughts were very much that my chances of staying with the Broncos were draining away too. I remember sitting there one day thinking, It's almost over – this is where it started and this is where it will end. But thankfully Wayne had seen something in me, and late in the year Shane Edwards (Broncos CEO) offered me a new two-year deal.

There is a description somewhere of the young Webcke, which suggests that I possessed a style 'akin to a battering ram'. That pretty much nailed it. It was all I had ever done as a footballer – just grabbed hold of the ball and run straight and hard. It was all I thought I had to do back then. Maybe I used to pass a bit, but not much – and the skills in the main came later, in the ongoing education process at the Broncos. Up to reserve-grade standard I got away with the bull-at-a-gate style, and I guess I must have had some ability at it. But when you play first grade the absolute certainty is that there are a lot of big strong men up against you. Keep running at them the same way, and they'll keep knocking you over. Through the years my style adapted to that reality. I developed a bit of a step, which I'd never had, learned to run some angles, put some deviation into my running and learned to offload. I can recall Wayne working hard on me to run different lines. I added stuff to my game which just wasn't there when I came to first grade in '95. And inevitably, as the seasons go by in a career you learn extra things, different skills, just by being around footy.

When I look back at the team list of 1995 I am struck with the realisation of how quickly eras come and go. Among the Broncos first-graders of '95 only three remained when season 2006 rolled around: Darren Lockyer, Brad Thorn and me. Lockey arrived from Roma that season ('95), looking right from the start like one of those young players who was going to make it. Brad Thorn falls into that category I talked of earlier – young fellas who were never going to do anything else but become first-grade footballers. Those sorts of players seem to bring with them the confidence that I lacked – at the start, anyway. Letting the negative dominate the positive was a big drawback in the early days of my career. It took me a long time to turn that around. Thankfully, today it is no longer part of me.

Chapter 6

SOME THINGS I NEVER HAD THE CHANCE TO SAY

Writing a book provides many opportunities – and one of them is the chance to put on paper thoughts and ideas that you may not otherwise have been able to make public. The manner in which I lost my dad, in a sudden accident when I was just 19, meant that I never had the chance to publicly say goodbye to him. His death in 1994 profoundly affected me, and ever since that time I have had a feeling of disappointment that I was not mature enough to deliver his eulogy. So I feel it is appropriate that these few words be included in my book – they serve to satisfy a long-held desire to describe exactly how I saw my father, as well as depict events and times that have shaped my life. It is not a traditional eulogy, given the passage of time since he died. So, I feel I have some licence. The time of writing is appropriate: Anzac Day (2006) – Dad's favourite day of the year.

My earliest memories of Dad revolve around life on our little farm and the wonderful childhood I had there. I recall those days when Dad would go over to our neighbour's farm to work and

I would always be trying to tag along. Many times I succeeded and immersed myself in whatever activity Dad and Kerry happened to be doing. I suppose I was a bit of a pain in the backside, but I adored my dad and just loved being alongside him and Kerry, doing all sorts of farm work. My father was a keen dairyman and we always had six or eight milking cows as well as endless poddies to feed, along with various other animals around the place – my dad was a real animal-lover. We always had a menagerie around the place. Dad was also quite a recycler, and would build sheds and enclosures from stuff he found at the dump or somehow gathered around the district. I'd imagine that to the rest of the Leyburn farming community Dad was a bit of a 'hobby farmer', but in fact he always harboured a desire to expand our holdings into a more viable operation.

Sadly, time and tide conspired against him and the financial realities of those early days forced him back into the workforce. The haze of time prevents me from remembering the details of all those years ago, but I can recall Dad being away for long stretches of time. And I remember that things began to get tough . . . really tough. I remember too how much we (Mum, my brother Dallas and I) would look forward to Dad coming home – but how his stays always seemed too short. Back home he would do his best to catch up on all the stuff that had fallen away at the farm before heading back to whatever job he was working on. 'Hardworking' is the perfect word to describe him. Dad could work unbelievably hard – and he had to, in the absence of the finance needed to afford the tools to make various backbreaking jobs easier. I remember him clearing most of our farm by hand, with just a small chainsaw. In the end the place was really neat and tidy, and it was a tribute to all his hard work.

There was a period where Dad had had enough of working away and decided he would stay home and damn the conse-quences. It was through that period that I believe he began to see some of his hopes and dreams dissolve. And he was a great dreamer, my dad, always cooking up weird and wonderful schemes to make money. Some of his ideas on farming were ahead of the times, such as setting up a cell rotation system on the farm. But dreams (mostly) don't pay bills or make money, and there was the sense of things just getting gradually worse. It was at about this time that Dad, who had always liked a beer, started drinking far too regularly . . . and his drinking became a problem. He would go to the pub almost every night – and then drive home, usually well over the limit. I would lie in bed those nights praying to God to bring him home safely. Then when he did arrive home we would just hope his mood was okay. He was never physically violent, but he could be mighty unreasonable. Eventually he would go off to bed, and in the morning and we would hear him in the kitchen, making coffee and singing. I suspect he was trying to quash the memories of the previous night and the things that haunted him. It was at those times that we had the old Dad back – at least for while – the man we loved and respected. It would never last too long, though, as I'm sure Dad was always plagued by despair through that period about what to do next. Our farm then was not viable, and in the wider picture Australia was not experiencing great economic conditions. Dad would have us out collecting bottles, cans, scrap and all sorts of stuff all to help make ends meet. He was a resourceful man but he lacked financial education. If he'd had that, coupled with his amazing work ethic, I believe it could have taken him anywhere.

Throughout all of this Dad fought a pretty public fight with alcohol, and I reckon people used to feel a bit sorry for us and probably viewed Dad as a bit of a loser. I never felt that about him. But through that time I so much wanted him to just always be the wonderful dad that we had at home most of our days together. If he had lived long enough I know that together he and I could have realised our common dream of expanding the farm.

It makes me sad to think that although he did live to help me invest some of my football money back into an agricultural enterprise, he was not here for the further steps, not here to see what we have bought and where we have ended up. I know that would have made him happy. I know for sure that things would have been much easier for me if Dad had lived; I know that having him to help me set things up in terms of hands-on labour would have made a big difference. It's odds-on that he would have been a better worker than anyone I could ever find!

One of Dad's great redeeming features was the love he had for Mum. He would embarrass us boys no end (and sometimes Mum, no doubt!) with unabashed displays of public affection. Dad was just being Dad – and as I have grown older and thought back, I'm happy to know that he was capable of that sort of thing and I feel happy for Mum too, because I know that she must have felt loved. I have always had the feeling that Dad was unhappy that he hadn't been able to provide Mum and us kids with a lot of the material things in life. But you know, in so many ways his life provided us with so much more. Life around Tom Webcke was always exciting and sometimes dramatic, but forever interesting.

One of his great traits was his generosity – not to do with financial matters, but of himself. He would help neighbours and mates at the drop of a hat. Whatever he could do, he would, and there are plenty of people out Leyburn way who would testify to that. One of Dad's favourite things of all was his occasional BBQ . . . and these were no ordinary BBQs! Dad would kill one of our sheep and we would have giant fry-ups of rough butchered chops and the like – all of it all cooked on a hollow 44-gallon drum with a BBQ plate placed on top. The fare was rough and ready but the company was great and the beer free-flowing. At these momentous events Dad would usually be drinking some of his famous home brew. Most blokes who brew their own beer take a great deal of pride in how it turns out and have all sorts of weird and wonderful theories about how it's done. But not Dad! To Dad, home-brewing was akin to a grand prix event – the object being to get it brewed and bottled as fast as possible . . . and then to get to the drinking. There wasn't a lot of science in it and there were times I saw Dad bottle in the morning and then drink the brew in the afternoon. It sounds primitive, but it was just Dad. He was a bloke who wasn't long on ceremony but certainly knew how to have a good time.

I hope I haven't painted a picture here that is too unkind to Tom Webcke. I'm sure he wouldn't mind me recounting some of his idiosyncrasies, given that he certainly had the ability to laugh at himself. The truth for me is that saying goodbye is a pain that wounds so deeply that the scars only fade . . . they won't disappear. As the years of my life unfold I know they will always be a little emptier for not having my father around. I know there will often be times when tears well inside me as I remember him.

It's been a wonderful experience, revisiting some of my favourite memories of Dad for the book. My motives in doing it were twofold. First, one of the great things about writing a book is that it's a chance to have an uninterrupted say – and I have valued that as I have long felt that my Dad was looked upon by some in a light that simply did not portray the type of man he really was. I hope my words here have addressed that at least in a small way. My other reason to remember Dad on these pages is to fulfil a personal desire to have my thoughts and feelings about my father put on some sort of public record – a record that my own kids can read and enjoy someday and come away from with an understanding of the type of bloke their grandfather was . . . and how I felt about him.

I purposely left this to last: the things that I cling to when I think of my father. Remembering him, I will always think back to the long walks around the paddocks and roads of our farm, talking about this and that . . . and the happiness that we all shared doing that. And I recall the early morning cups of coffee in the kitchen of our house, again as we talked about a whole lot of things. But most of all, when I lie down some nights I think of a morning shrouded in the mists of time. It remains the single most enduring image of my dad. It was a morning on which he was going away again – to work in some far-off place. As I lay in bed, the pre-dawn light made him just visible. He leant down and kissed me and told me he loved me . . . and he said goodbye. Because of how he died I never got to say goodbye then, and so this is the goodbye that I use in my mind as a replacement. Tom Webcke of Leyburn was a good, hardworking, honest man. He was and is the toughest man I have ever known – in the ways it's hardest to be tough. It is my great honour to be his son.

Chapter 7

KNEECAPPED . . . AND LIVING WITH IT

On a morning in mid-season 1996 I received shattering news from our club doctor. The real possibility existed, he told me, that I might survive only another 12 months as a footballer. In a Round 16 match against Cronulla at Shark Park I had partially torn the cartilage off my left knee. I can remember the moment clearly – of someone tackling me on one leg and me standing there, bouncing and balancing and trying to get a pass away. Then I got hit hard from another direction – and I felt my kneecap go. I came straight off – not because it was particularly painful, but because it felt *weird*. Early the next week I ran at training, but the knee didn't feel right. When the doc examined me he said, 'There's something floating around in there . . . we're going to have to get in and take it out.' When they went into the knee it was discovered that the damage was fairly extensive . . . and worrying.

I had done enough damage to potentially impact on my entire future as a footballer; I guess it's fair to say I've been on borrowed time ever since that July '96 day. I battled out the rest of the year on a knee that was swollen just about all the time. What happened back then was the start of the process of the progressive wearing down of the knee, something that became a growing reality for me as the seasons went by. The injury was a problem from that day at Cronulla right to the end of my career. But luckily the alarm bells that the doc had sounded back in '96 never quite rang out – although I have had my moments with the bloody thing.

In 1996 the doctor's words played on my mind, over and over. I would go to the physio at that time and always ask the question, 'Am I going to be all right?' It's funny how the mind works. I had just arrived at a point where, for the first time, I could see a future path as a footballer – and now this had happened. Things tend to loom very large in my mind at times, and I had by then allowed myself to dream the dream of being a long-term professional rugby league player, and of being able to retire one day far down the track and look back on having achieved something worth-while. Now, different thoughts were crowding in. Was I going to be a flash in the pan? It was an unsettling time, with the injury weighing heavily on my mind. Any day that the knee got particu-larly sore I would think, Oh, god . . . the end's coming.

I battled with it for a long while, mentally. But I gradually learned to live with what I had – and got better and better over the years at dealing with injuries generally. I learned more about my body and gained confidence in what it could and could not do. And I made small adjustments to cater for a knee that was not the same as it once had been. I think the thing that saved me was that I have big upper thighs with plenty of muscle there to hold up my knee so the leg itself does a lot of the work rather than all of the force going through the knee. Over the years numbers of people have commented on my 'limp'. And I suppose I do limp, and especially when I get tired in a match and the knee is bloody sore, which it certainly gets. The surfaces, where the parts rub against each other, tend to get pretty raw. For a long time after that first injury the knee would swell after every exertion. But then it settled down, and after an operation nine years later (one of several I had) the specialist told me that the bone in there was quite smooth and polished. After that it continued to function quite well. Touch wood.

The knee injury of '96 was a real blow, considering my increasingly professional approach to the game. In the off-season of 1995–96 I did exactly what I had done the previous year and trained really hard, determined that I would be in good nick when the New Year came around. But the season started in disappointment, with me being part of a first-grade trial out of town and then almost immediately learning that I had been put back to reserve grade. It was the only time coach Bennett ever did that to me in 13 years at the club. But I couldn't say I'd been 'dropped' – because I wasn't a regular part of the first grade team at that stage. I was to spend three months in the reserves, continuing to learn my trade, and it wasn't until Round 11, almost exactly a year after my brief first-grade debut, that I managed to win back a place in the firsts.

The game was in turmoil for much of that season. We Broncos were one of six 'rebel' clubs to forfeit our first-round game (against Auckland) as the fight for control of rugby league at administrative and corporate level reached bitter and then monumental heights, with the likes of Kerry Packer and Rupert Murdoch pulling the strings. Auckland picked a team from their local competition and were prepared to fly over and play in the scheduled match in Brisbane. They were told not to bother – that the Broncos had forfeited, along with all the other 'Super League' teams (or the mooted breakaway 'Global League', as I think it was known then). On March 11 the Federal Court had formalised orders to ban Super League until 2000 and had ordered that

League to pay its players to compete in the ARL premiership. The players dug their heels in and refused . . . until Round 2. It was a real shit-fight.

Again, much of the detail and drama of what became known as the 'Super League War' passed me by. I was, after all, a reserve grader again, and not really in the loop. The battle that was unfolding with so much rancour on both sides was almost entirely about 'elite' players.

For three months that season my career marked time. The success of the firsts after they finally got going in Round 2 contributed to that. They won nine games straight, which is as good a reason as any not to change a football team. When Norths beat us 16–10 in Round 10, Wayne made a number of forced changes brought about by Origin commitments – and with our front rowers Glenn Lazarus, the 'gun' prop of the time, and Andrew Gee out of the side I got my second chance. But as in 1995, it was not a particularly happy debut, with Manly beating us 18–4 the next week on our home turf, ANZ Stadium. I remember the occasion of my selection very well. Up to that point I hadn't had a single thing to do with 'Lazzo'. Probably he is a very different bloke now from what he was then – because then, and for whatever reason, he wasn't real friendly at all. He didn't interact with younger players. That was his choice, and I had no problem with it. It goes without saying that he would never have been over the moon about even the mere thought of a young bloke stepping into his position.

The bloke was a Colossus of front-rower play, and I had all the respect in the world for him. I don't know if he knows that. With Canberra, Brisbane, Melbourne, NSW and Australia he set the pace for front-rowers of that era. For sure in 1996 I wasn't getting around the place thinking I was the equal of Glenn Lazarus!

But I was excited to be tackling first grade as I had been that first day, back in '95. But I was more comfortable this time. I had had my brief experience of first grade the previous year and had been in the first-grade squad for the trials that year. I had at least broken the ice; everything was still quite surreal to me, but I was a little more at ease. We lost that game, as I mentioned, and the next (against Illawarra) – but I mark that mid-year point in '96 as the true beginning of my first-grade career. From that Round 11 match I went on to play 13 first-grade games, plus one off the bench. I even scored a try, against Wests when we beat them 36–6 at ANZ. August 10 it was – mark it down. It really was a red-letter day; I managed to win the Man of the Match award too. But I wasn't getting carried away. 'I coughed up one possession and gave an intercept pass,' I told the media, marking myself hard. It was through the '96 season that I struck up what has been a lasting friendship with Brad Thorn. We were a bit the same back then, I suppose – young, rough, raw players recently arrived on the scene. It was the first time we had played together on any sort of consistent basis and we developed a really strong friendship. Amazingly, ten seasons later we were still playing first grade together – although Brad went 'missing' for a time when he headed off to play rugby union (at the highest level) in New Zealand.

One of the papers described my 'circus-like juggling act' in scoring that first first-grade try, and oh yeah, I remember that. Kevvie Walters passed me the ball after I had trailed him through, and it hit me somewhere around the belly region, and immediately jumped out. I had something of a handling problem in my early days because I was brash and I just wanted the ball; I was a bit 'grabby', and now and then would put one down. Still do, in fact! This day the ball hit me and just bobbled up into the air and I'm bloody well juggling it, with the outcome uncertain. But I managed to rein it back in, and next thing I was over the try line and I just fell down and planted it. ANZ Stadium, it was – running north . . . on the right-hand side of the goalposts. I can report there was no backflip, no punching of the air and no shenanigans after the try. I was just pumped up and very happy. I don't mind jubilation at achievement on the sporting field, but I think it's overdone at times. And I really don't like the scripted shit at all.

When it comes to the subject of tries, I haven't scored that many for the Broncos – my memory tells me 16 or 17, although I did get a couple of 'doubles' and I'm quite proud of that. I've gotta say there was a bit of pizazz about that first try . . . but a fair bit of arse too.

ANZ was our home base back then. We were good at winning there and I've got tremendous memories of the place. I don't reckon a ground becomes your 'home' until you make a habit of winning at it. By the time I was a regular first-grader we were *extra* good at winning at ANZ and teams hated making the trek. There was a period of my career during which we won 20 or so games in a row there. The Broncos were really dominant in Brisbane in those days, which were before the Lions (AFL) and rugby union, via the Super 12s, now Super 14s, grew. League was undisputed king. We didn't have to share our crowds with the other codes as we do now. I loved playing at ANZ when the place was full, but the atmosphere does fall away at a big ground like that, at which the crowd is set a fair way back, when the numbers dwindle . . . and that happened – and ANZ no longer had what it once had. In the end, although I was sad to leave it, there was excitement in going to Suncorp, the brilliant development of the old Lang Park; it is a more spectator-friendly ground.

When I think of ANZ Stadium I am taken back to thoughts of my mum. In those early years after Dad died she would regularly make the drive from Leyburn, stay with us and then head out to the footy. Mum grew to love the football experience, especially at the junior league level, where everyone pitched in and made it all happen. At ANZ it was an exciting scene, every home match – and I'm sure being there was part of the process for her of getting over the death of my dad. And it was right and fitting that she was there. After all, Mum is the reason I played football. From the start she was the one who would always take us to the game, regardless of the financial situation at the time, or whether Dad was away. Of the many gifts she has given me in my life, that is a massive one. Without her enthusiasm and commitment in those early years I wouldn't have been a footballer . . . wouldn't have had my career . . . wouldn't have been who I am. In the later years, the gloss probably wore off a bit for Mum and she was not such a regular at the matches as previously. She got busier and moved on in her life. But I knew that she supported me and followed my career; she didn't have to always be at the game to do that.

The period in 1996 which marked the true beginning of my career was the first time I accepted that I was going to become a first-grade footballer, that I was going to be a rugby league professional. For the first time I felt comfortable in that role. I still got nervous before games, still worried that if I didn't perform I'd be gone. But I knew, at least, that I was on my way. Essentially I treated every game as a trial – and it is an approach that has stayed with me right through my career. I have never taken it for granted, felt I have some sort of 'right' to be in first grade. I like to think that has been one of my strengths over the years. If you never let yourself believe that something is automatically there for you in life and is going to be there for all time then you never let yourself get into that complacent state where things will happen that can steal it all away. That same feeling and belief was with me as I headed towards the end of my career . . . just as it had been at the beginning.

The ending to it all – as certain as death and taxes – always nagged away at me from somewhere at the back of my mind, and I'm sure it's the same with a lot of people in sport. I grew certain that I didn't want to put a blemish on a career in which I had never relaxed in my approach – where I had set out *every* match to confirm my worth to the team. I would hate to have started getting lazy and lackadaisical and thinking that the club owed me something when it didn't. It is a mistake a lot of players make – to believe that having been at a place for a long time provides an excuse for poor form or poor attitude. I have never accepted that. And as I got into the later stages of my career I had no qualms at all about Wayne demanding that I play well, regardless of what service I may have given the club. That, after all, is the business we're in. Loyalty is a great thing, and there is plenty of it at the Broncos – from club to players, and in return. But it goes only so far; you need to play well every week, and if you can't do it, you have to go.

That 1996 season ended abruptly for the Broncos after a campaign of great promise. We finished second on the ladder (behind Manly) and then bombed out two straight in the finals. Norths came to Brisbane and beat us 21–16 in the quarter-final and then Cronulla finished us off 22–16 at Sydney Football Stadium after leading 12–0 and then resisting our attempts at a comeback. The refereeing, by Martin Weekes, was controversial, and I remember that Wayne was filthy about it afterwards. That match and our disappointing exit was the catalyst for changes he made the following week. He let go Canny (second rower Alan Cann) and winger Willie Carne, among others. It was pretty clear that Wayne had reached the end of his tether the day of that loss. I remember him talking to Thorny (Brad Thorn) and me after the game and how upset he was – although he said to us, 'It wasn't the fault of you two blokes.' So we must have performed okay in the coach's eyes. But he was filthy on a few . . . and a decent shake-up followed. It was big news in Queensland because the sort of players he let go had been part of the successes of 1992–93 and were seen as Bronco stalwarts.

It was disappointing at the business end of the season,

particularly as the strong showing through the year had supported Wayne's stated hopes for the side. Right at the start he publicly declared that the aim for the season was: 'No more of that crap football we've played for the last two years. We just want to put the football right.' In an early interview the coach implied that the focus had wandered and players had been too involved counting the flood of money that the Super League had bestowed upon them and adapting to a sudden change in lifestyle. But for my part, to cement a place in firsts after the scratchy start I had had and the long period of reflection in reserves, made '96 a very special year.

For the first time in my life I attracted some media attention and began accepting the reality that when you are a first-grade footballer you are automatically in the public spotlight, and the media, so much a part of the mix in rugby league, will come calling. It was fitting that the first major feature interview/story on me was done by Tony Durkin, then Queensland editor of *Rugby League Week*. Durko has been a friend and supporter throughout my career. In that first story (titled 'Law of the Land') is evidence of the old saying that 'the more things change, the more they stay the same'. I told Durko of my love of the bush and how I knew that on retirement from football I would go back. I had just returned from a short break at Leyburn when we talked. 'I love it out there,' I told him. 'There's nothing like calling around to a mate's place, sitting in the sun and having a yarn over a mug of coffee. Only those people who have lived in the country would know what I'm talking about. I like to know and trust everyone around me . . . you can do that in the bush.' The philosophy I spelt out in that first interview has pretty much stood the test of time too. 'Even though I love playing the game,' I said, 'I'm not doing it just for that. It's a business thing – when I finish playing I intend to be on my way to having set myself up for life.' That set the scene pretty well.

The media were kind to me that first year – and generally my relations with them over the years have been pretty good. They are on the other side of the fence, but not so different. Like me, they are doing a job in rugby league. As we came to the 1996 finals, *Rugby League Week's* David Page wrote after a match in which we destroyed Penrith (50–20):

> *Shane Webcke will provide the Broncos with a new attacking dimension in this year's finals series. Webcke has cemented a place in the crack Brisbane team and looms as a potential game-breaker come the big matches in September. He is still a bit green but there is no denying the value Webcke's ability to stand and offload might present to the Broncos during the finals series.*

It was positive stuff.

It was in '96 that the media first tackled me on the subject of how things were for a country boy like myself living in the city. I told an interviewer that I disliked the city, and pined for the country life. Ten years later the urge to 'go back' hasn't waned. I still can't wait to live back in the country. But I know now what I didn't know then: that living in the city has been good for me, that through the chance provided to me by rugby league I have been able to experience many wonderful things and that because of it all I have a much better, broader perspective on life. I have been so fortunate. The country life gives you a wonderful simplicity, and that's comforting. But to move away and out of your comfort zone as I had the opportunity to do from 1993 is a wonderfully widening experience, taking you into new territory and making you a more rounded person, I'm sure.

There will never be a word of criticism from me about country people who choose not to take that path. But even if I wasn't thinking it when I gave that magazine interview back in '96, I am so pleased I have lived my life in this order: growing up in the country, the move to the city to chase opportunity, and then the chance to go back to the life that still calls to me. I know in future years that I can continue to experience the best of both worlds – to live in the beautiful Australian countryside, but with continuing links to the city and the chance to jump on a plane and head overseas to enjoy and learn of further cultural differences.

The interview in '96 triggered some sad memories for me when the subject came up of the land I owned in Leyburn. Mum and Dad helped me buy that when I was 19 and I viewed that 120 acres, adjoining the family property, as the beginning of the future I was to have. It was not a flash block by any stretch of the imagination, but it was a start, and it was my little piece of Australia . . . and I was so proud. It was the beginning of where I was going to go. My dad was gone by the time I cleared the land and re-fenced it. I sold it a few years later. To do that was part of the process of letting Dad go from my life . . . of moving on.

Funny thing is, the football of '96 is all a bit of a blur to me now, which I suppose doesn't say any more than there has been a lot of water under the bridge between then and now. But from that Penrith game a moment does stay with me – I remember an instant . . . passing a ball to Darren Smith down near the Panthers line, and Darren scoring a try.

But generally, it was just football, week to week, and I was happy to be there. I was surrounded by some terrific players – and I have to say I was in awe of the great halfback Allan 'Alf' Langer. He was a superstar of our time, and as I got older and more interested and started watching a bit of footy, I got to realise who he was and what he meant to the game. Now when I was actually out there playing with him it felt funny to be on the same field. He was a hard little bloke when the battle was on. One of his favourite sayings was, 'If you're fucked . . . get off!' He was a tremendous bloke, a magnificent footballer, and a wonderful competitor with it, and if he felt you were letting the side down he didn't want you there. Having him there was another spur to me. I certainly didn't want to be letting Alfie Langer down!

A few weeks after the Panthers match we were dead and buried in the '96 premiership, with all of us looking at a longer summer break than we had hoped for. Funny game, football. The season's summary in David Middleton's annual *Rugby League 1997* paid due credit to our skipper Alfie Langer, acclaimed as playing 'outstanding football week after week', which he did. Middleton added a generous tailpiece: 'Apart from Langer, the emergence of powerfully built forward Shane Webcke was a positive note to come out of the season.'

It added up to what I probably thought myself: that I had laid down a fair foundation when it came to the challenge of playing first-grade football.

My knee was now an ongoing worry . . . but at least I was in with a chance.

This was the first year I thought of myself as a genuine first-grader, more and more so as I overcame that first jolt regarding my damaged knee. I regard that time now as the true start of my major career, and the start of my inner acceptance of it – that this really was something I was going to be able to do, albeit with a bloody lot of hard work. Disbelief was still there in my thinking, and some lingering amazement that it had happened to me. I had come to first-grade football down an unorthodox path, but when it did happen there was a beautiful consistency about it.

My career just rolled on from that 'beginning', checked by injuries now and then as football careers inevitably are, but packing together a lot of football, club and representative, in a fairly condensed time period. The start of it all was rough and rocky, but once I got on track, I didn't fall off. It's a weird thing to reflect on really, considering all the self-doubt that had been in me. I think of it now in terms of arriving at a beautiful plateau. It had been a long climb, but once I got there I settled into a rhythm and routine that just took me on and on.

Chapter 8

MY TEAM

On a spring day late in 1996, I married Allison Knapp in a church ceremony in suburban Hendra, followed by a reception at the Brisbane Park Royal, directly across from the city's beautiful Botanical Gardens, where the wedding photos were taken later that afternoon. I have the feeling that a lot of my mates thought I was bloody mad. After all I was only 22, and many people will tell you that's far too young for a man to get married. But the thing was I didn't want to marry anyone else. I knew I had found the right girl. I was a fairly steady sort of bloke and I had no desire to hang onto the single life and sow my wild oats.

Ally and I had been together for a couple of years by then, and had bought a house together, a cheap little place at Bald Hills, a fair way out of town, but something that was a pride and joy to us both all the same. There, she had started her own business, as a beauty therapist. In our time together before that day we had been through rocky times, which had drawn us even closer. She had been there for me at the time of the biggest event of my life, the death of my father. And when you are with someone through hard times you get to know each other very, very well. Now and then she had seen me at my worst, too, and I thought if we survived all that, we'd be okay.

The beautiful thing about it was that Ally knew me when I wasn't a Bronco, was nothing really . . . someone with no great prospects at all. (She loved footy, though, still does, and that was a good start. Ally was a netballer and good at it, and had been involved in Little Athletics in her earlier years.) But she knew me – and we had grown together. And through all the successes since, I've been fortunate that she has been right there with me. Anything we have achieved we have done together.

To get married was a big step for me (and for her!) and I was scared about it, although happy. To me it just seemed like a natural progression. And the wedding day reflected the way it was, developing into a happy, good-hearted occasion with plenty of love and good wishes from everyone. Afterwards, it being footy off-season, we headed off on our honeymoon, a fly-drive holiday in Tasmania, a beautiful place to which I'll return one day. We had a great time.

When we got married, Ally and I already looked forward to having kids. I think, though, that Ally, who so wanted children, always harboured a little hidden fear on the subject – even if there seemed no reason at all to suggest it wasn't going to happen for us. Then, as the early months of the marriage passed with no sign of a pregnancy, a little worry started to creep in with both of us. One day we went along and had a yarn to the local doctor, who sent us on to David Molloy, a fertility expert and a past president of the Australian Medical Association. Both of us had tests done – and there seemed to be nothing wrong. That's probably the worst outcome, Doc Molloy told us: unexplained infertility is the hardest thing to find answers and help for. Ally was very upset . . . but life went on. Months went by with no sign that the Webckes were to become parents, and eventually we decided on the next step, which represented some sort of quantum leap for us. We began IVF procedures.

It was the beginning of a tough, testing, and at times heart-breaking phase of our lives. For five years we persevered . . . or should I say Ally persevered . . . she carried the entire burden . . . and I really can't find the words to express how I feel about her courage and perseverance. There was a time when I wanted to give up, seeing what she was going through. 'This isn't worth it,' I said. But we pressed on, Ally having her injections and other medication, a program that plays havoc with the body. She went through the cycle time after time, having the eggs harvested, inseminated, put back in, then sometime later . . . the disappoint-ment. It really broke me each time – to see her crying, again, when the time arrived at which we knew it hadn't worked . . . after all the hope. I wanted kids, sure, but balanced against that was the pain I was feeling at seeing what Ally was going through. To 'miss' each time is in reality losing a baby – and Ally went through it again and again. We were in what seemed an endless cycle of part hope and part grieving. Time after time we lived with these mini-tragedies and disappointments in our lives – and then moved on. Hers was the most amazing feat of perseverance; I can only liken it to going through extreme mental torture. It was horrendous for her, and hugely expensive. It cost us a fortune. Such an experience can bring people closer together, as it did Ally and I, although we had our bad days – but I can well understand how it can rip people apart. Every time the pro-cedure doesn't work, it just rips at you, drains you.

It was hard enough on me. I was trying to play footy and keep a balanced life together. But it was a bloody lot harder on Ally.

After five years of trying there came a day when we went to

yet another appointment with Dr Molloy. David is a dry bastard . . . he would give you nothing! This particular cycle had been very difficult for Al. She had been really crook, to the point where I don't think she had wanted to do it. And she had been so ill when they did the implant that probably neither of us gave it a hope. But she went ahead anyway, undergoing the general anaesthetic at the day clinic to implant the embryos as she had each time. A few weeks later, on this morning in David Molloy's office, he sort of stalled a bit, wandering around, fiddling at the filing cabinet, with us sitting there, busting for news – and then he finally turned to us with the words, 'Well, you're a little bit pregnant.'

Allison just burst into tears, and I was covered in goose-pimples . . . it was *unbelievable*. Although I guess right from the moment of realisation neither of us dared get too excited. We had climbed Mount Everest and at least reached high base camp. But there was still a long road to travel . . .

But, you know, Ally headed on with relatively few dramas although walking on eggshells through the entire pregnancy because of the years it had been and all the trouble we'd had conceiving. But at the end of it we got our beautiful perfect little baby, Erin Rose, born May 10, 2001 in the Wesley Hospital, Brisbane. The day she was born was one I'll never forget. In a single moment it erased all those years before . . . just washed them away.

If we could never have had another baby, it wouldn't have been a worry. But a couple of years later we decided we'd try again. I had serious doubts, because I didn't want to see Ally put herself through all of that again. But she did, and we went through the pain of losing a baby in the early stages after she had become pregnant. Then one later morning she was at Broncos training with the news that she was pregnant! Eventually, there was an wonderful outcome – a son. Hayden Michael Patrick, born August 5, 2003, after some difficulties early in the pregnancy when it looked like we might lose him too. At that stage we thought we were blessed, and we were. But it got even better when out of the blue arrived beautiful baby Grace Helene, born February 15, 2005 – no IVF, just making her own way into the world. I had learned the news of Gracie's unexpected presence one afternoon when I arrived home from training – and Ally held up a pregnancy tester, indicating positive! 'What's that?' I said (I didn't have a clue . . . neither of us had seen one of those before that day – everything had been done through blood tests) and when she told me, I was dumfounded. How on earth?

Grace was our biggest and tubbiest baby (at 8lbs 12oz) and for Ally it was a struggle. On the night we buried my Nan, New Year's Eve, Ally finished up in Toowoomba Hospital after a scare. There followed a difficult last couple of months of the pregnancy, with Ally unable to lift the other children or even walk more than a few metres without the onset of pain . . . and me doing what I could to help ease the load. But eventually, Gracie arrived safe . . . our beautiful 'bonus'.

I still find it all hard to believe.

Ally had gone through five years of hell in the lead-up to Erin's birth. Now we had three children! My admiration for her is unbounded. We're like any other couple – we get annoyed with each other. But what she went through for herself and for me and for our marriage was amazing, and I have her on the highest pedestal. What she endured, and the passion and determination she showed, was just enormous. I'll just say this: if I have a reputation in rugby league for toughness, it pales into absolute insignificance alongside what she went through over those years. It was only because of her determination that we got Erin, who kicked it all off and led to the family we now have – three precious kids, each one of them unique: Erin, the first after all our disappointments, Haydie, who was touch-and-go at one stage, and Gracie, arriving in her own sweet way.

Ally is a wonderful mother to them, takes wonderful care of them. I couldn't have married anyone better in terms of a lot of things, but particularly in terms of how she is raising our children. You may well understand that because of the way it has been with the Webcke kids, we are a bit more protective of them than some parents. We are not weird about it, just very careful with them. They are just so valuable to us. And ten years after that day we were married, life is fine, if very different – with three beautiful kids now running around the place.

One day no doubt Allison will go back to a career or an involvement in the community, although it won't ever be a thing about money. She is a very kind-hearted girl and she has ambitions to do volunteer work somewhere down the track. She has always been very good in the way she handles older people and maybe she'll do some of that – providing help to people who need it in retirement homes.

Meanwhile, life is full, with Erin, Hayden and Grace growing by the day and providing a challenge for her that is far more than full-time.

This chapter seems the ideal place to tell you a little more about the private life of Shane Webcke, footballer. As a kid, I never really had 'heroes', never plastered my bedroom walls with pictures of sporting – or any other – stars. But through my life there have certainly been people in the public arena whom I have admired – and they range across a wide spectrum of society, with more of them outside sport than in it. As a young bloke, as I mentioned earlier, I wasn't a huge cricket watcher, although my dad certainly was. But the style and the quality of Aussie captain Allan Border shone through to me all the same. He was enormous; he saved Australia on so many occasions and I became a huge admirer of his courage and his doggedness under pressure.

I got to meet 'AB', in later years of course, and to tell you the truth, I was a bit overawed by him. Isn't that ridiculous? But I still am. I feel a certain reserve, probably stemming from that deep childhood admiration I had for him. One day I might be lucky enough to sit down and have a bit of a one-on-one with him. I'd love that.

Many of the people I admire come from other areas of society. Quintessential Australians like RM Williams and Slim Dusty, two self-made men, always rated highly with me. In their different ways, both have made a strong impression on my life. For all their achievements they were modest men, with great gentlemanly qualities. I admire that a great deal. I regard them both as unique Australians with unique talent and ability. I have read their books and drawn inspiration from their stories. There is a great romance about those stories . . . how they dragged themselves up to become what they became.

I have respect for someone like John Singleton too. He's a bit of a knockabout and larrikin – and different from the other two. But he seems a man of generous spirit and I admire the way he has created a hugely successful life, by his own skills and abilities. I read a book about him too – and I respect him, if not in that same revered sort of way I do the likes of Slim and RM. Among other high-profile Aussies I'm an Andrew Denton fan . . . and Gerry Harvey seems my style of bloke.

You might identify a theme in some of this: my highest respect is almost always for people who have 'done it themselves'. There are plenty of stories of people who have been left empires and fortunes and who have gone on to make something even more special from the legacy. And good luck to them. But the people who really capture my imagination are those who start with little or nothing – and through the combination of talent and determination and a capacity for hard work make something great of themselves. In those sorts of stories I think there is inspiration for all of us. The message is straightforward: you *can* do it.

My interests outside football over the years have ranged over a whole lot of fields, and I'm really happy with that. There's always something new you can learn. Mel Gibson captured my imagination at one stage and I bought a book of his, and was interested in him and his life. I'm an admirer of Jimmy Barnes, a bloke who ranges across different styles of music unbelievably. He's a way-out bloke who has done all sorts of bad crap, I'd imagine, but he's a survivor. I think he qualifies as 'iconic' . . . and I'm a fan.

Musically, my tastes are pretty wide, although a lot of the really modern stuff is not for me. I can pick anything from the '60s through to the '80s – and that'll do me. But hip-hop and the like? Forget it. I find nothing in it. I like Australian rock 'n roll . . . The Hoodoo Gurus . . . I've got matey with a few of them . . . Cold Chisel, Australian Crawl. I love country music . . . Slim Dusty, of course . . . Lee Kernaghan. I think the liking for country music comes down the line from my dad, and, as he was, I'm a big fan of some of those old-style American country people: Johnny Cash, Willy Nelson, Kris Kristoffersen, Waylon Jennings, Kenny Rogers.

I love the books of Bryce Courtenay – I think he's magnificent. Colleen McCulloch too. Through their craft they open up a whole other world for people like me. I recently read Jared Diamond's *Collapse: How Societies Choose to Fail or Succeed*, and was pretty much gobsmacked by what I learned and by the messages it contains for this increasingly alarming world we live in. That's what books can do – open your mind . . . take you to other places. When I think back on my early life, I was always a bookworm.

I think there is an ever-present danger for those of us involved in high-level full-time sport that our focus can become too narrow, that we can fall into the trap of living entirely in the bubble of whatever the sport happens to be. I consider myself fortunate that my own interests have always been a lot wider. I attribute that most of all to books. It is said that the whole world exists in books and it's true – and I am probably at my happiest when I have a quiet couple of hours to spare (rare!) and can sit down with a good book. It is one of my favourite pastimes in the whole world and I have the sense that the reading habit I have acquired has opened up that world to me.

As time goes on my interests seem to broaden. I suspect that's the way it should be in life, and is for many people. I love Australian art and Aussie landscape painting particularly – and I would become a serious collector if I had the money and the time. Often, when studying a lovely Australian landscape painting I feel as if I have been 'taken inside' it, so familiar is the scene I am looking at.

Travel will be part of life for Ally and me, once these football days are over. I have tasted some other places already, thanks to football, and I am keen for more. In thinking about such things I know how fortunate I am. Inevitably I think of my dad and how tough his life was, and how his focus could never go much beyond making sure the bills were paid and making sure the family was all right. In saying that, I think my dad and I shared an ambition: to be a farmer, and to be a good one. Farming was his love and his passion. The great misfortune was that he never got to experience it at any other level than working his bloody guts out to try to make ends meet. I lived under the regime of those hard days at Leyburn and now I live under a different one, one in which so many more things are possible. It disappoints me so much that he's not here to be part of all that. And I sometimes don't know what to think about all of it, don't know where the good and bad of it start and end.

For Allison and me and the kids there is opportunity and possibility that my mum and dad never had in any way. I feel very

96

privileged with what I have now. Yet there is inevitably a pang of . . . *something* . . . is it guilt? . . . that my mum and dad, whom I loved, never had it. Yet Mum is here now, of course, and a wonderful part of our life. It is funny how the wheel turns: it was my dad's dream to be a (successful) farmer at Leyburn, not my mum's. Similarly, the dream that lives on in me, to farm out there, is my dream, not Ally's. But she is happy to share it, because she is my wife and she knows what it means to me. But I could never let her go through what Mum went through. That will never happen.

Yet that upbringing and background gave me so much too. It gave me the qualities I have, however they may be judged, and it gave me a sense of the value of the important things in life. And it gave me a broad range of friends for life who come from all sorts of weird and wonderful backgrounds. The fact of what we may or may not have become in our lives doesn't matter one bit. We are friends.

The good and basic things, and simplicity, are an ongoing theme with me today. For all that surrounds me, in terms of what I have built with the help of a career in rugby league, life's enjoyment is still most of all in simple pleasures: a night at the movies for Ally and I, a walk with the kids, a yarn with friends. I don't need extravagant holidays, I don't need to stay at lavish resorts to enjoy myself. My lifestyle is a fair way down on what you would call 'luxurious', and the acquisition of 'things' is not of much interest to me, although people may see *some* contradiction in me.

For example, I drive a Toyota Landcruiser, a bloody expensive vehicle, but that was the fulfilment of a long-held dream of mine – from childhood. Way back then I saw Landcruisers as a mark of success. It's stupid, really . . . it's a car, and means nothing. But for me it's a measure of something from long ago, a little gift I gave myself – in response to a kid's dream from way back.

I sometimes think of all those little dreams and ambitions of childhood and shake my head at the thought that I've bloody well made it. But I don't allow myself that thought very often. I know very well that life can crash-tackle you unexpectedly and snatch things away. I am never complacent about who I am or what I have. And I have all this energy in me for the future – football being a peculiar occupation in that it ends at 30-something for those who play it, a time in life when many careers are just seriously beginning. I've got all this good stuff in front of me and I really can't wait to get to it!

I have a number of business interests, property development being one of them. And people who know me – or think they do – may laugh at this, but in doing the things I do I am not motivated by money . . . not in the slightest. Money to me is purely a security thing. I want money so that I've got a nice home and a reliable car and I can look after my family and pay my bills. That's about it. I now own the best car I'm ever going to own; I'll never go beyond that – I have no desire for flash cars. My current house is as great a place as I'll ever own. I do not want to go to higher and higher levels in those things. I have no interest in being like a Rupert Murdoch or the late Kerry Packer and chasing and building more and more as if in some sort of never-ending game.

There has been mild speculation in more recent times that I might look to a post-football future in politics. To tell you the truth, I don't think I've got the stomach for it. I know the leader of the Queensland Nationals, Lawrence Springborg, pretty well – he's from out our way – and yes, he popped out to see me one day and we had a yarn. And we had a talk about what politics involved and I was offered the opportunity to learn more about it if I wished. I vaguely entertained the idea for a bit. And then, because it was in my mind, I watched the things that were going on more closely. The more I looked at it, the more I could see the frustrations that were involved. In many ways politics is the art of compromise and of sweet-talking people. And to be honest, there's too much bullshit for my liking. As we all have, I have formed particular views of politicians and the way it seems that most of them feel they have to conduct their lives. It seems to me that many of them often don't do things for the right reasons. Much of their lives seem to be taken up in deal-making. And deals shouldn't be done on things that are patently wrong. The thought of being bound by a party room, locked into decisions that I don't agree with, has no appeal to me. I'd go in, as an idealist, and I'd like to think I wouldn't be corrupted by the system; I have done enough things against the grain in my footy career to support that view. But banging your head against a brick wall has to wear you down. Politics seems to me an endless round of compromise, with many politicians being prepared to sell out their beliefs about an issue. I just don't think I could do that.

To be within a football club, as I have been these last dozen years, is a much more comfortable and healthy environment. If something is wrong within the club, we take steps to fix it. But if something is wrong with our state and we appeal to the politicians to fix it . . .

I think politics attracts a particular type of person – and I don't think I'm one of those. The pollies certainly need to be very dedicated and to be prepared to invest huge amounts of their time. I haven't shut the door on it altogether, but I can't really see it happening for me. After all, I have been busting to get back to the rural life for so long. If I did it – took on the political challenge – I might as well accept that the thing I have dreamt of doing is never going to happen. I have a vision of myself getting into politics and becoming all hooked up . . . and suddenly another 10 years will have passed by. I'm fortunate in that I have so many options to consider for my life after football. But above all else I harbour a desire to have a little piece of what I grew up with.

I think my upbringing gave me a sense of what *karma* is about – what goes around comes around. It is for that reason that I have tried to spread my good fortune in quiet ways that no one really knows about. There is an old saying: 'May good fortune revisit you when you bestow it upon others.' I'm a firm believer in that. And I never feel better in my life than when I'm helping someone.

If I can borrow a title from a famous book, I feel I am living a fortunate life.

Chapter 9
THE GETTING OF WISDOM

Very often in life it's the simple things that work best. I came to realise that early in 1997, a football year in which stress and worry threatened to weigh me down. I had come into first grade 'fresh' in '96, a newcomer to the team, with no great expectations. Everything happened so fast that I didn't have a lot of time to sit and worry too much about anything at all. I just went with the flow. But in 1997 I was an 'established' first-grader and suddenly life was very serious. As the season swung into action I started to have a real problem. Starting at two, then three, then four days out from a game I would begin worrying like mad, the match ahead preying endlessly on my mind. Fortunately, at almost exactly that time Wayne introduced into the Broncos support team a sports psychologist of note named Phil Jauncey, an Aussie with a Canadian accent. I was really having trouble by then. I was worrying all the time about my footy, thinking about the game ahead and about all the things that could go right or wrong, all the while knowing deep down that while it was natural to have some worry and concern about what lay ahead, to worry *too* much was not a good thing. And I knew I was worrying too much, burning up nervous energy, but I didn't really know what to do about it.

So I went to see Phil and he came up with a couple of deceptively simple pieces of advice, which changed things for me. Essentially they were these:

- It doesn't matter how you feel when you go to the football match – you do not need to feel good to play well, that's just a myth.
- In my approach to a match I should narrow my focus to just the first couple of things I was going to do in the game. Once I know whether we were kicking off or receiving I should think about no more than what I was going to do in the first couple of plays. 'After that, don't think of anything else,' said Phil.

It was so simple – and yet it was an answer. In my mind I had been thinking, Now what about if this happens? And what about if that happens? And so on, until it added up to a huge, wide view of the game. Phil stripped it down to basic, manageable things, and changed the way I approached playing football. Back then, through any week, the thought, Geez, I hope I play well, would circulate endlessly. Subsequently I could switch it on and off. Throughout a day, football quite possibly would not even enter my mind. But when I went to training it was there: 100 per cent. In our last session of the week, which was always followed by a barbecue, I'd be totally wrapped up in it. But I'd leave that session and not think about football again until I got into the car to go to the ground, or the team bus if it was an away game.

As far as I was concerned throughout my career, playing was playing. You can complicate a simple game too much.

And right to the end all I would think about before a game was what Phil advised me back then in '97: the first things I was going to do in the match. If we were kicking off I would focus on no more than making a couple of tackles (two of the first three in a match if I can) and getting myself thoroughly into the game. If we were receiving, I would do my hit-up and try to make it a good one – and then the kick-chase at the end of the set of tackles. I have found that if I kept it that simple, everything I practised, week after week, fell into place.

It is so simple – and I don't say this lightly – but what Phil Jauncey advised me on that day in 1997 changed my career. It changed my career because it made football, and therefore life, enjoyable. Phil now uses me as some sort of model to help convince the younger players to take the same approach. I honestly owe him a tremendous debt. His simple words rang true with me back then and made what could have been a very long and very hard road for me into something that was easy to do.

The question of worry and fear of failure was really taken on board by the Broncos. Throughout my career the undercurrent of that fear before matches was a constant travelling companion – although never to the point of actual physical sickness, like some players. Alfie Langer was probably the last one I saw of those; Alf would always get physically crook before a game. He'd just pull the wheely-bin out and go for it . . . you'd get crook just watching and hearing him. But you always knew that Alf was ready to play.

Phil explained to me how healthy that fear of failure is: it is actually a mechanism that drives you towards *not* failing and heightens the way you react and play. I have always felt some of that. I came to accept it as part of my career, and felt that if I ever lost it I would have lost something out of my game. It is perhaps hard to accept fear as being healthy. But in the football sense it is, as it provides the mechanism that enables you to succeed.

The advice about not having to feel good on match-day to play well is as true, and almost as profound, as Phil's 'second law' on focus. The hope of every footballer is to wake up on match-day and feel great and think, Right, I feel good . . . I am ready to go. I've had a good week's training . . . everything's right. But it's not always that way – there are days when you might wake up and feel not so great at all. But Phil's words are true. You *can* feel a bit off and still get out there and play a great game. There are countless instances of blokes being in doubt with 'flu or something and then making a late decision to play – and playing like champions. Again, that advice – and that truth – was a huge help in my career . . . and even more so in the years after Ally and I had our kids. As any parent knows, when you have children there can be bad nights – and mornings afterwards when you might be tired and struggling. But I wouldn't worry about it. Instead I'd automatically think, Well, okay, I don't feel real good, but that doesn't change what I can do on the football field this afternoon. It really 'uncomplicated' my life, made things much easier.

While I'm talking about the question of preparation for football I'll take you a little deeper into the way I did it over the years. Essentially I am a creature of habit. Once I discover something that I reckon works in my life, I stay with it. For years I ate pretty much the same things on game day, and at the same time. And I liked to be active. Early on in my career I used to believe I had to save up every possible ounce of energy for the game. But it became different. I found I enjoyed going for a nice long walk with the dog, or the kids – so that became part of my routine. Sometimes I would go by myself, relishing the quiet time. It would make me calmer. I'd certainly feel better, and I reckon I played better when I had that activity on game day. The other thing I tried to and do is keep busy. I used to be bloody awful – such a grouch on game day that nobody was allowed (or probably wanted!) to talk to me. But that changed too, and on any match day you'd find me doing some work – a bit of painting around the house or whatever. It came back to Phil Jauncey's first rule, that the way you felt didn't necessarily have any effect at all on the way you played. That thought became a thread right throughout my career.

Over the years I arrived at a nice even-keel way of preparing for my football, a process that made my career much more enjoyable. Once those elements fell into place, I didn't change.

On the question of food, I recall a conversation I had years ago with Ron Massey, a wise league man renowned for the work he did alongside the great coach Jack Gibson. Ron put forward the theory that footballers – and especially big men – should get lighter as they get older, and to do that would help sustain their careers. I took it on board, and among other things changed my game-day eating in the later seasons. For an afternoon match I'd have a couple of sandwiches at lunchtime and that would be it. I eat very 'normal' food – there is no science in it for me. A couple of ham and cheese sandwiches and I'd be off to the footy. Long ago I stopped thinking that there was some magic diet formula by which what you ate could make you feel like a million dollars. I certainly don't eat a lot. I didn't like to feel heavy going into a game.

Superstitions? Well, I don't really have them – although I guess you could say I was always a bit superstitious about routine. For me it was a case of the old slogan: 'When you're on a good thing, stick to it.' In football I believe routine in your life is a big part of being consistent. On tours, when life is different, you can still put in place mini-routines, which include the important items that you normally do. Routine is about having constants in a week of variables, and wherever I am I latch onto them. It's a very steadying and reassuring influence to have a set program factored in around the things you can't control.

It was suggested in a newspaper article years ago that I always wore black tape on my boots as some sort of gesture to the memory of my dad. It wasn't true. It's true that I have always worn black tape on my laces, but that was just a little superstition thing, born out of . . . I have no idea. I didn't need some sort of symbolic gesture to remember my father; he'll always be there in my memories.

Training preparation for matches always changes in the collective sense – in that a team prepares specifically for the side they are playing the next weekend. But for me, individually, the question of preparation through my career has always been the same. I took very little notice of who we were playing, other than the certain fact that I had respect for them. Some weeks there would be an extra spur, if we happened to be playing a side which had really good front-rowers. Then I knew it was going to be hard, and there would be some pride to be had in doing well. But I always respected everyone I played against, because I figured they wouldn't be there unless they could play the game. It was never a case of me thinking that I was going to get over the top of someone. There was more the concern that I might not.

What I once referred to in answer to an interview question as my 'maintenance program' was one of the fundamentals of my career and the sustaining of it. I am talking about getting out of Brisbane and going home to my property, which is 15 minutes out from Leyburn, on the Warwick Road. To get away for a day on the farm is still my favourite thing – always has been and probably always will be. For me, it is my little piece of heaven. Just to be there is great therapy – it is a place to clean out the cobwebs. There are a couple of aspects to that. One is the chance to have time away: the chance to have some thinking time and to put into context the things happening in my life. The other is the question of hard physical work (which I inevitably undertake when I go home). I love it; for me it is purifying. And out there at 'Wheatvale' there is always something to be done – fences to be checked, firewood to be cut and stored, grass to be slashed and the general running repairs that go with the rural life. Maybe there's a chance too to have dinner at Mum's and some corned silverside and white sauce – something she cooks beautifully. Leyburn and that country will always be home. These days my mother is there, and we've got the pub and seven or eight houses. It is a huge chunk of my life.

The different seasons out there all have their individual appeal to me. In summer I love the very early mornings and I'll be up before the sun, at the time of day I've heard called 'piccaninny dawn'. Equally, the late afternoon with the sun disappearing and the full sting of the heat easing just a little, is a special time. In winter, after a start to the day that can be bitterly cold, the mid-morning is a beautiful time, when it's warming just a little and the birds are starting to chirp. If I can be out in the paddocks at that time, I will be. These experiences breathe new life into me every time – and when you're playing serious football, you need that. At my home in the city I have some Australian landscape paintings, including a couple of Darcy Doyle's, and I love them. They conjure up those country images and sensations that mean so much to me.

The things I have discussed in this chapter underpin everything I was becoming (and then became) as a footballer, and season 1997 – such a fractured, contentious time for rugby league – was the year in which it all really came together for me for the first time. The rugby league world in Australia was split like a watermelon, the ARL playing their competition and the Super League teams playing theirs. And there was never a chance that the twain would meet, despite persistent suggestions that there should be a 'Super Bowl' at the end of it to decide which team truly was the champion outfit of the year. Nothing had ever been experienced like this in the game and there was dismay at the sight of rugby league seemingly ripping itself apart.

But as the saying goes, you can only play the cards you are dealt, and after three successive disappointing seasons, everything came together brilliantly for the Broncos. Rugby league waters had never been rougher, but we sailed smoothly through the storm. The side went through the World Club Challenge undefeated and won our last seven games, including the grand final against Cronulla, to clinch the Super League premiership. It was a helluva year and one in which I graduated to representative football, winning both an interstate jumper (Super League Tri-series) and an Australian one (second Super League Test v New Zealand). For the team, and for me, it was a season to remember. I doubt the wider world of league remembers it anywhere near as warmly. Along the way, in fact, it was called the 'season from hell'.

Chapter 10

LIFE IN LEAGUE'S WAR ZONE

We played 29 games of football in season 1997 and lost only three of them. In the words of the old song, it was a very good year. But for a bloke like me, who was part of all that and who during the year pulled on for the first time both the Queensland and Australian jumpers (Super League versions), it was a season that left a sour and lingering taste too, notwithstanding all the success we had. The whole Super League thing, the split, the damage it did to the game, is well documented. But what I'm still filthy about at a personal level is the lack of ongoing recognition for our (the Broncos) half of the rugby league world. Yeah, we played half a competition. But so did the ARL clubs. Yet the honours gained on that side of the fence, such as representative jumpers, are recognised – while the achievements of the Super League-based players are marked with an asterisk, and treated as if they came from some other planet.

I look at it this way: no one gave me a choice of where I was going to play in '97. I happened to be a contracted Broncos player, and so I played where they played. And all I did was train hard and give my best for the eight months of the season, and in doing it I made the Queensland side and then the Australian side. To me, the year marked the beginning of my representative career. But to anyone else checking the records, I am looked on as kicking off my rep career in 1998.

I am not one for records, but there is a strong principle involved in this. A sidelight is that if the three Super League Tri-series games I played for Queensland, off the bench, were counted in my overall record, I would now be equal with Gary Larson's mark of having played 24 consecutive games for the Maroons. But because the game had ripped itself apart for reasons that had nothing to do with me, the recognition is not there, and I suspect it never will be.

I can tell you that my life is not going to end if that recognition is never forthcoming, but I have to say that the asterisk that now accompanies everything we achieved that year annoys me more than a little. We didn't play any less hard or do any less work to get where we did than the ARL-based players, and I don't think there's a whole lot of justice in this continuing classification we have as some sort of 'outcasts'. Realising that everything on the Super League side of the fence from season 1997 is downgraded still makes me angry all these seasons later. Now, it is almost as though the events of the year never happened: the three games I played for Queensland; the premiership win in a competition in which there were some bloody handy football sides running around. Along the way there were some wonderful spectacles that showcased rugby league as it had never been showcased before, such as the Tri-series final, which was an amazing game that went for 103 minutes and 47 seconds.

Even if you regard Super League as a mixed blessing, or far worse, I think there would be agreement that the 'new game' at least opened some fresh frontiers and showed glimpses of what the game could become. We played an enormous amount of footy and loved it. Yet all of it is swept under the carpet and pretty much dismissed because it was 'only Super League'. I regard that season as such a valid experience of my career that to have it blown away as though it never took place is a huge disappointment.

The situation remains the one lingering regret I have from 1997. In personal memory it lives on as a wonderful year of footy – even if the ending turned out to be weird and disappointing for me. For all the negative things said about Super League, there were some wonderful initiatives in evidence that season. Maybe what was done and the way it was done meant it was never going to be sustainable, and the evidence since points that way. But what if the coup *had* been successful? It almost was. I think if Newcastle had fallen to the News Ltd forces the battle would have been won. What then would have been the makeup of the premiership today? Maybe the game wouldn't have had to go through all the pain that it did.

It's an interesting question, and my answer, which is crystal ball stuff, I know, is that we could be in a very different setup now. Very likely we would have had a proper national competition and the chance is that international football would have been strengthened. The World Club Challenge we played in '97 is remembered now as a bit of a joke by most people because of the lop-sided nature of many of the games – UK clubs v Australian clubs. Euroleague clubs won only 8 matches out of 60, a reflection of the gap between the two hemispheres, and we had some huge wins ourselves, including 76–0 and 54–10 (Halifax), 34–0 (Wigan) and 66–12 (St Helens). For some of the clubs it became a bit of a holiday, but we kept pretty well focused in the knowledge that one loss could put us out of the running. To be honest, the football wasn't hard for us. We were a good team, going well. At a personal level, I had a ball.

But even if the series revealed a great divide between the countries, at least it was a *beginning*. My belief is that the effect ultimately on the international game would have been wonderful, with a gradual building of northern hemisphere strength. Maybe the costs would have overwhelmed it, maybe not. But the theory that just taking the Australian team to England every year and beating them up is going to make them any better is a nonsense. A better pathway, in my opinion, was to do it via the clubs, with a bite of it each year, and gradual improvement. That sort of approach is about foresight and patience and long-term vision – good qualities, all of them. Everything in life suggests that the journey is not easy, and that good things only come after a long period of hard work. It's no different in rugby league, and I don't know why that's such a hard pill for the power-brokers to swallow when they are contemplating the direction the game should take.

We won that World Club tournament, bowling over the new Hunter Mariners side 36–12 in the final at Ericsson Stadium. The Mariners had given us something of a shellacking in the premiership game not long before (24–6), so the turnaround was satisfying. The ambitious tournament must have cost a fortune, and before it was very far down the track at all, plans were in place to amend it dramatically if it was ever to happen again.

But I really loved that year – and I really didn't give a shit about the politics of the whole thing. At that fresh, new point in my career, rugby league was the only sport in the world. And for all that was going on, I could never see it being under the slightest threat. Rugby league in trouble? The thought never even occurred to me. Asked about my personal plan in a late-season interview, I said: 'I am keen to work on my positional play and my durability. I intend to keep learning and improving until the day I retire.'

There were unquestionably visionary aspects of the Super League plan, which was built on a philosophy of elevating rugby league to a bigger stage. Prepared to throw large buckets of money at things, they dressed the game up with some razzamatazz and made the presentation different from the way it had been. I honestly think they were on the right track; I know for sure that Brisbane fans loved the entertainment that was part of every match. I had people talk to me about it in later seasons – how they were disappointed, having tasted that sort of experience (such as Olivia Newton-John at the '97 grand final, following huge parades), that it had subsequently disappeared from match day. The economic realities of the game no doubt dictated that. And while the truth of it is that the majority of people go to the game just for the footy, it's also a safe bet that some outsiders will come along – and maybe get hooked on league – if there are extra attractions provided.

To make my debut for both the Queensland and Australian Super League sides guaranteed that it was an extra special year for me, with it all beginning on April 11 at Sydney Football Stadium when the Blues, led by Laurie Daley, beat us 38–10 after running away to 22–4 in the first half. On what was a day of some significance in my own career, the Queensland team was: Julian O'Neill, Wendell Sailor, Steve Renouf, Geoff Bell, Mat Rogers; Kevin Walters, Allan Langer (C); Brad Thorn, Steve Walters, Andrew Gee, Owen Cunningham, Gorden Tallis, Darren Smith. Interchange: Peter Ryan, Chris McKenna, Paul Green, Shane Webcke. In our second game, when we beat New Zealand 26–12 at ANZ, I scored a try, so another small milestone was reached.

My kickoff as an Australian player came at Auckland's North Harbour Stadium on September 26. The Kiwis gave us quite a towelling in this game, which was characteristically physical in nature – and won 30–12. The Australian team in my first appearance was: Darren Lockyer, Ken Nagas, Steve Renouf, Ryan Girdler, Wendell Sailor, Laurie Daley (C), Paul Green, Jason Stevens, Craig Gower, Brad Thorn, Matt Adamson, Bradley

Clyde, Darren Smith. Interchange: Shane Webcke, Craig Green-hill, Brett Mullins, Luke Priddis.

It was a massive thing for me to pull on an Australian jersey for the first time that day, albeit the Super League version of it. I still have it among my souvenirs. Coach John Lang gave me a lot of game time and I came off the bench to play a fair lump of the match, including all the second half. How did I play? Well, I can't remember, to tell you the truth: that first Test is something of a blur. A win would have been nice – but the Kiwis were right on their game and were too good for us.

A week before that New Zealand Test we drew 60,000 to the Super League grand final against the Sharks, and it was a fantastic culmination to a great year for the Broncos. The match was played in rainy, slippery conditions and featured brand new footballs carrying painted logos – a certain recipe for handling problems, which there were. But it was a tough, hard game, a real grand final. Thankfully, we won 26–8, although I was filthy with Wayne. At that time the coach had a habit of listing blokes on the bench, and then starting them in the game. And he did that to me, therefore handing me the 'stigma' of being listed in the Super League grand final program as a bench player. In fact I started the match – a game in which the brilliant centre Steve Renouf ('Pearl') scored three tries.

It was an emotional game for both me and Gorden Tallis, who had sat out of football the year before, waiting to take up his Broncos contract, and who played in the grand final despite the pain of a rib cartilage injury. I can still picture Gordie straight after the match, with tears pouring down his cheeks. For me there was the ever-present memory of my dad. When the full-time siren sounded, I looked up and acknowledged him in my own way. I knew he would have been proud that day of what his son and the rest of the Broncos had achieved. I told the media guys that the occasion felt like the greatest moment of my life.

Afterwards there were media references to me conceding that I played like a 'madman' in the way I took on opposing defences. I credited my dad for my on-field attributes. 'He was as mad as a cut snake,' I said. 'And strong too – physically and mentally. He introduced me to the game and encouraged me. He just loved the footy.' *Rugby League Week*'s Tony Durkin wrote generously of my contribution: 'No player on the field made a bigger impact than prop Shane Webcke.'

I loved the fact that the game was national in 1997 – loved the chance to go and play in places like Adelaide and Perth, and play at famous grounds like the WACA and the beautiful Adelaide Oval, before crowds of 10,000 or so, which wasn't a bad start. Gee, I miss those days. Whether there would have been eventual success in those places, we'll never know. In the end all of it just became a real shit-fight and money way beyond counting got blown away on lawyers and managers and inflated contracts that could never be sustained. Some horrible things happened – and greed was right there in the mix. Clubs like Adelaide and Perth and Gold Coast were sacrificed in the political wheeling and dealing, and that was bloody disgraceful. I know some hard things had to be done to plaster things back together, but some of them were shameful, and for me that's one of the really disappointing things that came out of it. At the moment we are kidding ourselves calling the competition the *National* Rugby League. It's not.

And Melbourne? Well, I reckon if they drop Melbourne, they're wrong. In my view, if there is somewhere we need to preserve a (rugby league) team, it's there. But I am not filled with hope, and I think the chances are that eventually they'll fold. It's tough down there, you see. Well, bloody hell – what did people expect! It was tough too when the Brisbane Lions came to town up here – and look at them now. The league should forget about paying players more and increasing the salary cap – and instead put the money from their new television deal into development and the quest for a genuinely national game. And the game has to be strong enough and patient enough to 'carry' teams for 10 years in other places while the development process is in place. We are told endlessly that rugby league is a 'business' now and I accept that to an extent – but it can never totally be a business, because it is a game. Rugby league must always be a lot more than just a business. Now and then there have to be decisions, which are not instantly business savvy – such as starting franchises in places like Perth or Adelaide where money will be lost for a period of time. If it's for the greater good of the game, it should happen. And forget about News Ltd and the business side of it; rugby league is still the game of the people. Without the people, we don't have a game.

And it is such a great sport, evidenced even in a year like '97 when the opposing sides snapped and snarled at each other all season long, with most of the nastiness going right over my head owing to the fact that I have never been a big reader of the league media and was far removed from all that and just enjoying my season. No doubt it was the fact that rugby league *is* such a good game that saved its skin at that time. It appeals to people who play it and it appeals to people who watch it – and that's obviously been the way ever since 1908. It's a better game than rugby, for sure, so much simpler. My own career as a player never took me anywhere near a rugby field, and I'm not sad because of it.

It was thanks to the World Club Challenge that I got to go to England for the first time in 1997 and it was an unreal experience. We arrived in spring, coming into summer, had three weeks there, and it was just beautiful. There were even sunny days. We stayed for much of it at a place called Mottram Hall at Prestbury outside Leeds, a golf resort in the Yorkshire countryside, and one of my first thoughts was that we were in *All Creatures Great and Small* country – that show having been a favourite in the Webcke home back in the Leyburn days. On a later trip to the UK, I hired a car and drove to the little town where the show had been based, and stood outside the vet's surgery. I loved England, loved the great sense of history. We flew to Dublin and checked out the pubs, of course, and in London I went to St Paul's one morning and felt I could have spent the whole day there admiring the place and reflecting on the life's work that went into it. I found it awesome. The memories I have of trips like that one add to my feeling that I owe a tremendous debt to rugby league. I have travelled the world because of this game – and many of the values I now possess I have because of the education the game has given me.

When I was picked in the Australian squad for the Super League series against Great Britain in late '97 it seemed I was headed for my second trip to the UK in a single season. But I never made it. On a Sunday night in late October I was sitting at home with my bag packed, as excited as could be, and ready to leave the next morning. Then in one of the weirdest events of my life, fate crash-tackled me.

On that evening in late October before the Australian side flew out to do battle with the Poms in a three-Test series, the big green Nike bag I had been given as a member of the squad rested in a corner of our lounge-room at home. We were off on the big adventure the next day and I was packed and ready to go. Late that afternoon Ally and I had headed down to Sandgate for a feed of fish and chips. I was excited; I had thoroughly enjoyed the English experience mid-year when the Broncos campaigned over there in the World Club Challenge. Now, I was going back – into the late English autumn, and a different experience.

Well, that was the plan.

I was sitting on the couch not long after we arrived home when I started to feel a bit squeamish. I was a little apprehensive, as you are before a big trip, and I didn't worry too much at the start. But then the feeling turned into a throbbing pain . . . the sort of pain you get when you get hit in the balls during a match. And then I started to feel *really* sick. 'Have a shower . . . you might feel better,' Ally suggested. So I did, but the feeling and the pain only got worse. It felt like someone had hold of my nuts and was squeezing them – hard. Before long I was in really serious pain and Allison, being something of a wannabe doctor, had the medical journal down from the library shelf. She studied up for a bit and then declared: 'I reckon you've got testicular torsions.'

'What are you talking about?' I said. I'd never heard of it, but I was in no state to argue. 'Whatever it is, I'm really crook,' I said. 'I've got to get a doctor.' So we went to the local emergency centre and a doctor there examined me and delivered her verdict.

Testicle torsions. As was explained to me, a man's testicles move around in the scrotum – more so in young men. Sometimes they can twist too much and the glands that supply blood can become obstructed, starving the testicle of blood to the extent that it can 'die'.

'You're going to have to have an operation right away or you'll lose this,' the doctor said.

'Righto, let's go,' I said. Half an hour or so later I was under the knife. I will spare readers the full details. Suffice it to say that it involved some cutting and some untwisting and then some stitching to ensure it couldn't ever happen again. So, with the team getting ready to go to England, I was in hospital having an operation of the most delicate kind.

I was out of the tour.

I made the hard phone call to Johnny Lang, the coach of the side, and he understood straight away, the coincidence being that his son Martin had encountered the same problem. That was a stroke of luck for me. Imagine ringing a coach unaware of such a condition (as most of them would be, I reckon) and telling him at the last moment that you're out of an overseas tour because you've come down with 'testicular torsions'. That at least made it easier for me and in a fairly difficult climate in which there had already been a few dropouts, including the likes of Alfie Langer and Steve Renouf, creating something of a perception that the Broncos were not too keen on the tour. As far as I was concerned I was very disappointed. But I had been overtaken by a freakish event – and the big Nike bag in the corner of the living room never did get to go to England.

Being something of a homebody then, as now, I soon enough came to terms with what fate had dealt me . . . and set about getting well for the Brisbane summer ahead.

Chapter 11

LET THE GOOD
TIMES ROLL

In 1998, the good times rolled. The game was (uneasily) back together in a 20-team competition, providing once again the chance for players to win full-scale, fair dinkum state and Australian jerseys. I managed both. And the Broncos won the premiership, thumping Canterbury 38–12 in the grand final and earning the rating from at least one scribe that we had 'earned a place alongside some of the great club outfits in premiership history'. Along the way I played 33 games, all, bar one, that it was possible to play that year . . . and Wayne Bennett coached every single one of them. Yeah, in the words of the song . . . in many ways it was a *very* good year. There was magic in the air for me that season and I barely had a niggle right through. The only (possible) game I missed was the first Test against New Zealand, the reuniting of the Australian side after the split season of '97, when Bob Fulton was coach. I honestly can't remember if I was injured. I suspect I just didn't get picked. It was the night that Lockey (Darren Lockyer) had his shocker, dropping some balls as

Australia went down 22–16. After Fulton stepped down as coach, for personal reasons, I played the second and third Tests late in the year, with Benny as the new Australian coach, and we won both games (30–12 and 36–16).

At the club we always gave ourselves a great chance of winning the '98 premiership. If you can win *one* premiership you are generally in with a chance of winning another if you can maintain pretty much the same side. Honestly, we were never going to lose that competition. For the first time in my career I had absolutely no doubts. We just had a really dominant side that clicked right from the start, winning seven of the first eight games and giving all the others something to chase.

It seems funny to say it, but when I look back on that 1998 achievement it doesn't mean as much to me as the '97 (Super League) premiership. And it certainly doesn't mean as much to me as the next one (2000). To win the premiership was still wonderful, still top-shelf of course, but it didn't match the others: the achievement of the first one in 1997 and the great journey of 2000, culminating in my 'broken arm' grand final. In '98 we were just so superior that *no one* was going to get up and beat us. It was something that was expected, more than revered for the achievement it was. But it was very special all the same. Mum was there at the grand final and so too was my Nan, who died in 2004.

Grand finals are a strange, nerve-wracking experience; they go by so fast. In '98 we got out there and just ripped in. I knew we weren't going to lose. It was a really, really good Bronco side, and one full of good blokes. We played at the Sydney Football Stadium (SFS), a place I love – I much prefer it to today's home base, Telstra Stadium.

Much of the time in '98 the enjoyment factor was high – but I don't think there's any doubt that real sadness within our ranks helped bind the club even tighter. The battle waged by Kevvie Walters' wife Kim against cancer, and then her death fairly early in the year, were truly shattering events. I remember talking to Kevvie after Kim had died. He was struggling and I talked of my dad's death and about my experiences in trying to come to terms with tragedy. When Kim died the whole club attended the funeral, of course – and I remember Kevvie coming straight back to training, the next day, and staying on. That was remarkable. And I remember at different times looking at him in the sheds after we'd had big victories, and he'd be close to tears. Part of the reason we had such a great season was Kevin Walters; while it wasn't done for him, I think we were all very happy for him in the light of the tragedy he was wrestling with. The club rallied around Kevvie, as clubs do at such times, and he had a mile of support. But in the end he had to find his own way through it, and he did. And it wasn't an easy road. It said a huge amount for his ability and character that in such a year he was able to construct the best representative season of his career. He was a source of inspiration to our club.

In 1998 Locky scored 272 points, Thorny had a good year, Petero Civoniceva came into the side, ready now to make his mark, and I pretty much came of age as a footballer. It was the start of the next generation for the Broncos, with a younger group of players arriving to take the club on to whatever might lie ahead. As I write these words, heading along the track of season 2006, I see a parallel situation at the club. The wheel turns . . .

Petero was one of those late starters and late bloomers in football – and I think Wayne Bennett wondered at the beginning if he would ever come through. History now records that he just got better and better, building a no-frills career that blossomed a lot later than happens for some players, but just as fruitfully. He's a great fella, 'Bulla', a gentle bloke – and you wouldn't meet a nicer one. His father is a huge man who was a rugby union player of note, and I'm sure all the family are very proud of

Petero, who worked at his game and grew to become a great player.

Like me he had chosen the hard road of being a front-rower.

In an interview around Origin time in that 1998 season, I mused on the deeper subject of front-row play (or my philosophy of it) at that time: 'Front-rowers don't get paid to make breaks – our job is to take the ball forward, bend the line and tackle. If I make one clean break in a game, that's a bonus,' I said. My dad's philosophy on it right from the time I started football was that front-rowers get the ball and run hard and straight up the middle. When the other side had the ball you knocked over anyone with the footy that got near you. Of course it's not quite *that* simple, but in essence it's pretty easy to be a front-rower in terms of what you have to think about: that is, get the ball and go forward. That has changed to an extent in recent years, and now more is expected of front-rowers. They expect you to pass and be a bit clever now and then. From the beginning in rugby league the forwards, and especially the front-rowers, have been described as the 'labourers' of the game. That hasn't changed – but it is good how we are now encouraged to be a bit more skilful. It is becoming a bit more appealing to be a front-rower these days. I have never been coached *not* to make use of skills, just to play ball-under-the-arm barging football, although there has been an occasional individual day when I have struggled with my hands or my passing and Wayne has told me not to pass again that day. But that's generally been a context thing – related to the way the particular match is going.

We play a game that is not too complicated at all, really. It's essentially a game of momentum and pressure. You use momentum to build pressure and eventually the other team will make a mistake under that pressure and (hopefully) you will score a try. That is how all coaches coach their teams. The game is so hard and fast now that momentum is absolutely vital. None of it is rocket science.

When it comes to the blokes who play in the front row, there is almost always mutual respect. It's probably always been a popular discussion point amongst the fans – who's the dominant front-rower and who isn't – but really, all of us in that club just scramble to be the best we can. I think at the end of the day just about all front-rowers, realising how tough the job is, have respect for the other blokes trying to do the same job. I have had some wonderful things said about me over the years, which is all very flattering, but I think the one thing that has saved me is that I never really believed it, certainly never got carried away. I have always been much more inclined to look at others, blokes like (Glenn) Lazarus and (Paul) Harragon and think, Geez, what wonderful players. I have always been like that when it comes to football – quick to look at other players' strong points rather than my own. I think my approach has been a fairly well-balanced one, and whatever ego I have (and we all have a bit of that) has been safely kept in control.

Right up to the last years of my career I continued to admire the good things in other front-rowers. I look at a young bloke like Mark O'Meley (Bulldogs), obviously the next really strong player in our category, and greatly respect what he does. And I don't feel threatened in any way. I have had my day in the sun and I am perfectly at peace with that. Statistics do not always tell the full story. If you looked at my record over the years and the stats for 'metres gained' – a statistic that I think is bullshit, incidentally – I would be lower than many blokes. When it has come to tackles, I've got my share on the board, but if you did a stat for my 'one-on-one tackles' there'd be bugger-all, because the fact is that most blokes don't run at bigger blokes. So the majority of my tackles would always be 'assist' tackles – effectively doing what I have to do.

As for that 'metres gained' measuring stick, well as I built some notoriety in the game I became more heavily marked, and most times I'd take the first hit-up and get absolutely smashed. Yet I could come out of a game having run only 90–100 metres and still have people saying I'd had a 'dominant' game. Stats are good in some ways – but they need to be viewed with a certain perspective. There have been players who have consistently averaged better metres than me and haven't had some of the wraps and rewards that I've had over the years. If that is unfair, it is just the context of the game. The fact is that statistics never tell the full story of a football match. In some of the better games I have played I haven't gained a lot of ground, but I have done good things in tough situations, maybe a hit-up through heavy traffic for 4 or 5 metres and a quick play of the ball – setting the next bloke up for 15 metres and building the momentum. When you learn what rugby league is all about you come to understand that the important things aren't always the classic things.

There is a real bond that exists among the blokes who wear 8 or 10 in a match: those in rugby league's Front-rowers' Club. In some ways we've got the hardest job on the field and in others we have the easiest. We are not expected to be flashy and flairy – but we are expected to work very hard. A bond inevitably develops. As with all things that are tough, you are drawn together by the shared experience of what you do. The job is a hard one, no doubt. We've got to be big enough and strong enough to handle it – and we've got to be fit enough to carry out the task. Through all the adversity of trying to get to that level, you develop a natural mateship. Andrew Gee, who I played front row with at the Broncos, became probably my best mate in the game. We played the same position and we were the same sort of bloke, and we were drawn together by who we were and what we had to do as footballers.

So when it comes to football, I have to say the blokes I like best of all are the front-rowers. I've never found a front-rower I couldn't cotton on to, although they'd be out there, no doubt. In my career I roomed with some of the young guns like Jason Ryles and Luke Bailey and they are wonderful fellows. At the Broncos in these recent seasons, I have developed a great mateship with Bulla, who is a fine bloke.

Of course forwards would much rather mix with their own kind than have to spend time in the company of the backs! The division has always been there. We see ourselves as hardworking and them as bludgers. I reckon that about sums it up!

Among the current crop, Luke Bailey is a wonderful player and he's been a strong and respected opponent of mine over the years. It's a funny sideline of football, how you develop these little presumptions about players you don't know. A lot of that is to do with the competitive spirit (and you shouldn't be in the game if you don't have that), about not wanting to give too much credit to an opposing player. Generally, when you get to know them it all changes – although I have to say Luke was a terrific player from the start, a very methodical one who always got the job done. Mark O'Meley is certainly one I struggled with early on. To be honest, I thought he was a bit of a dickhead – and then I met him and found him to be a really nice bloke. I like watching him play because he's got that 'mongrel' quality about him, and I like that. Once I got to know him I felt really comfortable about playing with him. We get on well . . . we can have a laugh together.

That is the reason I love meeting footballers and yarning with them. Most of the good players are good blokes too, just out there to do their best in a hard game, and I find that reality quite relaxing. I could just focus on my own game and be comfortable with who I was playing against. I think that's an important part of growing up in football. As I got into my later seasons I didn't feel 'threatened'. If someone was to say I had been overtaken by Mark O'Meley, or whoever (as they probably will . . . or already have), I didn't see that necessarily as a slur. For a long time you work hard to be the best footballer you can be and when that starts to wear down a bit and other blokes come along, to be able to accept that is very important. You just have to be accepting of the likelihood that it's going to happen. To be otherwise would leave you bloody bitter and twisted.

I have certainly mellowed over the years. Once I'd go out there deadset disliking some bloke I wouldn't know from a bar of soap, just because he looked a certain way. Inevitably I'd meet the same bloke socially at some stage and find that in fact he was fine, and just like all of us – out there doing his best.

When I got my head around all that that a few years back it allowed me to be very complimentary where I should be about other players. It supersedes that other side of me where I might be a bit tight-lipped, thinking, Well, I don't want to give this bloke a wrap because I'm doing my darndest to get the better of him. Later I was more comfortable (older and wiser maybe?), and I'd happily give Mark or Luke or Jason Ryles a wrap because I didn't feel threatened by them.

And if and when it comes that they – or others – are rated as better players than me, well that's fine too, because I have had my day in the sun, and football was always going to end for me one day.

Mind you, there was never any chance I'd go easily!

Please excuse my diversion here from the unfolding story of season 1998, a year I look back on with real pride, but it seems timely to talk about something that has been so much of my life: playing prop. I was 23 in '98; young for a front-rower and still learning the craft and thinking a lot – and I hope learning a lot – about the game, and especially about the nuances of front-row play. We won the Origin series that year, travelling to Sydney for the third game and beating them decisively there, 19–4. The wear and tear of the campaign had taken its toll on the Blues and they were without the likes of front-rowers Rodney Howe and Harragon, plus tough little Geoff Toohey. We were able to apply the blowtorch to them in a three-tries-to-one win – and afterwards Alfie Langer was named man of the series.

Much has been made over the years of the problems faced by the Broncos in 'backing up' for the premiership after the annual Origin series, which inevitably features a large contingent of Brisbane players. In '98 we were premiership favourites from March to September, won the Origin series and barely missed a beat along the way. A record contingent of Broncos involved in the representative program was required to play two games in the space of 48 hours on four separate occasions. Four of our six defeats for the season came in this testing mid-year period, and at one point we slumped to sixth on the ladder. But it was only a glitch, and we came out of it powerfully to go undefeated for 11 weeks in the lead-up to the finals series.

I never found good form too hard to sustain in that period. The Origin series was mentally draining – no doubt about that – and you would use up plenty of that side of your makeup. But the positive spin-off for me was that I would go into post-Origin (or Test) or club games feeling very relaxed and with a feeling of, Well, I've just played an Origin game . . . whatever happens here is just going to happen. Some of my better games came, somewhat unexpectedly, at that sort of time, especially when I was younger. Physically it was never too bad, although I have to say that there was some sort of 'catch-up factor' later in seasons, via the accumulated tiredness and mental fatigue. I have a theory that footballers only have a certain number of games in them per year and there is always going to be some price to pay for backing up the way we had to, season after season, squeezing representative football in amongst the premiership matches . . . but the game goes on.

Recovering from the four matches we lost in five weeks mid-season we built a season of tremendous achievement. We came charging out of the Origin 'hangover' with wins over Penrith (44–4) and Wests (56–4), and in our last 15 matches lost only one (to Parramatta 10–15), plus a draw with Balmain (10–all). The rest was the sweet taste of victory – all the way to the grand final. The loss to Parramatta in a quarterfinal, our second that season to the Brian Smith-coached team, stung us into action for what was to follow. We had talked up the game after the Eels had given Norths something of a physical bashing in the preliminary qualifier. I told the media: 'I know I speak for all the other guys in our forward pack when I say we'll be ready for anything Parramatta throws at us. We have a score to settle with them. This is a body-contact sport – the best team at the end of September will be the one that can absorb the most pressure and remain standing.'

Well, for all the enthusiastic words, we came unstuck, and Parramatta beat us again, 15–10, in front of our own crowd at ANZ. The word 'embarrassed' became a recurring theme of Wayne's post-match discussions. And we were. We were down on discipline and up on mistakes, and had played well below our best. But the next week, with our anger (at ourselves) still apparent and pride in ourselves as a team, we were back on the rails, beating Melbourne 30–6 in the second elimination semi at the SFS.

I struggled with an ankle injury almost as old as my memory in the days leading up to that game. I had done damage to the ankle way back in the dim country footy past, weakening the joint and making it increasingly vulnerable to injury. Neither the club nor I made a fuss about it in the lead-up to the game, because that's the best way. I didn't train with the side until the Thursday, got through the match okay – although with the thought that one day I was going to have to get the bloody thing fixed – and lifted my gaze to the grand final qualifier against Sydney City.

We smashed the Roosters, 46–18, nine tries to three, leading them 18–6 at half-time and 40–6 with 25 minutes to go in the second half. They had been impressive in beating Melbourne and Newcastle, but we were just about on fire that day at ANZ, with Darren Lockyer right at his top and running in three tries from fullback. The showdown would be with Canterbury or Parramatta and when the Eels led 18–2 with 11 minutes to play it looked a certainty that we would have one last chance to square accounts with the team, which had already beaten us twice during the year. But miracles *do* (occasionally) happen in football and somehow Canterbury climbed off the floor to draw level with three minutes to go and then proceeded to run away with it in extra time. At the end the scoreboard read 32–20. Amazing!

The media tends to make a big issue of 'rivalries' between particular clubs and it was certainly that way between the Broncos and the Eels in 1998. But more often than not I think if rivalries do exist, they are more likely to be between the coaches (Brian Smith and Wayne Bennett on this occasion), not the players. There was certainly a time when the Broncos were seen as the rich, arrogant high-fliers of the competition – the side that everyone wanted to beat. It was like that in the early years of the club, when the Broncos team was pretty much akin to the great Queensland Origin side. Later ill-feeling no doubt followed the club after the Super League dramas – because of the now accepted truth that virtually the whole idea for the concept that eventually split the game down the middle came out of the Broncos boardroom. But in recent years I don't think the Broncos have been seen as the 'villains' anywhere near as much. The Roosters have probably got more of that about them than we have now, and I don't know how many times I've heard whispers involving the Roosters and the salary cap.

Now and then in any season you hear rumours of clubs cheating on the cap, but those honestly don't concern me much at all, mainly because they have absolutely nothing to do with the job that I'm trying to do for my club. As for the Broncos and the arrogance that was perceived to exist in the early teams, I don't think people see that in us any more. I know that playing for the club through the years of my career I have not felt any special animosity towards us.

Anyhow, in 1998 we had no further need to think about Parramatta, the team which had beaten us twice and with whom there was supposed to be some sort of feud. They were dead and buried in the premiership thanks to Canterbury's miracle fightback and now it was the Dogs we had to get over. On the afternoon of Sunday, September 27, 1998, we trailed them 10–12 at half-time at Aussie Stadium and then turned the match around spectacularly in the second half. We took the lead within two minutes of the resumption, via a Tonie Carroll try, had the match won at 26–12 by the 20-minute mark and in the end scored five second-half tries and conceded none to record the biggest grand final win (38–12) since 1975, when Easts thrashed St George 38–0. It was a fantastic ending to a really fabulous Broncos year. If we had only won 'half' a competition in beating Cronulla in the Super League grand final of 1997, we had now gone all the way – in a manner that wasn't much short of devastating.

The Sydney-based media wrestled with the implications of such a victory and questioned whether the dominance evidenced in our premiership win was good for rugby league. 'There is a resignation from Sydney-based fans that it's futile trying to compete with the Broncos, basically just a haven for Queensland's State of Origin players,' wrote Darren Hadland in *Rugby League Week*. Another journo, Tony Megahey, summed up the '98 Broncos this way: 'As a team, the Broncos have the balance and the class to be rated with the finest of any era. An undisputed champion play-maker in Langer, the try scoring potency of Renouf, the spectacular rising talents of Lockyer, the finishing prowess of Sailor and Hancock and a young forward pack rising in status every season.'

Brad Fittler went even further, writing: 'Invincible ... unstoppable. Call them what you like, but as far as I am concerned the Brisbane Broncos are the best club team I have seen.' 'Freddy' went on to rate the 1998 side better than the champion back-to-back Bronco teams of 1992–93.

It had indeed been a magical time for Broncos football. In the previous 18 months we had won the Super League premiership, the World Club Challenge, the 1998 minor premiership and premiership – and Queensland, built on a foundation of Bronco players, had won the '98 State of Origin series. I had the time of my life that year. In 13 seasons at the club I was lucky enough to be involved in some great ones and this sure was one of them. For a player to be able to be part of such dominance right across the spectrum – to win a premiership, the Origin series and the Test series – is pretty rare.

Chapter 12

ALF, KEVVIE AND THE GREAT BRONCO DAYS

Season 1999 was the Bronco year that had a little bit of everything. Ten rounds into the competition we had managed to win just a solitary game (20–10 over Souths at ANZ) and had gone from odds-on favourites for the premiership to being a shorter quote for the wooden spoon than for the title! Then we scraped in against Balmain at Leichhardt one Sunday in May (12–10) after they had led us until six minutes before full-time, and from that point proceeded to go on and win 10 and draw one of our next 11 games! The fairytale finally fizzled out when we fell, 42–20, to Cronulla in a quarterfinal, with Sharks coach John Lang declaring that probably we had 'run our race' in all we had achieved thus far – but the rescuing of the season to even that level was a pretty remarkable achievement. It was a season which featured maybe the lowest point in Broncos history to that time: when Melbourne travelled up to ANZ and whipped us 48–6 in Round 3, the worst loss in the club's 12-year existence. But like all experiences in life, sometimes it is good to sample adversity and the other side of the tracks, and there was a great deal of good that came out of the season in that we were able to overcome that humiliating loss, and some other jolting setbacks, and still rebuild a season of some respectability. It was enormous to do that and I certainly felt pride in what we had achieved. But Johnny Lang was probably right. We used up a lot of juice getting as far as we did, and we couldn't take the next step . . . and the next.

I remember how disappointed Wayne was that we bowed out against the Sharks. At the start of that season he had stepped down as Queensland Origin coach so that his season-long commitment could be to the Broncos – and he had it in his mind that we could do something really special and go right on with it and win the title. To take the line that we had achieved some success probably *is* a weak way of looking at it. I am a believer in the theory that as a footballer you can always find that little bit more. But honestly, we'd been looking over a cliff week after week after somehow clawing our way up the slope, and we had used up a helluva lot of petrol getting there. Perhaps the feeling existed that even to have made the finals was some sort of resurrection after the terrible start we had had. I don't think we ever dared dream beyond that. Meanwhile, the coach was thinking at the next level . . .

After a decade of achievement it was bitterly disappointing for the team to go out with a whimper rather than a bang. And a scoreline of 42–20 is a fair beating in any language. The Sharks led us 16–2 at half-time, and 22–2 just after, and we were never again in the hunt. One report talked of us being: 'out-muscled, out-skilled, outplayed, out-enthused and out-sped'. That was about it.

Notwithstanding, the 1999 experience was a good example of how adversity can sometimes draw a team and a club closer together. To be really up against it can bring out a whole range of feelings and reactions. We were cocooned tightly in there when the going was bad and we could have pulled the plug – but we didn't. We were really together. We knew we were struggling but we just hung on. In the world outside, the controversy and the criticism raged. But in our own little environment it was good. I think every single Bronco player from that year would agree it was a good learning experience. In those sorts of circumstances you learn to think in a completely different way – and I don't believe any one of us lost hope, or admitted defeat. We just worked away and waited for it to turn around, and when it did we just put our foot to the floor, and away we went. My own experience is that adversity brings out pretty good things in me. A dose of it every so often doesn't do anyone any harm . . . it reminds you what the good times are about.

As our fortunes fell in those early months of '99, the fans voted with their feet. A Saturday afternoon game against Penrith drew only 9790 people – the smallest crowd ever to attend a Brisbane home game. But when our run of success began and then continued, the fans came surging back and by the end of the year we had averaged more than 23,000 per home game, our best figures in years. I guess that says a whole lot about something most of us already know: that the only thing the supporters want is success, or at the least the hope of it. At the Broncos that year it might even have been a bit more subtle than that. Crowds dropped off early in our struggle, but in the latter stages of the run, they started to come back. On the day we played Sydney City at ANZ in early May we had won one football match in our last 10 – and yet almost 30,000 came to the ground. When the realisation sank in that a winning club like the Broncos was genuinely in a bad hole, it was as if the fans said, 'Hang on . . . these boys really do need our support.' And they came back.

Just days before that match, on Wednesday, April 28, 1999, at a media conference televised live throughout Queensland, Allan 'Alfie' Langer announced his retirement from football.

The shock news came in his twelfth year with the club and in his ninth season as captain. It came three days after the game against North Queensland in Townsville in which we had fought back to grab a last-minute draw, 20–all. I remember the match well. We hadn't played well and Alf, in particular hadn't played well, and it sticks in my mind that when I came off late in the second half, he was sitting there on the bench – and I thought to myself, My god ... I don't think I've ever seen that! In the night that followed, the usual letdown with a few beers, the whispers began ... 'Alf's retiring' ... 'Alf's retiring.' By the morning, it was a bushfire.

But when the official announcement came a couple of days later, I still couldn't believe it. Alf hadn't been going great, but I didn't think he'd been going that poorly either. But obviously he was feeling the heavy load of leading us through that period. That was just Allan Langer: he felt he couldn't do it, didn't want to let anyone down, and so ... bang ... decided he wouldn't do it any more. It meant walking away from a fair bit of money. It was no empty decision by Alf – there were huge ramifications for him, professionally and personally. The decision said a lot about Alf – that he stepped away because he felt he could no longer do the job for the team. He is not the sort of bloke who could have just limped along, getting his money. Pride and competitive spirit always existed in very large quantities in Alf. The decision came as a huge shock, but none of us in the team held it against him in any way. The thing was, though, that no one wanted him to go. It wasn't his time. Alf, of course, subsequently went to England for two years, returned to play a hero's role in the deciding State of Origin game of 2001 and then signed on for a full season with the Broncos in 2002 (18 games) and played bloody well.

Alfie Langer was the greatest player in my experience. When you line him up against someone like Darren Lockyer, a wonderful player, you'd probably arrive at the conclusion that Lockey is technically the better and more skilful footballer. But Alfie had that little winning edge that the vast majority of players don't have. When he was our halfback and we were in trouble late in a match, we'd give the ball to Alf every time. And more times than you could ever remember, he found a way. Nine times out of ten he would conjure up something and we'd get home.

I would never take anything away from players like Lockey and Andrew Johns. They are champions of the modern game. But give me Alfie Langer any day. The little bloke had a huge array of skills – although he probably fell short technically and aesthetically, and in the 'classical' sense as a footballer. For me, though, when I look back over my career, he'll be the fella I remember, the best player I ever played with . . . and such a great, unassuming bloke off the field.

Season 1999 produced a big development in my own life off the paddock. I never set out in life to own a hotel, but on June 29 that year I took over the Royal in Leyburn – Queensland's longest continuously licensed hotel still operating in its original structure. I probably had my first beer in the place when I was 15 or 16 and it was certainly part of my consciousness in my growing-up years. I never had any sort of plan to buy the Royal, but since my teenage days I have always loved the thrill of the deal. I bought my first tractor when I was 15 and a block of land when I was 19. And what did Shane Webcke, at 15, need an old run-down tractor for? Well he didn't, really, he just happened to like tractors. Being poor affects people in a lot of different ways, I'd imagine. For me as a young bloke there was this burning desire to accumulate things. That first tractor set up a pattern in my life. I love machines – and I continued to, buying tractors, motorbikes, little bulldozers.

By 1999 I had put a fair bit of money through the Royal Hotel over the years. There were occasions when my mates and I had done our best to drink it dry, and I had long before then realised that it was a very, very good business. At the time there was an owner in the place who probably wasn't so well suited to the business and I saw an opportunity, so I wrote him a letter in which I suggested that if he ever wanted to sell the hotel, he should contact me. And he wrote back and said, well, as a matter of fact he *did* want to sell the place. We talked and agreed on a price, and I bought it.

So I became the owner of a beautiful old colonial hotel (built in 1863), but one that needed plenty of work. In the years that followed I put quite a bit of money into the hotel, focusing on a restoration program to bring it back to what it used to be, and an extension, so it could grow as a business. Years before, the beautiful original bricks had been painted over, so we sandblasted all of that and took it back to its original form. The timber doors were all in poor shape and had to be replaced, we re-roofed the whole building and ripped off a façade that had been tacked onto the front in the '70s. At the end of it I had spent a bloody fortune, but I had a beautiful pub that was a third as big again as it had been, and which has grown into an excellent business. We went to great trouble to retain the character of the place, matching the bricks as closely as we could. It was a long and difficult operation, but the outcome was seamless and it is now a magnificent hotel.

There is still more work to be done – and for the time being, while I am playing football, I have leased it out. Like all of us, I only have enough time and energy for a certain number of things in my life, but I have heaps of ideas and further improvements will come down the track. Our dining room overflows at weekends, and I have plans to make use of the huge roof capacity for a nice little nook/eating spot. The only rule I set down for the dining room was that it must present the sort of tucker I enjoy. That means the best meat available, such as prime Darling Downs beef and big servings, with plenty of garden-fresh vegetables.

I love the place – it's a hotel with a real sense of history, with its beautiful fireplaces and all the other reminders of the way it was 140 years ago. I think people love the atmosphere of the place. I went to the local Historical Society and they dug out a heap of old photos, which I had blown up and which now hang around the walls. We've got good local support, but we get great weekend trade too, with Leyburn being just a nice distance for people wanting to run out of town at the weekend.

Ultimately I want to run the business for myself. I'll have a manager in there but will have greater control over it than I do now. I regard it as a challenge and I want to see where I can take it. It's going to be a real project for me when I finish football. It's not a billion-dollar city hotel or anything like it – and it's never going to make me a fortune. But it's a very stable bit of income that will be there forever. I take a certain amount of pride in owning it because it certainly is to me a 'grand' hotel, and one with lots of history. And I think it's a great 'overnighter' for Brisbane people, with a nice little motel across the road offering really good accommodation.

My link with the Royal is in line with a real love I have for old buildings and historic architecture. If I had to rank my interests outside the game, those things are right up there. There is something special about things that have stood the test of time. A really good memory of the 2004 UK Tri-nations tour is a trip I did with Scotty Hill and Billy Johnston (team trainer) and a local bloke, a real character, into Scotland – all the way to a small fishing village called Applecross right up the top, eight or nine hours' drive from Leeds, where we were staying. We stopped on the way at a little hotel in the woods in some tiny backwater Scottish village and it was fantastic, 500 years old and with an amazing atmosphere. When you walked in the door you felt you were stepping back into an earlier century. We were going to have two beers . . . but we stayed and stayed.

In Australia we have nothing to match that, of course, from a European settlement point of view. But sometimes, in a similar way, I have stood out the front of the Royal in Leyburn, just taking it in – and marvelling at the fact that someone built it 142 years ago and it's still standing, as solid as it ever was, a happy meeting place for people now as no doubt it was back then.

With its history came a message for all subsequent owners. The original licensee, builder and owner in 1863 was a bloke named James Murray, whose tenure lasted just six months.

He died from the effects of drinking to excess . . .

In the wake of 1999's topsy-turvy season we began the 2000 campaign by tackling what the media delighted in calling a 'torture course' at the Army's camp at Canungra, south of Brisbane, out Beaudesert way. The journos weren't far wrong. As a break in training in earlier seasons we had now and then been to the camp to do a one-day course, which was tough enough. But this time Benny upped the ante. For the first time we camped there for four days and the Army guys took us through some really tough stuff that asked deep questions of every one of us. They broke us into little teams and set us a variety of challenges, such as hauling heavy carts minus most of the tyres up steep slopes and heading out on marathon marches carrying heavy army gear . . . and all of it in sweltering summer heat. There were 3 am hikes through the bush and the challenge of negotiating Canungra's notorious tunnels – Canungra being the place where they trained soldiers for Vietnam. One task was to crawl through a 3-metre tunnel underwater, a great challenge to anyone who was even mildly claustrophobic. But by the end of the course every member of the team had successfully negotiated it. Over three days we hiked more than 40 km through rough terrain in temperatures hovering in the mid-30s. At all times we were on limited rations. Canungra is a tough environment, and the good thing was that as a team unit we came through it very well, rediscovering the truth that everything is possible if you work together, help the bloke next to you and have faith in him.

Wayne viewed the experience as a genuine marking post to us having a great chance in the 2000 premiership. We'd had a tough year in '99 but the coach headed home from Canungra convinced that the experience there had represented a turning point, and that the team could do great things in the season ahead. I think Benny looked at the group of blokes that had gone to Canungra, reflected on how we had gone and came up with the answer that we might be onto something special this year.

What we had encountered was bloody hard work. I love that sort of thing, but like everyone else I found it tremendously testing. Within the team environment it tested us in different ways. We had to work together over a period in which we were all fatigued and heat-stressed and irritable. But we came through it, and I think every one of us learned something extra about ourselves, and something about the blokes around us. To challenge yourself physically in a way that is different – as that experience was – tends to show up any failings. There's nothing like being under the pump (and we were!) to identify your weaknesses.

Variety is, without doubt, an essential part of good coaching. To do something completely different, as we did in 2000 – with the Canungra camp and later having fun with a couple of very competitive Skirmish events at a place on the outskirts of Brisbane, Oldies v Youngies – can be a big refresher, and break the monotony of the hard grind. In Skirmish, I started with the Oldies but shrewdly switched sides to the Youngies. It was good fun. From outside, the life of a professional footballer probably looks pretty glamorous, and for the first 12 months or so of a player's career, that's the way it seems. But after that it becomes drudgery: endless training sessions with the necessary repetition and sameness. It is the way it has to be – the perfecting of routines, the boring monotonous things that prepare a team each week and help them reach their potential. Repetition is the key to making things happen automatically in matches, and therefore that is how we must train. Coaches mix it up as best they can, but there are only so many different drills and different ways in which to present the things we (the players) have to do. Monotony is ever present, so the things that must be done become second nature. When something rehearsed comes off in a match and looks great, well, it's because it's been done countless times at training.

The only pay-off is success – never easy to achieve – or at least the encouragement of a strong finish to a season, providing hope for what lies ahead. There are personal rewards along the way, but in a team sense, in any season the goal sought can only ever be one thing: to win the title. This is particularly true with the Broncos, a one-town team around which the expectations are always sky-high. If we don't win the premiership people think we're 'busteds'. To come second is nowhere near good enough. The culture of pride within the team has almost always matched that expectation – a determination never to drop our heads or look over our shoulders. Alongside that, the strength of our club has always been that we enjoyed what we did, enjoyed our footy.

After the NSW Blues had won the first two games of the 2000 Origin series (20–16, 28–16), Gorden Tallis went public in calling for the third game to be dumped, because it was meaningless. Players had had more than enough football and there was now no real motivation with the series already decided, said Gordie. It wasn't dropped, of course, and NSW thrashed us 56–16 to really rub it in. His suggestion really stirred the pot, though – and just about the only person who wasn't dragged into the controversy that followed was the big bloke himself. It was a very characteristic Gorden Tallis operation: to start a raging bushfire, then shrug his shoulders and walk away unconcerned and get on with his life. And, you know, he wouldn't have given it two more thoughts. While the rest of the league world was in a mad, blustering panic about the idea, Gorden would have been at home having a sandwich. That's just how he is. He's a passionate man about issues, on the one hand – but on the other, things can be one layer deep and he'll just walk away. He's a funny fellow . . . a good fellow.

I loved the fact that I played with Gordie and I love the fact that we're mates. He was a real enigma, the big fella. I probably had the feeling that the latter part of his career, particularly the last two seasons, was a real letdown to him. Maybe not enough is made of this aspect of it – that he managed to play at all. From what I know, Gorden Tallis was within a fingernail of being in a wheelchair through a neck injury he suffered in 2001. There is no doubt that that played on his mind in the rest of his career, as it would. I just think he was incredibly brave to come back from what had happened to him. To be honest, I wouldn't have done it. I'm bloody certain of that. I take my hat off to him. I prefer to think of the five or six cracker seasons he had before the last couple . . . to think of those as the true mark of Gorden Tallis the football player. But it was a measure of him too at the end, that he kept playing under such a shadow.

He never 'leant' on the injury when things weren't going so well. He acknowledged that he wasn't playing well, but he never blamed his neck. And he was probably entitled to. At his peak he was such a powerhouse . . . he could bust open anyone. Apart from the pleasure I take from having played with one of the great second-rowers of the modern era, I'm just fortunate to have known him at all. He's a tremendous fella. He makes his fair share of enemies because he's so black and white. But that's just

Gordie's way. He's an extremely generous bloke – but to cross him is a bad move, as some have found out to their discomfort.

Gordie has been a great character in rugby league – and any game needs those. He has really kicked on post-footy: among many other new directions he's taken was being added to the NRL Board in 2005. He's a witty bloke, and the few speaking jobs we have done together have worked out very well. I'm more straight-laced than he is. I don't try to be funny . . . but when we work together, he puts a great deal of shit on me, and it somehow ends up being very funny. I expect we'll be doing some more of it.

Kevvie Walters was our captain at the Broncos in 2000, and for him to be given the honour was a great note at the end of his career. I developed a real affinity with him in 2000 that had not been there previously. I had always respected the bloke, and through my years in the game I had grown up, so I imagine he started to have a little more faith in me and my ability. Whatever it was, we drew closer that season. As we edged closer to the goal of winning the premiership, the motivation of sending him out a winner was ever present, although we made no fuss about it.

This was a great Bronco year. We were undefeated for the first eight rounds, led throughout the 26 rounds of the competition proper and didn't lose a game at home. Four of our six losses in the year came either when we had players missing through Origin commitments or were backing up after an international commitment (Anzac Test). We had lost two champion players in Allan Langer and Steve Renouf but managed to set, and maintain, a standard of excellence that must have been deeply satisfying to Wayne. The transformation of the team was a tremendous credit to the coach after the events of 1999 – and especially our horror start to that year, losing nine of the first 10 games. Late in season 2000 journalist Darren Hadland wrote: 'Bennett has turned the Broncos into the most physically dominant team since Warren Ryan's "Dogs of War" (Canterbury) in 1984–85. It has been a remarkable coaching feat.'

In Round 7 I reached the milestone of 100 games for the Broncos. It was personally satisfying, but I asked the club not to make a thing of it. After all, there were players around, like Cronulla's Andrew Ettingshausen, who had played more than 300 games.

Every time I have passed one of these milestones I have allowed myself the luxury of a little bit of reflection, even though the time to think about those things isn't when you are still in the game. It is later. But I do it anyway, and I inevitably think, 'Oh my god. How did this happen? How does it *keep* happening?' I don't dwell on it for too long in case it stops. I just shake my head and move on. Disbelief is in the mix somewhere.

On the day I played my 100th first-grade game with the Broncos I was quoted as telling the media: 'At times I have found it hard to accept all the outside things that go on around footy, but I have grown to accept them.' It's an interesting quote, which says something about my journey. It's hard for me to remember exactly what I was thinking at that time, but it was certainly tied up with what I had come to know: that playing professional football was about a lot more than . . . well, just playing footy. I suspect at that stage of my career I was still fairly confused about how I fitted into the whole picture . . . the media stuff . . . the silly stories that get put out at times . . . the weekly hoopla.

I had long since realised the way it was – that the newspapers liked rugby league and chose to run a lot of stories, and that in the main that was good for the blokes who played the game. But I also realised that in a world in which there were so many genuinely serious issues, a lot of the football stuff was nonsense, and far more was made of things that happened in league at times than should ever be the case.

Simplicity came for me with the passing seasons. The chatter of other voices about me or the game was no longer of concern to me. It came pretty much down to this: if Wayne was happy with the way I played in a match, I was happy. I grew up, I guess. I accepted that there would always be varying opinions. But I preferred it simple. If the coach was happy I didn't have to concern myself with outside views. He is the one big chief a player should listen to.

The milestone of 100 games came and went. Something that took place later, in Round 24 that year, was to have a far more profound effect on my season.

Chapter 13
BUSTED

Just after half-time in our Round 24 match against St George Illawarra at WIN Stadium Wollongong, Sunday, July 17, 2000, I went in hard for a tackle on Dragons front-rower Luke Bailey. The boys on the sideline reckoned they heard a crack at the moment of impact, with my left arm cannoning into Bailey's elbow as he carted the ball up. Funnily enough, I can't remember any noise, but I knew I had broken the arm all the same. My arm just went floppy. I've done something serious here, I thought. I left the field, and in the dressing room the initial expert diagnosis supported my diagnosis: a probable broken arm. This was not good timing.

We beat St George 44–14 that afternoon and went on with the job to finish six points clear of the field as the season's minor premiers. The Broncos' fifth premiership beckoned.

We flew home to Brisbane that night and I headed straight down to the hospital for X-rays. The verdict was that the bone in my forearm hadn't broken right through, although it was bloody close. But it was deeply cracked. It would take six to eight weeks to get it right, maybe longer, I was told. The grand final was exactly six weeks away, August 27, earlier than for many seasons because it was Olympic year, with the premiership shuffled forward to clear the decks for Sydney's huge September carnival. The news was promising enough. I decided then and there that six weeks was possible for me . . . and it began.

There is not much you can do specifically to speed things up when it comes to a broken bone. But I knew that if I was to be a chance I would have to keep up with my fitness, so I put myself on a really tough training regime, working in isolation at Gilbert Park while the team headed on towards the finals. It was bloody hard going. I told one journalist: 'At the moment I feel terrible, like I'm on another planet watching everyone else.' On the eve of the finals I was able to resume weight training and also to take part in some full-contact drills with the team – wearing a strong protective guard.

In the meantime I was getting all sorts of therapies on the arm. They cut a hole in my plaster and I had regular treatment from an ultrasound-type machine, which was screwed into the gap to deliver its (hopefully) healing rays. Anything I thought might help, I did. I certainly drank heaps of milk in those weeks. None of it probably made any difference, but at least I *felt* I was doing something positive.

The days and weeks ticked by. We stumbled in the last round of the competition, beaten 28–0 by the Sydney Roosters at the SFS, but regrouped strongly for the finals. In week 1 of the finals we knocked over the Sharks 34–20 after they had rocked us in the first half and all but silenced an ANZ crowd of 25,000 by leading us 20–6 at the break. One more win and we would be in the grand final.

On Sunday, August 20, in the match that would make or break the season, we would line up against Parramatta at

Stadium Australia. That would be five weeks to the day since I broke my arm.

The doctors would not give me a clearance, but early in the week before the game Benny pulled me to one side. 'If you want to play in the grand final, you have to play this game,' he said. I was far from convinced. By then I had tried it out in some 'contact' work at training and had a real scare. I took a knock right on the spot and thought, Shit . . . I've done it again! I went back inside and tried to do a push-up – the Webcke theory at that time being that if I could manage push-ups, I was okay.

I couldn't do a push-up.

I headed straight out of the ground and off for another X-ray. While it showed clearly the crack in the bone, there seemed to be no further damage. The pain had just been my body's normal reaction – a warning to let the bloody thing heal, and not to use it. It was a little lesson I had learned: that if I felt that same feeling again, it was okay.

I drove back down to training.

Late in the week I flew to Sydney with the team. 'Bring your stuff,' said Benny, 'We want to play you.' We stayed at the Swiss Grand at Bondi and I remember very clearly the breakfast on match morning when the other players had moved away in the room, leaving only me, Benny, Kevvie Walters (our captain that year) and Ron Massey, one of the wise men of the game. Benny was doing his best to convince me, because he felt I was right to play. But I was sceptical – not because I was scared about the pain factor, about how sore it might be. My worry was that I didn't want to go into a game, particularly a sudden-death preliminary final, re-break the arm five minutes in and leave us with only 16 men. Kevvie remembers the tension of the occasion, of how I was sweating as we talked about it. I was very nervous. But I left that meeting with the final words, 'Yep, I'll play.' It was an honest meeting, as they tend to be with a bloke like Wayne Bennett.

He wanted me to play but he also knew that if the move back-fired, the criticism and flak would be aimed at me. There would be talk of a 'foolish gamble' and of my 'selfishness' in taking such a gamble. There would be no backlash against the people who had encouraged me to play. Benny and I talked about that and in the end it was my decision.

Before that breakfast get-together, a bloke in Sydney had been commissioned to make up a guard for me (just in case!). It proved to be quite good, though not exactly right. It was made of plastic and resin and foam and was a pretty solid piece of work. The league had a look at it and gave it the okay. I was ready. Well, as ready as I could be . . .

And so I played – against Parramatta at Stadium Australia. I subdued my worries as best I could and did my utmost just to do the job I normally set out to do for the team. In the end my personal verdict was that I had got through it okay. The match statistics showed that I made 24 tackles, hit the ball up 14 times and played my normal match time. Later, the media made a fuss of me having played in 'obvious pain' – and, yes, the arm was still pretty sore. To be honest, I couldn't use it. I couldn't properly set myself to make tackles and I carried the ball in my right arm when I ran it up. The battle was as much a mental one as a physical one: I had to constantly keep telling myself that I was okay. It was a very uncomfortable way to play football. But I got through – and most importantly, we won the preliminary final in a tight game, 16–10, after we had galloped away to lead 12–0 in the first 15 minutes. We were in the grand final.

Playing in the premiership decider grew to be an even tougher experience for my mind than the Parramatta game. This time I didn't have all the emotional buildup; people just left me alone, presuming I was okay. But the fact was that heading in to grand final week I was still only five and a bit weeks on from the day of the injury. I was defying medical advice in playing and had signed an official form to that effect. The arm hadn't healed, was still bloody sore, and no way did I have full use of it. But I had the chance to play in a grand final, and I was so pleased to be there that I didn't care about the rest.

There was some bullshit in the press, and one of the game's 'Immortals', Johnny Raper, was in the thick of it. He talked about how our opponents should 'target' my arm. 'If Webcke played in my day he wouldn't have lasted 15 minutes,' said Raper after the preliminary final. 'That arm would've been looked after in the first scrum. Forget about the illegality – Parramatta should have worked the arm.' Roosters skipper Brad Fittler declared his forwards would run at me and observed how he had found it strange that the Parramatta forwards hadn't done that. 'Go for your life . . . best of luck,' Wayne Bennett responded to the 'target Webcke' calls. And I got my back up a bit when someone showed me the comments. 'Bugger it,' I thought. 'I don't care if they *do* target me.'

In the end I got lucky. We won the big football match that day and I didn't re-break my arm, though the recurring nightmare of that happening, of me letting the team down, had been with me in every moment of the buildup. It was like an old movie played over and over – me re-breaking the arm early on, and the Broncos down to 16 men in the game of the year (not that you can't win matches with a 16-man squad!). That thought churned over end-lessly in my head – how much I would hate to be a factor in losing a grand final.

I had no painkillers for either match. The doctors ruled against giving them to me and I was fine with that. There were no great heroics in what I did. While it is not exactly the natural thing to do – to play football with a partially healed broken arm – it didn't occur to me to worry too much about it once I got out there. In the end it was just a case of putting up with it, treating it as an annoyance rather than anything more serious. History says we got away with it. I came through the grand final and played my role and that was wonderful . . . but geez, it was risky. The relief at the end was huge and twofold, first, that we'd won the premiership, and second, that I had 'survived' and not let the side down. It was like winning Lotto twice, like putting your house on a horse race . . . and winning.

The experience gave me an interesting insight into how the mind works. The thing I remember most from both games is not feeling tired. That really showed me the power of the mind; I was so intent on what was happening with my arm that I wasn't worried in the least about what was happening with my heart and lungs! The game was going on around me and I was just praying I'd get through.

The grand final scoreline was 14–6 our way over the Roosters, in a match described as being 'as clinical and predictable as they come'. In the end it was comprehensive, although the score indicates a tight game. There was talk of our precision and control and how we had 'pounded' our way to victory. 'Defence was the bricks and mortar of the club's fifth premiership . . . and it is the foundation for the club's future,' wrote *Rugby League Week*'s Darren Hadland. I had always thought we would win the game, despite my own personal distractions, but was never as confident as I had been in 1998. I knew we bloody well had to work hard. And we did.

Chapter 14

FEAR ON THE FOOTY FIELD

Any first-grade player who says he has never felt the cold breath of fear on a football field is a liar. I feel confident in saying that, although I concede there may be blokes who are different from me. I got frightened, and I have no problem saying it, and feel no shame in putting it into the public arena in this book. Rugby league at the level we play it is a hard and painful game. Sit up close one day at a first-grade match and you'll hear the smack of the tackle and the oohs and aahs of the wind being knocked out of blokes, and now and then you'll hear the cries of pain.

Fear comes in different forms, and I'll do my best to take you through what it's like. I'll start with this: I loved playing footy, and throughout my career I always looked forward to the game. But when you are in the sheds on match-day and then you get the call to take the field, there is always that little whisper of apprehension, the hope that today is not the day when something bad is going to happen. And as you walk onto the field it's in the back of your mind just how painful the next hour and a half is going to be. It might be a little different for the backs, I'm not sure, but what I do know is that when I played footy, and the other forwards feel the same, the whole time you are out there it's about feeling like absolute shit. There's a feeling that comes when you train really hard and are absolutely buggered – that's what you feel like the whole time in a game. And that's what you have to learn to live with if you are to be a footballer. The moments of joy you get from a game are when that feeling is superseded by something great that happens – something you might do, or a try that is scored provides a break and a temporary uplift. Those moments can lure you into temporarily thinking that you are enjoying it! But I have to tell you that for most of the time you're out there, you feel terrible. You are sick because you are physically exerting yourself so hard. And always there is the mental battle – forcing yourself to keep going when your body screams out: 'No! Stop it! I'm buggered!'

The first kind of fear you feel is the strictly physical one. And the way the game is played today the front-rowers are guaranteed to get an early taste of that. If your team is receiving from the kickoff you know (in my case, anyway) that it will be your job to take the ball up against three or four charging opposition forwards hell bent on 'burying' you. The fear is a natural one. As human beings we are told by the inner messages of millions of years to try to protect ourselves, and the innate fear of someone smashing you is a fundamental one. People have talked to me about the way I took the football up and have told me how much they admired the way I was 'fearless'. Well, that's bullshit. Just because I charged into the tacklers doesn't mean I wasn't thinking about them . . . not potentially scared of what might happen. And if I draw some attention because I'm saying that, well, I couldn't care less. I am just being honest. Sometimes when you're tired and sore and you have to do it all over again you just think, Shit, and you get this little moment of hesitation and a voice somewhere deep inside asks: 'Do you really want to do this?' And that's just natural. But you ignore it and you do what you're paid to do as a professional footballer.

For the front-rowers of the game there is never any sort of easy passage. We are always in the 'hitting zone' where the defenders are tight, and in numbers. With those numbers in close, blokes are more inclined to feel safe about coming out of the line and giving you one. Out wider on the paddock, defenders tend to be a bit more measured in their tackling because if they miss one, very likely there is going to be trouble.

Fear is very natural – as the great coach Jack Gibson declared when talking about football years ago. Confronting it and dealing with it is the challenge. Good players do that and then get on with the business at hand. I've never run onto a football field without a nagging thought of what someone else might do to me. But I have learned to handle it.

Oh yes, there's fear in football. It's the mechanism we (players) have developed to overcome it that makes us different from a lot of people. There are players who never overcome it, although you don't see a lot of them in the higher grades. I remember kids from earlier days who just couldn't beat the fear, who were just too scared they were going to get hurt. Ultimately they couldn't play the game. And that's fine – absolutely nothing wrong with that. Plenty of blokes just aren't conditioned to play football and they head to other worthwhile pursuits and use the different skills they have. That's just life sending people down different paths.

And I do think there are some players, even at first-grade level, who have never really managed the fear thing as well as they would have liked and who feel a bit less for it. It is a part of the game that barely anyone wants to talk about – because it is seen as some sort of weakness. But I see it differently: I think it can be used as a strength if you use your knowledge properly.

I share an opinion with Jack Gibson about players who overtly display bravado and who deny the existence of fear and are inclined to mouth off: that there is a big question mark over them. For my own part, I like to think I displayed enough courage over the years in the way I played – and yet, right through, I had this underlying fear. In talking about it here, I wonder how that could not be the case with everyone who plays such a game.

The other kind of fear in football is very real too. It's an ongoing one about not wanting to bugger things up in a match. Before any big game I'd invariably be thinking, I want to play well tonight . . . I don't want to make a mess of this. And I'd think about the individuals on the other side, how I was playing against this bloke and that bloke and they are hard men, and for sure it wasn't going to be easy. But those thoughts had the positive effect of adding an edge, knocking any complacency out of me. Often in the room before a game I'd look around at the little blokes, look at someone like Darren Lockyer, a skinny little bugger who is assured of being a target every time in every match, and I'd wonder, Shit – how do you do it?

The collision factor between the big men of the game is enormous. I remember a moment in the Tri-series tournament of 1997 when Solomon Haumono was playing for NSW. Solomon was a big hard man whose career could have been better than it turned out. Back then I knew virtually nothing about Haumono, because I have never made too much of a fuss about individuals on the other side. I ran straight at him, and in those days, even more so than later in my career when I had some variation in my running, I ran *really* hard and *really* straight. We collided, and he went a bit that way and I went a bit this way and managed to unload the ball to Peter Ryan. Both of us finished on the ground. I was deadset dazed. He had hit me very hard, with a full body shot, and he could really hit. It was a momentous collision, and in my half-groggy state I just thought, Bloody hell! That was my first experience of the bloke, and after that I tended to be a bit wary of him. The fact that I was dazed and probably he was too showed the force involved. After all, there had been no head contact.

I suppose all players remember the blokes who manage to bring off a really big shot on them – 'bell-ringers', they used to call them. My own list is fairly short. A bloke named Matt Rua from Melbourne could hit like a freight train and he got me a few times, although he never really hurt me. But you knew what he could do and he was the sort of player that blokes stayed away from.

Ruben Wiki, who became an inspiring and outstanding New Zealand Test captain and the team's spiritual leader, was another. He was (and is) as hard as a rock – an aggressive player, but a good clean player in my mind. He was another one you would think twice about, particularly early in his career. We played against each other plenty of times, and later, as his career rolled on, I had the sense he was leaving me alone a bit . . . maybe it was just a little showing of respect. I certainly had high respect for him – a dignified, respectful sort of bloke who in his home country is the hero he deserves to be.

Carl Webb (Cowboys) is moving strongly into that category. I had enough to do with him in his time at the Broncos to know that he is a bloke who deserves to be treated with some care and caution. He can really hit, really inflict some damage – as NSW's Luke Bailey found out in State of Origin 1, 2005.

Generally you remember those sorts of players; they are etched fairly deep in your memory bank because they have smashed you at some stage. Some weeks in a season I'd glance at the other team and think, There's no one really to worry about there, but most weeks there'd be someone. And I'd think, Oh, shit . . . you and take a little air of caution with me into the game. With those sort of blokes it's not as if you lie in bed worrying about them. It's just the fact that you know they're good at what they do, so there's a healthy and human quality of slight unease in the equation. You don't look for them in matches, and you don't dodge them, and if you've got nowhere else to go you'll run into them, albeit with some apprehension. It might be surprising for people to read these things, but it's true.

I remember an event in 1996 which showed the reality that hard and painful things happen in football. In September that year North Sydney beat us in a quarterfinal at Suncorp Stadium – and I was knocked out early in the game. This story is a good example of how you get better at handling things as you go along in your career. In a match in 2005 against the Warriors, Richard Villasanti got me with a good shot and knocked me into dreamland. Ten minutes later I was back on the paddock and I played out the whole game. The Villasanti incident was a good deal worse than the one back in '96; it was a head collision, I think, which hit me in the mouth and knocked me clean out.

But against Norths back in 1996 it was early days in my career and I was a little softer than I became later. That day at Suncorp after I had been KOed, I think Wayne really wanted me to go back on. I was playing in good form at that time and he wanted me in the match. But I stayed off. We lost the game 21–16 – and I guess no one felt good about that.

A day or two later Wayne pulled me to one side and asked me the question: 'Were you scared out there?' I remember reacting. 'Fucking scared? I'm not scared,' I said. I suspect that would be the reaction from any footballer when they were asked *that* question. And Wayne just said to me, 'Look, it's all right to be frightened on a football field . . . it's fine. I was sometimes scared as a player. Footballers get scared; it's not something to be worried about.' Wayne talks about the subject in one of his books – of coming to terms with his own fear as a footballer. He had obviously thought it might have been fear that had stopped me going back on against the Bears. But it wasn't that – I have always been in control of my fear in so far as it would never stop me going out to play. I was just very crook. And that's why I got the shits with Wayne when he posed the question. But it was interesting that it was brought up at that early stage of my career. I'm at peace with it all now – it just doesn't worry me.

I think most players get progressively better at handling fear, and also at handling the inevitable injuries and pain that come with the territory of rugby league. It's a maturity thing more than anything else. To play with the pain of an injury is a mental thing. It's really got nothing to do with the pain itself – and I know the pain factor has never worried me. The bigger worry in playing with injury is that you're not going to be able to perform at your peak and that you're going to be limited by it. That's the real worry: buggering things up for the team. The other fear you have is that whatever the injury happens to be, maybe that part is not going to 'work'.

In 2004, when I had an arthroscopy on my crook knee one Sunday and then played a final the following Saturday, I had a genuine fear of falling over and my leg breaking in half, because the bloody thing was giving way on me a bit. Gee, I can tell you that you suck up some energy thinking about things like that! Once you get into the game, it's not too bad. Everything moves so quickly that you just don't have time to think about it, and if the injury is *just* good enough, that's okay.

And as you go on in your career you develop little ways to deal with the problems you have. You learn to deal with pain and to understand that pain doesn't necessarily mean danger. But it takes time, because the instinct is very deeply instilled in all of us to protect our bodies. Self-protection is a very powerful, fundamental human thing. And to go against the grain – as professional foot-ballers must sometimes do – takes learning and mental strength.

It takes real courage to referee rugby league too, and especially at the highest level, where the pressure is relentless. The refs have the toughest job in the game. Most of them are now full-time, and should be – and as far as I'm concerned they deserve whatever they get out of their careers in football. On my reading of it the NRL seems a bit smug about referees going full-time and what a massive step that is. But it should have been done 10 years ago! Because if there was ever anyone in the game with a need to concentrate 100 per cent on being good at it, it was the bloody referee. I think they've got a hard gig!

I'll put my hand up and admit that I have 'given it to' enough referees in my time, but I think they understand that and don't mind too much. After all, they are out there with us, in the middle of the pressure cooker. They understand the heat of the moment. Very often they get a hard time: they get the double barrel of being abused by fans when things go wrong in a match and then hammered by the media the next day.

We can never expect perfection from referees. We can just hope that on a given day or night they will be as good as they can be and they will be honest, which I believe they are. I have heard some of the old stories of 'cheating referees', but I'd like to think those times are long gone. I've seen some pretty ordinary referee-ing performances at times but I don't recall ever having the suspicion that a ref might have been 'crook'. I have never been in a match where I thought deliberate actions by the referee changed the course of the game. I have, of course, played in many games where a refereeing decision has had the effect of turning things around. But I always think at times like that, why would a referee do a thing like that on purpose, knowing the shit he is going to cop over it? They are just human . . . they make mistakes like all of us.

On the subject of the refs I'll pose the $64,000 question: where would we be without them? We can't put robots out there to run football matches.

Like everyone and everything else in the game (except maybe some administrators), the refs have changed. When I started out in football the ref called you by your number or maybe your surname. Now at the top level of the NRL the referee is more likely to call you by your nickname: 'Webby! Come here!' Some people see that as being too matey, but I don't mind it; in fact I think it's quite good, a reflection of some rapport between ref and players. Most of the refs are pretty civil too, as they should be, where years ago I know some of the top blokes were renowned as 'sergeant majors', barking out their instructions.

Now and then I can get dirty on a ref with the best of them – but overall, I trust them. And one of the basic things about football is that I really believe if you are bloody well good enough to win a football match, you'll win it, even if the ref has hammered you 8–zip in the penalties . . . no matter what the ref has done to you.

Another (of the many) negatives for a referee is those times when he finds himself used by a coach as a scapegoat for a losing performance. That's a handy tactic for a coach trying to deflect some pressure . . .

No, as far as I'm concerned I've never had an axe to grind with the refs. And I'm speaking from some experience. When I was about 16 I did the course and became a QRL badge referee. I used to handle some of the junior games, and quite enjoyed it. Even then there'd be irate parents on the sidelines jumping up and down when they thought you weren't doing your job properly. So I had a taste of what it can be like for the blokes with the whistle. And what it can be like is bloody nerve-racking and bloody tough.

Chapter 15
WAYNE

As much as any man could possibly be, Wayne Bennett has been like another father to me. You will understand that that is something that could never be said lightly. Wayne was coming into my life just at the time that my dad left it, in 1994. He's been there ever since, coach of the Broncos, a mentor and a mate, and a profound and positive influence on this 'second half' of my life. We really clicked from the start. In a lot of ways our backgrounds aren't dissimilar, although his was probably quite a bit tougher than mine. In essence they are constructed of some of the same stuff.

Wayne could never replace my father. No one ever could. Affection-wise, he could never be the same to me as my father Tom was; he wouldn't expect that, and I never have either. But in terms of guidance and mateship and loyalty, I couldn't possibly have found anyone who could be closer. Particularly in those early days and months after Dad's death in 1994 I leant on Wayne a lot. I have continued to do that over the years. I trust him implicitly.

The things he has taught me over the years about the way the world works have been wonderful – wise and positive philosophies. I have certainly taken on board a whole lot of things of value over the seasons; other people perhaps have not so much. I think with some of the younger players at the Broncos that there is that old thing about not wanting to be seen as being too friendly with the boss. For that reason some of the messages he offers are sometimes privately laughed at or scorned. But either way, I think that anyone who gets the chance to play football under Wayne Bennett soaks it all up. There is so much common-sense around the man that whatever public face blokes put on it, they can't help but think, Bloody hell, that's right!

In my life, both in and out of football, I ask him about everything big that I do. It doesn't mean I always do what he advises, but I have a great deal of faith in his perspective on things. I find his judgement is right most of the time. And sometimes I have gone against things that he has said . . . and he's been right. If Dad had been around I think I still would have gone to Wayne and asked him things. No one could ever look as good in my eyes as my dad did. I worshipped him in so many ways. But the grown-up part of me understands there are things that he certainly wasn't an expert on. To have a bloke around like Wayne who I can go and bounce things off is an invaluable resource for me. It's been wonderful, and as my career has rolled along I've been more than happy to be seen as a strong supporter of the coach and his philosophies. I am very well aware of the benefits I have gained from my association with Wayne. In all these years, he has never given me a bum steer. I talked earlier about the gratitude I feel towards the game for what it has given me and to the club which provided me with my chance. Well, I owe an even greater debt to the coach. I wouldn't be the bloke I am today (or the bloke I hope I'm becoming) if it wasn't for his wisdom and influence.

Someone mentioned to me once how Peter Sterling had written years ago that of all the reasons he wanted to win football matches at Parramatta, the one that stood above all others was to win for the coach (Jack Gibson). I felt that way to an extent about Wayne Bennett. On the day of any victory I am always happiest for those who mean most to me – and he is one of those. But – setting aside winning – I always just wanted to play well to please him. That was really important to me. Praise from him means a whole lot to me, much more than any words in a news-paper could ever mean. If he told me I played all right, I was happy. But you have to earn it with Wayne. He doesn't go out of his way to make me or anyone feel good if we've had a shit game. And that's as it should be. With Wayne the praise is dealt out pretty sparingly, although I think he has softened to an extent over the years in his approach, and that's fine. People change.

But he'll still make the hard calls when he believes they need to be made – and there have been some tough ones in his years at the Broncos, leaving a fair few blokes walking around with chips on their shoulders. People seem to tell me things . . . sometimes I wonder whether I've got a sign painted somewhere on me which reads, 'Talk to me, I'll listen!', because many times over the years I have been told one side of a story from within the club, some of them to do with decisions made by Wayne, and then almost inevitably I'll get the other side and be caught in the middle, with neither party knowing it. I have stored up some information over the years!

I always hoped I would not be one of the blokes who Wayne would feel the need to make one of those tough calls on. But I was realistic enough to accept there might come a day when he tapped me on the shoulder – and how I dealt with it would have been a great test of who I was. I think the hardest part about being truly honest with yourself is acknowledging your deficiencies as much as your accomplishments. I suspect not many of us are much good at that. I have always admired Wayne for his ability to make the hard calls. But would I have gotten the shits if he made one on me? It would have been an interesting day! If you are loyal to Wayne, that includes knowing when it's time to go – and that is bloody hard. I certainly can't suggest that all would have been fine if it had happened to me – I'd definitely have had to work awfully hard to put it in perspective. But knowing and respecting Wayne as I do, I would also understand a certain truth: it would have been bloody hard for him too.

There have been dilemmas through the seasons that he has agonised over, things that have been very hard on him. Outsiders would never know what he was feeling; he has that impassive quality about him, something I suspect he has worked hard on. But if there is a tough decision to be made he just does it – and that's the essence of his strength and character. I think it's one of the qualities of the great men of history: the ability to be strong and make the tough calls when they need to be made.

I will do my best to profile him here, in the different areas of his life, from the perspective of a bloke who played under his guidance for a decade and valued the experience immensely.

Bennett the man

Wayne's exterior tends to block him off from the world to an extent, but it's something of a façade. Underneath he's a bloke who cares deeply about his football players and about his fellow human beings generally. He just doesn't allow people 'inside' too often.

I love talking to the bloke. He seems to have an understanding about the way the world works, a certain wisdom. I feel we are very good friends, and I value that a great deal. To have had the chance to play at his club and play under his coaching has been a wonderful thing for me. To have also been his friend has been a privilege. I think about those things in the quieter moments. The part he has played in my life has been so strong that I feel in debt to him, and I know it's a debt I'll never be able to repay.

Perhaps the greatest thing I can say about him from my very personal perspective is this: that through his teaching and his guidance he has made me a man I don't believe I could ever have become had he *not* been involved. I could almost write another book on the bits of advice he has given me over the years. I use him as a sounding board – even if Ally and I happen to be struggling a bit at home. I'll run something past him: 'Wayne, am I being a chauvinistic arsehole here?' and almost always the answer will be a wise and helpful one. *Always*, it will be an honest one. And that's another great thing about Wayne: he never tells you what you want to hear; he tells you what he knows you need to hear.

There should be no misunderstanding: Wayne Bennett and I have had our heated moments. There are certainly times I have been pissed off with something that's happened and others when he's been pissed off with me. I don't want to suggest that we never have a cross word. But I feel quite comfortable disagreeing with him, because I know the sort of man he is. With him it's never a case of, 'I'm right and everyone else is wrong.'

A good example of that was his ill-judged decision to sneak out an airport back door and fail to meet the waiting media on the return home of the 2005 Tri-series team from the UK. I thought straight away that he was wrong – and he quickly admitted as much himself. No, Wayne is not without his chinks. And there would be some things that his detractors could pick him to pieces on. He's like all of us: nowhere close to infallible and no Nobel Laureate. But I'd suggest he's got a lot fewer flaws in his makeup than anyone else I know, and more basic common-sense than most.

Wayne Bennett and Tom Webcke of Leyburn had certain things in common. Fundamental to them both was a great work ethic. I saw my dad do it many times in the physical sense, just working on and on to get something done that had to be done. Wayne is the same, although the challenges for him are not necessarily physical work – he can just push on and on. Obviously he would never have got to where he is in his life without that quality.

The public view of Wayne is probably a bit of a mixture – although I'm sure the *Australian Story* piece the ABC produced shed new light on him for many thousands of people. The wider public probably have a perception of him as a man of very few words, and I'm sure he loves to feed that. He is anything but: he is a man who loves a joke and is warm and easy-going in many ways.

I'll tell you a story about Wayne that says a lot about him and certainly something of my respect for him. Because he is a great coach and a special human being there is a tendency among some people to try to pull him down. Once at a function in Sydney I did something indirectly concerning Wayne which I was in no way proud of. In the company of a couple of other rugby league blokes, one of them a player-manager, I joined in this bit of bagging that was going on about Wayne. The next day, when I thought about it, I felt really terrible, felt that I had let him down. So I went and told him when I got back to Brisbane. 'You may never get to hear about this,' I told him, 'but I owe you an apology.' I went on to let him know what had happened. 'I owe you more than that,' I told him. 'It was a real bloody weakness, and I apologise. I don't know why I did it. It was a weak moment and I don't believe for a moment a couple of things I said.' In response he just shrugged it off, thanked me and told me not to worry about it, and life went on as before.

Bennett the coach

Call me biased if you like, but if there has ever been a better coach than him, well, I'll take plenty of convincing. His record is sensational; in almost 100 years of rugby league in Australia he is the only man to coach more than 400 games at the one club. I don't see Wayne as a 'Superman', but his qualities add up to someone who is as good as a football coach could possibly be. He is an unbelievable communicator, hugely knowledgeable about rugby league and deeply passionate about the game – and whatever he does in the game he backs with a hard edge unmatched by most. He is street-smart, business-smart, a very, very savvy bloke. He is a man from the school of hard knocks, building the life he has created from the shaky base of a bloody tough beginning. I think the revelations about those early years are one of the big reasons that the *Australian Story* profile on Wayne was so popular. A man viewed as enigmatic and grim and uncommunicative was seen in a completely different (and true) light.

As a football coach he is very good analytically. At a video session he can pull a game down to exactly what needs to be focused on. But what he is *really* good at is getting a room full of footballers ready for a match. Not for Wayne the old face-slapping ways of the old Wests Magpies sides or of the Churchillian, rabble-rousing coaches of the past. His way is with measured words; he is a wonderful orator who gets right to the heart of things and says it straight without the need to cover it all in flowers. And he has the knack of putting things in such a way that you can't disagree with him. Wayne draws on a lot of outside inspiration – the lessons of great past events or the words of some of the legendary NFL coaches.

There have been some match-days on which we have gone into the final meeting with Wayne before the game still sensing that we needed something special. On plenty of those days when

Mum and Dad and me in very early days on the farm at Leyburn.

This was the greatest Christmas of them all for Dallas (white hat) and me. New pushbikes! I can only imagine it must have been a very good year on the land.

This pic of Dallas and me feeding a lamb brings back very strong memories of those days on the farm. It's the way it was . . . we always had animals around.

This is a pretty rare shot, really, owing to the fact that Dad hated having his photo taken. He is probably expressing his disapproval to the photographer – my uncle Leon Webcke.

It could be said I was a little the worse for wear here. 'Blind' might be a better word. I'm with Mum on the night of my 21st birthday party. The previous week I had been as sick as a dog with some bug and the doc had placed me on medication, with the strict instruction that I was not to drink. But I did.

There's some history here . . . it's the day I played for the Allora Clifton Wattles in the Under 18s grand final, in 1992 . . . the day that Wayne Bennett first saw me play rugby league. It was to be the start of something big in my life. That's me, fourth from the right, back row.

On the steps of Parliament House, Brisbane on the day in 1996 that I married Allison Knapp.

The life I love – a day out there on the farm, with just enough room on the bike for Pompous the pooch (named by my father) and me.

With my Nan and my Mum, I'm all dolled up – ready for the wedding day of my brother Dallas.

I'm in the classy company here of Allan 'Alfie' Langer and Anthony Mundine as we bid to monster a Sharks opponent in the Super League grand final of 1997.

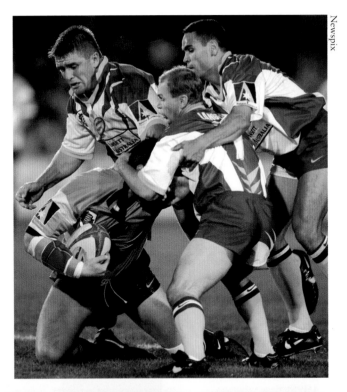

How sweet it was. Super League grand final 1997, Brisbane 26, Cronulla 8, ANZ Stadium, Saturday night, 20 September.

A fractured game is back together – well, more or less – and we've won the premiership. Hoisting high the new NRL Trophy after we beat Canterbury 38–12 in the grand final at the Sydney Football Stadium in 1998.

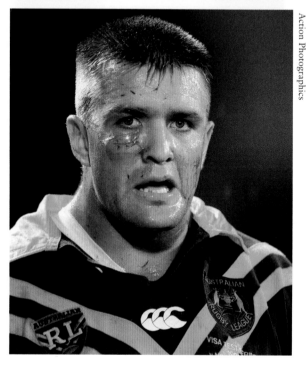

Kiwi Jarrod McCracken made sure I bore the scars of battle from my debut Test match in the rejoined game (second Test, 1998). I copped McCracken's knee in the face.

The aftermath, as I nurse my sore head. Thanks, Jarrod!

Newspix

The guard on my busted left arm shows up clearly in this shot as Roosters Luke Ricketson, Bryan Fletcher and Ryan Cross give me a hard time in the 2000 grand final. Luke Priddis (left) is there to lend a hand. It was a great day; we won the grand final, 14–6.

Action Photographics

In the glow of a Grand Final victory, 2000 . . . and a moment of thanks to all the fans. Tonie Carroll on the right.

Action Photographics

I played one of the very best games of my life in this 'one off' Test against Great Britain in Sydney in 2002. It was an ill-conceived match, however – the Poms flying in a few days before the game to take a 64–10 thrashing.

With my front row mate Petero 'Bula' Civoniceva, going hell for leather in a wrestling drill at Broncos training.

Eat your heart out, Glenn McGrath! In action in our annual social cricket match at the Gabba, 2004. You will notice the ball is pitching a trifle short. I suspect the following scenario: that one of the backs was at the crease and I was doing my best to bounce him.

Origin 1, 2004 and Bulldogs duo Mark O'Meley (left) and Andrew Ryan have me in a spot of bother. The Blues pipped us 9–8 at Telstra on the back of a Shaun Timmins field goal.

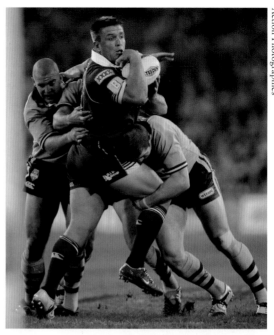

Action Photographics

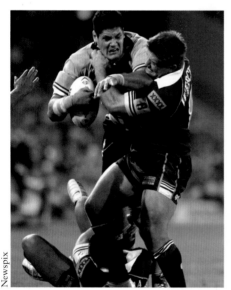

Newspix

Newspix

I didn't realise it, of course, at the time, but this was to be my last hometown Origin game. It's Game 2, 2004 at Suncorp and I'm doing my best to throw a very big Blue, Willie Mason. We won the match (22–18), but lost the series.

It's the last roundup – and that's maybe why I'm looking thoughtful. Taking a break on the bench, Origin 3, 2004 at Telstra Stadium. I would never play Origin football again after this night.

Ally and me, Broncos presentation dinner, 2004.

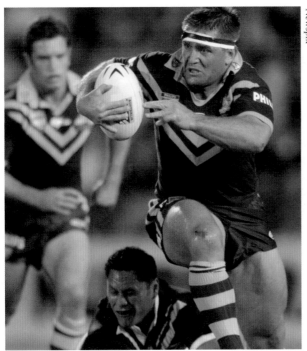

Newspix

With the defensive line breached I'd like to think this was the start of a 50-metre gallop upfield. Perhaps not, though. It's my last 'home' Test, v the Kiwis, 23 April 2004 – a game we won 37–10 at EnergyAustralia Stadium, Newcastle.

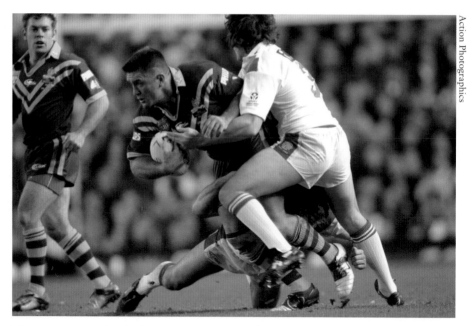

The Tri-nations final of 2004 was a match I will never forget. On a bung knee I was privileged to play in an opening 40 minutes which has been suggested as the 'greatest half of rugby league ever played'. By the time my knee 'locked' just after half time and ended the game for me, we had it won. The score was 40–4 at the end, an amazing result against a talented Great Britain side. This was my last game in the green and gold.

A photo I value greatly – sharing the moment with my mate, mentor and coach Wayne Bennett at Leeds after the Tri-nations Final of 2004.

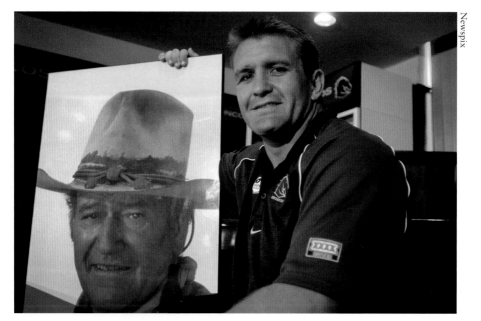

Newspix

John Wayne, the quintessential cowboy, has been a great favourite of mine (and was of my Dad's) over the years and on the April day in 2005 that I announced my retirement from representative football, the cameramen got me to pose with 'The Duke'.

Newspix

The fact that I have let go of Jake Webster's leg does not alter the reality that this was an awful moment. It happened in an instant in the match v Melbourne, 17 July 2005, as David Stagg and I tackled Webster. It was a tackle gone wrong in the blink of an eye, and right at this moment I was not feeling real flash at all . . . I could see where he was headed. Thankfully, Jake was okay – and that was a huge relief.

There are many things I'll miss about football, but off-season training on a scorching Brisbane summer's day? Well, I won't miss it one bit.

The day after this photo was taken in April 2006 I was booked in for a 'sitting' for a portrait that was being painted for charity. They reckoned the facial scars made me look 'rugged'. Hmmm.

Action Photographics

A later career pic – as I prepare to take it up to the advancing forwards, ball in hands. Early in my career I would just tuck the ball under my arm and charge. But I learnt as I went along in the game, as you should, and took pleasure from the times I could hit the line and slip the ball away to a support.

Action Photographics

There was some genuine pain here. I tore a rib cartilage early in the 2006 game against Manly in May . . . and it bloody well hurt! Trainers Tony Spencer (left) and Ken Ragh were there to help me off the paddock. We had the bye the following week so it turned out I didn't miss a game, although the thing was still sore months later.

Newspix

The Crew . . . the reason for it all. I love this photo of us together – Ally, Grace, Erin and Hayden. This is my future.

And this is part of the future too – the beautiful old Royal Hotel at Leyburn (built 1863), which we have faithfully restored and which will be a centerpiece of the ongoing Webcke years post-football.

his words have reached even deeper than normal, I have left the dressing room ready to tackle trees! Yet the buildup has never been about pumping us with ridiculous notions. All is done in a calm, commonsense way, nailing the direction that we need to take. That is his great gift.

Men of special wisdom are not in great supply in rugby league (or in plenty of other areas of society, for that matter!). Wayne Bennett is one of them; another is Ron Massey (Jack Gibson's renowned 'offsider'). With 'Mass' you get pure commonsense. He's a mate of Wayne's and he was always around us in the later years of my career. Apart from his wisdom, I used to marvel at his ability to eat . . . he's up there with the best I've ever seen in that department. A few years back, if you showed him a buffet break-fast, he'd be at it like a tornado!

In 1999, when we lost our first three games, and were whipped 48–6 by the Melbourne Storm, adding up to the worst start in the club's 12-year history, Wayne was his usual implacable self. In the week following the Melbourne game there was no revisiting the nightmare that had taken place. Instead, the videos we watched were of some of the team's magic moments of the previous two years – strong, positive reinforcement at a difficult time. The coach knew that confidence was down, and set about rebuilding it. 'You achieve nothing by being destructive,' he said at the time. The day after the Melbourne match, we visited kids in two Brisbane hospitals. It was business as usual. 'We have no more right to success in this game than any other team,' said the coach. 'The advantage we have is that we know what it is like to be there, and if personal pride – and embarrassment – are not the triggers to get us going, then I am a poor judge of my players.'

Inside and outside football he is a respectful man, too. It's interesting to see him around someone like Ron Massey. He almost defers to Mass, a great football man whose status in the game should never be underestimated. And when it comes to respect, Wayne respects the game he is involved in as much as or more than anyone else around, I'd suggest. He respects it both for the great sport it is and also for what it did for him, providing him with an opportunity to build a new foundation above a very tough early life. When I think about Wayne Bennett, 'respect' is one of the key words that comes to mind. He is a very respectful man, too, in terms of how people should be treated, and he instils that in his players. Of his pet hates (and he has a few), one of the strongest is any real or perceived lack of respect shown towards people in the general public or anyone trying to help the Broncos. He despises that – hates the thought of decent people being 'used up' by footballers, or anyone else who might see themselves as 'celebrities'. As a player, if you want to piss him off, just bite the hand that feeds you . . . he'll go nuts. He is 100 per cent right. There are wonderful people around rugby league who bend over backwards to do things for us (the players) simply because they love the game. If any of us disrespect them and what they do, we are bloody idiots.

Footballers who do not fit into the Bennett framework are probably not going to be in there with Wayne too long. But he is a giver of chances, all the same – even though he cops some flak for it at times. When a high-profile player went after Wayne had flipped him to reserve grade, people really gave it to Wayne. Yet the bloke had been given chances long after what would normally be considered normal. He has done that with a lot of blokes – the likes of Julian O'Neill, who had his problems – cut them some slack, did not make knee-jerk decisions, gave the players their opportunity. I think he really loves picking up discarded players and making something of them. He has done that many times, and always such players leave us better than when they came.

I have a great jumble of memories about the coach, most of them good, but some with a bit of an edge too. In a match in 2005 against a team which has faded from my memory now I got a knock, probably my knee, I think, and was sore and hobbling. We were slipping behind on the scoreboard, and about five minutes into the second half he took me off the field, and didn't put me back on. I was *filthy*, sitting there thinking, I'm not bloody well helping anyone here. I felt like I hadn't played at all, and by the end I was as cranky as I've ever been in my life. Not for the first time, walking off the field, I was thinking, I'll tell him to piss off. I want nothing to do with him. I'll tell him to stick his football team up his arse. He wants me to play with a broken arm, and now I can't even play with a sore knee!

There had been commonsense and purpose in what the coach had done, of course. He took me off that field because he didn't want me hobbling around on an injured knee when he knew we couldn't win (and we didn't). That's why he did it, and I knew it. But human nature takes over and I wanted to blame him because I didn't feel at all good about what I had done in that match. I barely talked to him that night at the after-match thing and I was snapping and snarling and whingeing to Kevvie (Walters) all night and whingeing to Andrew Gee. I was carrying on, I really was. Later in the evening, when he was leaving he came over to me and said, 'See you later', and I ignored him. And he turned away and then came back and said it again, and I just grunted in reply.

The next morning I felt really guilty and knew I had acted childishly. So I picked up the phone and rang him. 'Wayne, it's Webby. How're you going mate?' I said.

'I thought I might hear from you today,' replied the coach (he knows me better than I know myself sometimes!).

'Wayne, I'm a dickhead,' I said. 'I was carrying on . . . I was whingeing to Kevvie about you because you didn't let me back on the field. I went on like a damned fool and I'm ringing to apologise.'

'We're mates,' said Wayne, 'don't worry about it.'

And that was the end of it.

That was a hard phone call to make. But I had to do it. I respect the bloke far too much to have anyone else telling him that I had been carrying on. My realisation in the cold light of day was that no way in the bloody world did he deserve either that, or what I had served up the previous night.

I know that in having Wayne as a coach I have been privileged to have the very best of what a career in sport can offer.

Messages from the coach

At the Broncos Wayne taught me life skills such as thinking like a winner and the importance of being of good character. Right from the start of my career in those seasons of the mid-1990s I enjoyed and admired his coaching. I think it was in 1995 or '96 that I first received and experienced one of the coach's inspirational documents. The subject, from memory, was 'courage and character'. Right through the years I have known him Wayne has been a great collector of sayings and stories and quotes, clues to success and winning and being a decent human being. Over the years he has equated the gladiatorial nature of our sport to many different fields of endeavour. The war analogy is one he has returned to now and then and I believe it to be quite legitimate, in that we go into a 'mini-battle' every time we take the field – with the big difference being that the consequences of our actions do not equate in any way to what happens in war. I have valued and enjoyed the 'Bennett Papers' over the years and kept a lot of the material. I think smart people learn from the ideas and the good thinking of others. And there is no shame in using someone else's thinking when it is sound and appropriate. It was no surprise when he put some of his thoughts together in a book – and it became a bestseller!

I remember that before we played Cronulla in a match in the mid-'90s, Wayne encouraged us to make small sacrifices in our lives. Blokes were giving up things like beer and chocolate . . . I think my sacrifice was a pledge to spend more time with the tackling bag. The coach was just making a point that sometimes you had to pay a price to achieve things that you wanted to achieve. I think it was probably part of him pointing the team back towards the solid things that go towards success after the surreal period everyone had been through (well, the senior blokes anyway) with the Super League dramas. This was his way of saying: put footy above the other things in your lives. That philosophy became part of my life.

The ability to sacrifice is the ability to think that something is a bit more important than you yourself are. It's a big part of being in a team sport. From a man like Wayne, such a request to players came from a very strong base. After all, he is a man who has made sacrifices all his life. People watching the *Australian Story* program came to understand the sacrifices he has made for his family. One thing I learned very early about Wayne Bennett is that he will not tell you to do things that he won't do himself.

Origin and Test coach

Wayne coached the Queensland Origin side in seven series and lost only two: the first (1986) and the last (2003). I'm presuming he won't throw his hat into the ring again, but with him you never quite know. I was in the Broncos team in four of those years (1998, 2001–03), and in looking back I'd have to say that his Origin commitments had an effect on us at club level. It was a case of something having to suffer. Wayne is not the sort of bloke who is ever half-and-half when he takes on a job – he's such a competitive bugger. And it was a logical outcome that him being away for a period and stand-in coaches taking over the club reins was going to be to the detriment of the club. But it's one of the wonderful things about Wayne that doesn't get talked about enough is that he has always been about doing the right thing for the *game*. He loves the Broncos, and they are always his first focus. Stepping back into the Origin breach, and especially in those later series, was very much about the wider good of the game.

When he came back in 2001 it was about saving the Origin series. We had got our arses kicked in the 2000 series (beaten 3–0, 112 points against 42), and the edifice of Origin football was starting to look shaky. If it ever gets back to what it was before 1980, where Queensland can't compete, it will be the death of Origin and a crushing blow to rugby league generally. I think it was a wonderful thing that he returned for season 2001, on a mission to try to help the cause. And the club gave him the green light to do it, knowing that his absence and involvement over those six weeks would probably damage our campaign. I think that said a lot about the Broncos too – evidence of their belief that the club has to help look after the game as well as conduct its own affairs. Queensland won in 2001 and drew (so retaining the trophy) in 2002 and all was well with Origin football again.

There was a presumption when Wayne stepped down last time that it was a signal he had finished forever with Origin football. I'm not so sure. Wayne (55 as I write this) is a bloke who retains his enthusiasm and passion for the game. When he has stepped into the breach as Origin coach (1986, 1998, 2001), he has breathed life back into it. Who's to say he couldn't do it again? I have no doubt he could reinvent it all again if the time came when he was needed once more.

The absolute bottom line with Wayne Bennett is that he loves rugby league, and his affection for the game goes right across the spectrum. So it was regrettable that his campaign as Australian coach ended (almost certainly) as disappointingly as it did in late 2005. When the Kangaroos lost the Tri-nations final against New Zealand in the UK, inevitably he copped some of the flak. A football match lost against a good and committed

Kiwi side was a positive result for the international game – but Australia had been beaten, and out here the unforgiving media much preferred to accentuate the negative. It got worse when Wayne made a poor decision and ducked the media at the airport on his arrival back home. He knows he erred in doing that and I'm sure there was a moment that very night when he thought, Shit! I shouldn't have done that. But the tour organisers have to carry some of the load for the stuff-up too. Surely the matter should have been taken right out of the coach's hands? Of course he should have met the media, but it should have been done at a formally arranged press conference for which he was fully briefed long before. And even after he made that mistake, it could have been so easily and quickly fixed by having him back at an all-in press conference the next morning where he could have said, 'I'm really sorry about that, guys. Now what would you like to know about the tour?'

A few days after that drama he was gone as Australian coach. Moving swiftly, the ARL appointed Ricky Stuart. I felt it was rather sad to see Wayne depart on that note. It would have been so much better if he could have gone out on his own terms. The really sad thing was that he's a bloke who cares so much about international football. I accept that there are things about Wayne that people don't like and that he has his detractors. So do we all. But one thing that has always shone through is his love of the game, his feeling and passion for it as an international sport.

I think that maybe most of all he loves what young men can become when they embrace what the game is about – and where it can take them in their lives. I know that just as I do, he credits rugby league with so much of what his own life has become. For my part, I'll fight tooth and nail till the day I die to convince people of just how good a game it is. Rugby league has enabled me to become a much better person than I would have been – and I'm happy to shout its praises from the rooftops. I'll be more than happy if my son Hayden chooses one day to play the game, although there will be no pressure on him about that. And if he does make that choice, he will be fortunate indeed if he chances to find a Wayne Bennett in his footballing life.

Longevity as a coach

I believe that in the late 2005 sacking of assistant coach Kevvie Walters from the Broncos lies at least one important clue to the secret of both Wayne's longevity and his success as a football coach. And that's not the slightest reflection on Kevvie. The point I am making is about the *principle* involved. Wayne, the coach, is willing to bend, willing to learn, willing to use other ideas. He is open to debate at all times on whether his way is the right way. But once he's confident he's doing the thing he believes is right, you won't stop him. The fact that he did what he felt he had to do in showing the door to Kevvie and 'Badge' Belcher after a disappointing Bronco season showed him yet again to be a bloke prepared to make the toughest possible calls and not let anything prevent that if he believed the decision was for the greater good of the club. I mean, he sacked Wally 'The King' Lewis, for heaven's sake, because he felt it was right for the club! Over the seasons others have felt that same sting . . .

Wayne is a tough, hard professional who is immensely loyal to his players while they are doing the job he wants them to do. When he makes the call that it's time for blokes to go, some get really pissed off, and I have to say I can't understand that attitude, although I can accept their natural disappointment. Some seem to have expected the loyalty to go on forever. It is my view that a coach owes no more than that. But loyalty is a two-way street. And the second part of that is about reality – about accepting that if a coach who has been loyal to you (and you to him in return) decides one day that your time has come in the evolving interests of the club and the team, then I think players have to accept with some grace that it's time to go. It's not easy, though. It's a very human thing for blokes to want to hang on at a joint they have been part of, and at the Broncos there have certainly been those who have been very crooked on him. Anyone who thinks that Wayne makes such decisions easily is way off the mark. Those sorts of calls hurt him too, but he makes them anyway. In that lies one of his great strengths as a coach and leader. Interestingly, just about all the blokes who have been dirty on him at different times have come around to accepting what happened and are back on more or less normal terms with Wayne.

The great strength of Wayne Bennett, the man and the football coach, is not only that he recognises the right thing to do, but he has the courage to do it, regardless of the fall-out.

I hope we'll be friends for life.

Wayne has a farm only 15 minutes from where our place is, and I harbour a little dream that sometime in the future there'll be days when he'll wander over and he and I will sit out the front and have a cuppa and a yarn about football and life and all that sort of stuff. I look forward to that . . .

Chapter 16
MY NIGHTMARE

This book being as honest a recall of a career in football as memory will allow, I will share here for the first time a story that represents the worst experience of all in my long stay with the Broncos. It happened in 2001, the same season in which rugby union's Ben Tune made unwelcome news after he had unknowingly breached the code's drug laws by taking the banned drug Probenecid in an attempt to speed his recovery from a knee injury. The story of Tune's 'positive' broke after the ARU anti-doping tribunal decided not to punish him; the Wallaby winger was dragged into the headlines, and by 2002 was under serious threat of being suspended for two years by the International Rugby Board, according to the newspapers.

The tale I am going to tell you has many similarities. What happened was this: in early 2001, after returning from the World Club Challenge game in the UK, I developed a knee infection, a week or so before the season began. We had been training on various different fields – in England and back here – and I picked up an infection serious enough for the doctors to be extremely worried about it. In fact, I was told that the infection could be life-threatening if it got a hold deeper into my knee. I saw the orthopaedic surgeon Peter Myers and was told I needed to be in hospital and on strong antibiotics if I was to get rid of the bug and play in the opening round. With the antibiotics I was given Probenecid, the same drug as Tune had been given (also by Peter Myers) – it had the effect of accelerating the body's acceptance of antibiotics, but it was also (as I was to learn) a popular masking agent for anabolic steroids.

The treatment worked remarkably well – well enough for me to play the opening round of the 2001 premiership, a game that we won 18–17 over the Cowboys in Townsville. In the dressing room that night I was one of the players selected for a random drug test, an event that is nothing unusual in today's closely monitored game.

I told the testers that I had been in hospital during the week and had been on medications, but that I didn't know what they were. I noted that fact on the testing sheet. And I did my test and walked out of the ground that night with a clear mind and without a worry in the world. Drug tests never bothered me. As far as I was concerned they were only of concern to players who might have been taking something, and that had never been my way.

Two weeks later I fielded a phone call from a woman from the Australian Sports Drug Agency. The news she conveyed was the most shattering thing I had heard in my years in senior football. 'You have tested positive on the sample taken at Dairy Farmers Stadium, Townsville on February 17,' she told me. She named the drug: Probenecid. Shocked, I argued the point. 'No, that can't be right . . . you are wrong,' I spluttered, almost swallowing my tongue. But she was adamant, and went on to calmly outline what would happen now.

The moment our conversation finished, I rang Wayne. His was the first advice I needed – I had to get to him and find out what the bloody hell I was going to do now. My opening words to him were along the lines of, 'Wayne, you're never going to believe this, but I tested positive to that drug test two weeks ago.' At that stage I hadn't even given a thought to how this might have happened.

'What do you mean?' he said. I think he was as stunned as I was. But he told me later he knew straight away I wasn't going to tell him I had taken something. That was a measure of his faith in me, I guess. 'What's happened?' he persisted.

'I honestly don't know,' I answered. And I didn't. I went on to tell him how Peter Myers had put me on some stuff in hospital, and maybe I should check that. I was thinking a bit more clearly now and remembered as we talked that I still had the bottle they had given me in hospital. I hung up the phone and went to the cabinet and checked. It was the drug she had named. Probenecid.

I rang Wayne back and told him the news. And straight away he went to work.

Things were going particularly well for me in my football career then and the first thought that entered my head was that with this news everyone would be thinking that the only reason I had been playing well – now, or ever – was because I was taking something. I would be branded a cheat. This is how you think when you're panicking. I had never been so scared in my whole life, and night after night through that period I lay awake thinking about what might happen.

It affected my whole life at the time, and later, when it was over, I wondered if people around me had noticed how I was. I had never taken drugs, and my whole philosophy was against them, to the point that I had taken a public stance on the subject. I was like just about all the players I know: feeling abhorrence for the use of drugs, whether recreational or performance-enhancing. Now I could see this blowing up to become a huge public controversy, with me pinned like a rabbit in the headlights . . . and with the mud sticking.

Probably only Allison knows the hell that I went through in the period that followed. It was nothing short of harrowing, day by day.

Wayne was my best ally, of course, and he investigated all the available channels.

The result of it all came as a blessed relief. It was deemed that Pete Myers, the doctor, had done nothing wrong . . . and, of course, he hadn't. The drug in question wasn't a steroid or a performance-enhancing substance but it *was* on the list of those that could be used as a masking agent. What had been done at a time when there was genuine concern about potential danger to my health was perfectly legitimate. Peter is an outstanding doctor and his only concern at that time was that my health was at risk.

After days of agonising, I learned my fate . . .

The decision arrived at was that what had taken place was not a notifiable offence, and that my positive test would not be made public. I had a lot of people to be very grateful to for that outcome, the NRL included – and I was especially comfortable in the knowledge that everything had been done through the right channels. To me, rugby league showed its true colours in the way it was all handled. The investigation was thorough, the facts were treated on their merits and the whole process remained 'in house', out of respect for what public disclosure could have done to me – in relation to an accusation of which I was completely innocent and unknowing. There was no underhandedness and nothing sinister. Everyone who had to be notified was notified. The whole thing was kept quiet because of the understanding that to not do so would be to risk having the truth twisted. I am quite sure that sections of the media would not have been content with letting truth ruin a good story. And once it's out there, it's very difficult to live down a lie.

This was a bloody tough time in my life, and probably the most terrifying experience of my football career. Through those bad days and nights I could see all that I had worked for crumbling around me, including the reputation I had for conducting my life in a fair and straightforward way. That reputation was built on what I believed was respectable and decent in terms of conducting one's life. For this to go unfairly or badly would have planted a seed of doubt in people's minds – and I don't know how I could have lived with that. No doubt my resilient and stubborn side would have kicked in and I would have survived, but I know for sure it would have taken a great toll on me.

I tell the story now because it is part of my life. It is Shane Webcke history. It is probably a cautionary tale, too, for all footballers. These days all of us are extra careful about what we take, whether supplements or medications. But there is a need to be questioning at all times, to make sure that anything we put in our bodies is okay on the drug checklist. A single slip can bruise a career forever. I am fortunate that it didn't happen to me.

I will never forget the drama and angst of those days. Everything had been going so well for me that year, but then came a single phone call bringing news of potentially the biggest crash-tackle of my football career.

What a contrast it was to the lighthearted way that season had started . . .

The premiership defence of 2001 kicked off with the team 20,000 kilometres from home – and with the extraordinary sight of players running around like lunatics, throwing snowballs at each other. It snowed heavily in Wigan the day we arrived in the English north to ready ourselves for the World Club Challenge against St Helen's. Being from Queensland, where snow is not a major annual attraction, plenty of the boys had never seen the stuff. So there we all were one late January afternoon, a few million bucks worth of Aussie footballers, tearing around like schoolkids and pelting anyone who came within range.

The weather gave us a hammering during the match, when a fierce hailstorm descended on Reebok Stadium Bolton. Before the wind and hail arrived we had crafted an 18–6 lead in bitter conditions. But with the storm, St Helen's came rushing back to win the game 20–18 and take the trophy.

The match was an early-season trial for us (and we wanted to win it!); there had been personnel changes at the club, headed by the departure of 2000's skipper, Kevin Walters, who was to return later in the season on a request from Wayne Bennett to help out the club at a time of need. Ahead, unknown, lay a season that was to ultimately be crushed by injury. To lose to St Helen's was disappointing, but we had a great time over there anyway; the trip was effectively a celebration for winning the 2000 premiership.

But we had started the serious business earlier than any other club, and back home there would follow a season of declining fortunes, most of it centred on an injury list that just grew and grew. Phillip Lee lasted only three matches, Ben Ikin six and Gorden Tallis (with a serious neck injury) 10, and as the season unfolded, the likes of Shaun Berrigan, Scott Prince and Michael De Vere were all missing for extended periods. The wear-and-tear factor was huge, with 12 of our players involved in the Origin series. Wendell Sailor announced that he was going to cross the bridge to rugby union and the promising Justin Hodges was dumped to first division after it was announced that he had signed a three-year deal with Sydney Roosters. The Hodges decision, which no doubt perplexed some people, was characteristic of Wayne. He had a tough call to make and he assessed the situation and made it . . . and we just got on with business at the club. Once it was done it was not even talked about any more.

On the question of high-profile league players jumping the fence to rugby union, I don't hold anything personally against the blokes who made the switch from rugby league to union: Lote Tuqiri, Wendell Sailor and Mat Rogers, for instance. But I am dirty on the *principle* of players turning their backs on rugby league. I am fiercely loyal to league for the game it is, and the opportunity it has provided for me. And when the likes of Tuqiri and Sailor and Rogers leave to go to the other code, I believe it is a kick in the guts to rugby league. In switching, they are taking away from the game that gave them their chance – while adding to another, opposing game. I don't respect it and I know for sure that I could never go and play another football code, certainly not professionally.

The historical fact is that rugby league and rugby union have battled it out for almost a century over the issue of which is the better rugby code. There has been bitterness and ill-feeling along the way. The tussle continues today, although in a more amicable way. They (rugby union) have a better international setup and we have a vastly superior domestic club competition. To drain one (rugby league) to bolster the rival code seems to me nothing less than disloyalty to the game.

When you look at someone like Lote – a wonderful fellow against whom I hold no grudge – rugby league fostered his talent, instilled a professional approach in him and provided the platform for him to become what he became. And he just trotted across to union, as Wendell and Mat Rogers had done, and got the big dollars. Whenever it happens there is a lot of airy talk about the 'challenge' of playing rugby, but when you pull it down to its bare bones it's about money – and if they were going to be fair dinkum honest, that's what they'd tell you.

I have no problem using the word 'defection' in relation to blokes who choose to hop the fence. The question needs to be asked in our game: 'What price do we put on loyalty'? In my view, players have to accept that publicly contemplating and/or transferring to union hurts our game. It gives the other code a whole heap of free publicity. Look at the Mark Gasnier circus in 2006. The 'will-he-or-won't-he' speculation around that went on longer than any soap opera – and even dragged on when all seemed dead and buried after Gasnier and his manager had failed to respond to a signing deadline set by rugby union. It was a huge distraction for rugby league at an important time in the season. I know I could never have made the switch to rugby – although I don't think any less of players who do it. That decision is theirs alone and they have to live with it. I just hope that when players receive these kinds of offers in the future they can look beyond the dollars and reflect on what rugby league has meant to them.

I have talked to Lote and I've talked to Wendell about it – and I'm not giving too much away to reveal that neither of them professes to liking the game of rugby union better than they liked league. If it came to pure football, I think they'd both come back tomorrow. But there is a certain lifestyle in rugby, with its superior international game (although to me there are still only a handful of real quality sides in the world); and the chance to travel and play overseas is an attraction. The other thing is that rugby is not as physically confronting. I don't believe that union is as hard or as tough a game as league. The club commitment is essentially non-existent, so they are free of the week-to-week load. How different league is, with the weekly battles of NRL club football, absolutely full-on every week, then the step up to Origin, which is even tougher, and then the final step up to the international arena, which is getting better all the time . . . as the 2005 Kangaroos learned. In a rugby league season there is no rest zone.

Along the difficult journey of that 2001 season Wayne used 13 different combinations at halfback/five-eighth. All of it added up to a crumbling Bronco year, which, unfortunately, was mirrored in a series of seasons that followed. In 2001 we lost six of our last seven games in the premiership proper, limped into the finals, rallied promisingly to beat St George Illawarra (44–28) in the first semifinal, with Wendell Sailor scoring four tries – and then departed, beaten 24–16 by premiership favourites Parramatta in a tight grand final qualifier.

The snapshot of the season was that we made the finals . . . and bombed out. It was the start of a pattern that would stretch as far as 2005 – hopefully, no further. The letdown in '01 was huge, just as it was to be in the following years. The expectations of Bronco supporters are never less than sky-high. Up here, you either win the premiership or you have failed.

I know that Wayne was very disappointed in the way we bowed out. I think he had the feeling – again – that we could have done something really special. But really, nobody who loses seven out of eight games at the end of a season can be expected to win a premiership – even when some of the losses were close, as ours were, and when we were continuing to put in plenty of effort. After we bounced back from that horror stretch, to beat St George, I honestly think he believed we could do it. But we were too mentally fragile. Let's say it straight: we were mentally *weak*. We just didn't have the mental toughness to get through. After we limped into the finals and beat St George we gained some confidence, and thought we mighta, coulda, and shoulda done something. But we didn't. We had our chances against Parramatta and didn't take them, so the season ended in a whimper rather than a roar.

But in the midst of all that, season 2001 turned out to be a standout personal year for me, individually, blunted only by the shadow of my drug-test drama. All up I played 29 games, and at the end of it was named both Broncos Player of the Year and *Rugby League Week*'s Player of the Year – the first prop to win that honour since Arthur Beetson back in 1974, the year I was born. To be linked to Beetson, such a legendary figure in the game, meant a lot to me too. Overall it was a nice feeling. Although I am never the sort of bloke to get too carried away, 2001 ranks pretty close to my finest year. I was consistent and free of major injuries – and those factors are important in any season-long award. And it was a season in which the gladiatorial aspect of the game came back to an extent, thanks to the dumping of the unlimited interchange rule – and that suited me too.

It was in 2001 that Gorden Tallis and I penned an open letter to our fellow players. I had the effect of rattling the cage a bit, no doubt upsetting a few of them. The game had been attracting attention off the paddock for the wrong reasons – with such things as John Hopoate's notorious finger-poking escapades and some other off-the-field incidents. The letter found its way into the public arena – and that was not the intention. But probably it was a good thing anyway, guaranteeing that it reached all players, whatever they may have thought about it.

Gordie brought up the idea, and being on pretty much the same wavelength as him I was happy to be part of it. We did it at a time when the game was starting to unravel at the seams after all the turmoil it had been through in the years that followed the Super League split. As I mentioned earlier, Gordie had been particularly upset at the realisation that recreational drug-taking was part of the lives of some players. Wayne got involved in the discussions and we reached a point where we said, 'Well, we should do something.' So we wrote the letter, which read:

A yarn on the way home from Sydney on the weekend got us both hot under the collar. We asked each other the question 'What is going on with our game?' We have both played rugby league since we can remember. So did our dads, and their dads before them. We have played with blokes from all walks of life, all shapes and sizes, colours and religions, and with different skills and personalities. But there has been one common denominator – we all play rugyby league because we reckon it is the best game there is.

Rugby league has given us just about everything we have – friends, camaraderie, a career and financial security, unbelievably happy moments, fantastic memories and heaps of travel. Neither of us would be where we are today, nor have what we have, if it was not for rugby league.

This game has also given us a focus, has taught us about commitment and discipline, something we would not have achieved in any other walk of life. We are better people because of rugby league, there is no doubt about that.

We want the thousands of young kids who sit up on Friday nights to watch us play, to aspire to be like us one day. We want them to be given the same opportunity that we have been given. We want the game to be there for them, and not spoilt by the tiny minority that seems hell-bent on ruining rugby league.

Fellas, the ball is in our court. Whether we realise it or not, everyone playing in the NRL has the ability to change the future of our game, to take the responsibility in our own hands and make sure we do the right thing.

This isn't about us, and it isn't about you. It's about the game we play, and it's about the living we earn. It's about being a positive influence on every kid who asks for our autograph.

We don't have to be angels . . . just fair dinkum.

Gorden Tallis and Shane Webcke

My own thoughts at the time were expressed pretty bluntly in the media: 'I just felt that the public needed to see that all footballers aren't a bunch of low-down drug addicts who get on the piss and play up. Obviously the things we do get exaggerated, and that's our responsibility, of course, but maybe something like this will show the public that most footballers are aware of their responsibilities to the young players who look up to them.'

The letter was probably seen by some players as fairly tacky. And maybe some of them questioned our motives. But where Gorden Tallis and I have common ground is that we both have a deep love of the game and a respect for it and a knowledge of a certain truth: that when players harm that game, they harm us all. Individual things that happen have a tendency to come back on the whole group. We wrote the letter as a reminder that all players had a responsibility and a commitment to the game – and a responsibility to enhance it, rather than inadvertently or otherwise drag it down by their actions – and that to regularly remind each other of that could make a difference.

I suspect that the letter and its messages largely fell on deaf ears, but who knows? Maybe some of the younger blokes thought about it and took at least some of it on board. I hope so. It came straight from the heart, and people who knew us realised that. Gorden and I are normal Aussie blokes who enjoy a beer and a good time as much as anyone; we are no angels, but I can say with some certainty that we have always tried to stay within certain boundaries, out of respect for the game and for the community. I feel very strongly about that. By now Gorden and I were getting into the territory of being senior players, and in any generation of a particular sport that carries with it the responsibility of enhancing the game in whatever ways are possible.

There has at times been insular thinking along the lines that we can live by different standards within the game. I have never agreed with that. The game overlaps with the wider community in many ways and the standards of that community should be respected and adhered to.

The question of 'role models' is much discussed in sport. It is one subject (there are very few) on which I disagree with Wayne Bennett. I have heard Wayne several times raise the rhetorical question: 'Just because you're a rugby league player, why do you become a role model?' Well, as far as I'm concerned, whether we like it or not, once we reach a certain standing in a high-profile game such as rugby league we inevitably assume a position where kids look up to us, and people (although not all) admire us. We wield some influence, no doubt about that. My view is that we are mad if we don't work to enhance both our own image and the image of the game. I think the 'role model' thing comes with the territory these days, is part of the responsibility of being an elite sportsperson. When you are in a public position where a lot of people see what you do, you have a decision to make. You can act like an idiot or be a rude bastard, and disappoint everyone, or you can act responsibly and reasonably and with some care for both the game you represent and your own place in it. You don't have to go out of your way to become some sort of saint. Just lead a nice quiet existence. Like everyone else, I may not always get it right, but at least I can sleep well at night knowing I have tried.

I have disappointed myself at times, notably in being caught on camera in the heat of battle, mouthing profanities. I have been bitterly disappointed when I have seen that – and angry too that television coverage seems to make those occasions such a focus. Most of the disappointment is with myself, though, and with the certainty that there will have been impressionable 10-year-olds out there watching. And I think to myself, What message does that send them? Notwithstanding all the heat-of-battle excuses put up every time it happens, I honestly think that as players we have to work at building in some sort of mechanism which reminds every player instantly that they are probably on TV right now and triggers the immediate question: Do they really want to appear on national television saying *that*?

But if we have to accept our responsibilities, so too should the broadcasters. They choose to air the footage of those moments on many occasions, when the option is always there not to use them.

The Wests Tigers players who dropped four-letter words on national television after their grand final win in 2005 did the image of the game no good at all. Their words stirred up a hornets' nest of public controversy and were seen quite reasonably as reflecting badly on rugby league in comparison with other sports. It should never have happened, and I think the blokes who run the club should have put up their hands straight away and copped a fair slice of the blame. I'd imagine if it had been us in the grand final we would have been given a bit of a talking to before the game along the lines: 'Look fellas, if we win this, let's remember who we are and that we've got millions of people watching us.' After all the publicity, we can be sure that the Wests Tigers blokes involved won't ever come up with a repeat performance if they happen to win another grand final. It wasn't good. And while it was probably a product of them not having been 'schooled' right by the club, it was also a hangover from that bullshit belief that just because you win a football grand final you have completely open slather on what you can do. You haven't.

I don't believe I could ever get so excited that I would drop a four-letter word while I was doing an interview. It's a funny thing about me and swearing – sometimes I swear like a trooper. But I pick my mark and I certainly don't swear in front of women (which is what you do when you come out with four-letter words on national TV!). I can sit and talk with someone for hours and never use a single swear word. But if I happen to be with mates in a knockabout situation, well, it's different. I don't ever find myself swearing when I shouldn't be.

Chapter 17

THE YEAR THAT TERRORISED RUGBY LEAGUE

There were very few things in my career that upset me as much as the mess that unfolded in rugby league in the wake of the terrorist attacks on the World Trade Center, New York on the day now imprinted forever on global memory: 9/11. I found myself the victim of what I regard as a significant weakness in our administration and it really angered me. I'll tell the story the way I saw it. After what happened in New York that day in 2001 I think it's fair to say that the feeling generally among people everywhere was one of uncertainty and confusion. I'll be very honest: following what had happened I had reservations about the tour to Great Britain that lay ahead. Allied to those reservations was another factor: I was a very tired footballer after a couple of big years of footy, dragging some lingering injuries after playing 29 games during the current season. On September 22, I offered my opinion publicly – I believed the Australian Rugby League should consider rescheduling the tour in view of the fraught international situation.

This was a really uncertain time in the world. None of us had ever seen anything so shocking, anything of that magnitude. It was no light undertaking for us to head off to England in such a climate to play a few games of footy. Every day it seemed there were different theories abroad about what might happen next in the world. But no one really knew. The ARL announced, reasonably, that they would be advised by the Department of Foreign Affairs as to whether the tour should go ahead.

We got together as a team in Sydney a while before the tour and there was much discussion amongst the players on the subject of what lay ahead and whether we should go or not, and what we all thought about it. I could see no great problem in putting the tour off for a year. After all, we had been in the UK at length only 12 months before, for the World Cup. There would be no big deal about rescheduling the tour for 2002, I reckoned, and I could see quite strong reasons for doing that. But when that idea was aired publicly, England jumped up and down about it. They were very keen to have us over there in 2001.

By the time I came back home from Sydney to Brisbane after that preliminary meeting it seemed to have been settled. Pressured by the English Rugby League and having got positive guidance from Foreign Affairs, the ARL decided that the tour would go ahead. I accepted the decision and was fine with it. The advice had been sought, the decision had been made and I certainly wasn't going to miss a tour because of any personal misgivings I may have held. I want to make that point very clear here: I was ready to tour.

At that stage we were only a matter of days out from departure and I had my bags just about ready to go. I had organised things to do with the family and with the business side of my life. I was set to tour and well prepared for the five or six weeks away. But suddenly the issue of whether we should go or not re-emerged publicly. On October 4, Australian coach Chris Anderson admitted publicly that there were genuine fears about the tour because of the uncertain nature of the global situation. Four days later speculation intensified that the Kangaroo campaign would be cancelled following UN-backed military strikes on Afghanistan. On October 10, the Sydney *Daily Telegraph* carried a major back-page story in which Brad Fittler's fiancée appealed to him not to go on the tour.

That very day the ARL Board met and called off the tour, announcing that 12 members of the 24-man squad were unwilling to make the trip. Before that meeting I had spoken by phone to Ross Livermore, Managing Director of the Queensland Rugby League and an ARL Board member. 'Mate, I don't think we should go,' I told him. 'But I'm fine with going if the decision turns out that way.' And I remember him saying to me, 'Well, the rugby union are due to tour in a couple of months – and we'll look silly if we don't go and they do.'

I was annoyed about that comment. It was the sort of thinking that would consign us to always playing second fiddle. My opinion was, why should we give a shit *what* they (rugby union) might do? We were the first national team going anywhere after a major terrorist strike, the likes of which had never been seen before. We were entitled to have reservations about it. I did no more than convey those reservations to Ross, and around the same time blokes like Freddie Fittler and Robbie Kearns were making their doubts known too. I think most of us shared the same feelings, that we would be safe, but we were naturally worried about other aspects, such as getting home if another major event took place.

At that point the ARL decision-makers sat down and tackled the subject again. This time they decided that the tour was *off*. The Kangaroos would go instead in 2002. It was a measured decision on a particularly difficult subject, and deep down I applauded the ARL. I thought, That's good strong leadership . . .

they have considered the situation and the players and their concerns.

As soon as the news was announced, all hell broke loose. The backlash was unbelievable. The English media were scathing in their criticism, and here at home there was a barrage of criticism from media commentators – and from radio talkback callers who called us cowards and said we were giving in to terrorism. There were suggestions that white feathers should be sent to the Australian players and a good deal of other bullshit was talked. Inevitably, there were analogies drawn about war and football. I spoke out: to compare us as a football team going to England with soldiers going to war was absolute nonsense. We were a *sporting* team with a choice of whether to go or not to go in what could fairly be considered dangerous times internationally, when events of a far more profound nature were unfolding. We were not soldiers.

Meanwhile, English officials claimed that cancellation of the tour would cost the game over there $9 million.

It was now a huge drama, with newspaper reports appearing that the ARL was under enormous pressure to rethink (again!) and reschedule the tour. Chris Anderson publicly advised the ARL not to reverse its original decision. Meanwhile Australian selector and former national coach Bob Fulton declared that the tour should go ahead. In the midst of all of that I remained at peace with the decision that had been made. It was a shit fight now, but a tough decision had been taken after due consideration, and that was that. After all, the ARL must have known they would cop some flak. Any tough decision made in any public arena can expect that sort of reaction. I'd like to think I have always been pretty good in those sorts of situations. If I lock in a decision and I'm comfortable with it, it's done, and I don't give a damn what happens. It's an at-tribute that I'm pleased I've got. It's really helped me to be solid in a lot of situations where it would have been easy to be otherwise.

In the midst of it all I received a phone call from ARL chairman Colin Love. The ARL needed the senior players to come out publicly and support them, he told me, because with the heat on the game, the players needed to present a united front on the issue. I agreed with their decision and was happy to provide support. I sat down and wrote an impassioned letter which appeared in the *Courier-Mail* explaining the reasons why and reminding people how serious a step it was from the players' point of view *not* to be going on a tour and playing for our country and how no player would ever give up lightly such an honour. Once my thoughts were out there in public I had made my final decision. For me it was now long past the deciding stage.

This is the letter I wrote:

It was with great relief and disappointment that I awoke today – relief that I would not have to leave my young family and travel into what can only be described as an uncertain world and disappointment that I had to be part of the first postponement of a great sporting icon, the Kangaroo Tour. It is as a result of this disappointment that I feel compelled to publicly explain the fears and concerns that led to me and several other members of the selected touring party voicing our opinion that the tour should not proceed.

The most poignant concern was the extreme uncertainty concerning the final outcome and the retaliation that may occur as a result of current military action in the Middle East. I think it is fair to say that most players believed that our own personal safety was not in immediate danger but that any actions against Great Britain by terrorist forces could result in extreme difficulty for our return trip to Australia being completed safely. It has been suggested to me that the likelihood of action against Britain, or us directly, is extremely remote, but then did any of us believe that terrorists would ever fly planes into buildings containing thousands of innocent civilians? I think on that dark day the parameters of what could be considered impossibility were altered beyond anyone's comprehension. Therefore it was felt that the tour should not proceed given that we had no way of properly defining the nature of the risks we would be taking.

Naturally enough it would have been our families, should the tour have gone ahead, who would have suffered a very different and some ways more difficult set of consequences. It would have been those families, many containing very young children, who would have spent what may have been the longest six weeks of their lives watching news reports and unfolding events, hoping that none of us would be in harm's way and forced to stay away longer as a result. I, for one, consider not being able to play a few games of rugby league, albeit extremely prestigious and important ones, a small price to pay not to have put my family through that torment.

I would like to publicly thank the members of the board of the ARL who ultimately made the decision for the tour not to proceed. It is they who have spared players the onerous task of choosing whether or not to partake of the tour. It had been publicly suggested that players would have the choice of going or not going. Choosing not to go, given our concerns outlined above, would on the surface give us a chance to show the courage of our convictions. But it would also mean that we would give up the opportunity to be part of a Kangaroo tour – and it is here that the real heart of the matter lies and why expressing an opinion of not wanting to go on tour with the 'Roos is so difficult. As rugby league players, the ultimate honour is to represent your country and I can assure you that there is not one player who did not dread having to decide between going on tour or staying home with family. Faced with that scenario I would most likely have chosen to go, such is my desire to be part of a Kangaroo tour. As it turns out the ARL has made the decision for us, and we as players are grateful. Form permitting, we may get another opportunity next year.

While I am relieved we don't have to tour at this time I would like to apologise to rugby league supporters who, I would imagine, would have been looking forward to the games – but I ask for your understanding given the circumstances. I will make as my final point a response to an email sent to the Broncos website. It was addressed to all our players involved in the Australian tour and reads as follows:

You are all a disgrace to the old Green and Gold tradition. My late father-in-law – a Cairns Queenslander, veteran of Gallipoli and the Western Front – will turn in his grave at your cowardly behaviour. You only deserve the White Feather.

Keith Gorman

Mr Gorman, I will say this to you. It is beyond my comprehension that you can equate the actions of thousands of young Australians who so courageously gave their lives for our freedom and way of life all those years ago to a group of sportspeople who feel it a mite dangerous to be travelling overseas at this time to engage in sport. For us to go on a sporting tour will not save anybody's way of life, our freedom or anything terribly important. It would simply bring pleasure to those who play and support rugby league. If it makes me a coward not wanting to take part in the tour for the sake of my own safety and to spare my loved ones a great deal of anguish – then call me a coward.

Shane Webcke

A couple of days later I was up at Leyburn, and from all I was reading and hearing I had the strong sense that the ARL were getting antsy about it. On the critical day I had various phone calls at different stages of what was now a continuing deliberation: from Brad Fittler, Chris Anderson and Colin Love. Would I consider changing my mind? 'No, stuff it,' was my message. 'I've made my decision now . . . I've been in the paper; I won't be changing my mind.' Freddy Fittler called. They'd been talking to him too. 'No . . . I'm not going,' he told me. 'The decision has been made and that's that.'

Three hours later the Kangaroo tour of 2001 was back on, in reduced form, down from seven weeks to two.

Freddy now was going, and so were all the other players. Looking back, I hold nothing against Freddy because of it, or against anyone; everyone had to make their own decision. Their actions were not the action that I chose. But I am not critical of the other players.

In the hectic hours following the new decision I took a succession of phone calls. From memory, Colin Love, Geoff Carr (Chief Executive of the ARL) and Chris Anderson all rang me. 'Opes' (Anderson) was good. 'Look, mate . . . we're going to go now . . . any chance you could change your mind?' And I told him: 'Mate, I can't do it. I've gone out on a limb publicly. I've written a piece for the papers explaining why I'm not going. I can't change now; my credibility would be zero.' He was fine. He understood.

Colin Love also tried to persuade me. 'Everyone else is going,' he said. 'We need you.' And I told the ARL chairman, 'I don't give a stuff, mate. I am not going to go back on this now. I've been all over the media supporting the fact that we *weren't* going. If I go now, I'm as weak as piss.' Colin was pretty good. Like Chris, he understood my position and accepted it.

I'll admit I was tempted to roll over. But only for an instant. What was at stake here was my word, my integrity, my credibility – and I wasn't prepared to sell out any of those. I couldn't possibly go. The media chased me hard.

And so the Australian team of 2001 went to England . . . and I didn't.

One bloke who remained terribly undecided was Locky (Darren Lockyer), who held out for quite a time. I remember we went to a golf day in the middle of the drama and I said to him: 'What are you going to do, mate? You're going to have to make a decision.' And he told me he was thinking about me and considering staying home to give me support. And I said to him: 'Don't worry about me, mate. You have to make your own decision. I'm fine – I don't need anyone to stand with me. You've got to be happy with what you want to do yourself.' Maybe that cleared the air a bit for him – and he duly decided that he would tour.

I felt very let down by the game at that time. I wrote the newspaper article and supported the (ARL's) original decision specifically because they asked me to. And then I got left like a shag on a rock when they changed their minds. It was a monumental backflip.

I lived with my decision and the whole issue for months afterwards. People either loved what I did or hated what I did and it just went on and on. Maybe in some ways it helped me. I guess a lot of people understood and appreciated the fact that I had at least taken a principled stance and stuck to it. In a lot of people's eyes what I had done was a show of consistency and strength.

But years later, I still have moments of anger when I think about it, still feel very let down. There are three Test matches that are gone forever from my career. They were Tests I could have had – and I blame the ARL for costing me those games. Okay I made my own decision not to go and I made it twice. But it would have been a different outcome if they hadn't about-turned the way they did. It's the point I want to make strongest of all here – that, yes, I had reservations but *yes*, I was ready to tour. And I had arrived at that position because the ARL had made a well-balanced decision after taking on board all the right information. It was always going to have to be something valid for me not to go. As soon as they deemed it safe, I was right.

And then they succumbed to pressure and turned 180 degrees. Because of it there is a potential experience of my rugby league career that I was forced to forego. By staying true to my principles I paid a high price.

Chapter 18

THE PRICE WE PAY

It is my opinion that as footballers, playing rugby league at the top level, we age 20 years faster than 'normal' human beings. Everyone who plays the game in a serious way lives with the wear-and-tear factor. During a season you are sore *all* the time. And as your career continues, the accumulation of all the knocks and sprains and breaks you have endured mean that you probably stay sore all *summer* long too. I know I'm that way – with my back and my knees and my ankles (with one of my ankle problems going back to days long ago, when I was playing in the bush). It is not something I talk about much or plan to dwell on too long here. It is just part of football. Suffice it to say that there are many mornings you wake up feeling not so good – but then maybe there's a fair proportion of the rest of the population who feels that way too. For footballers, it is the price we pay.

Money is good in the game now, and that's as it should be, because the long-term price of playing elite football is particularly high. And for all the things that are possible in this modern world, we still cannot renew our bodies. So almost inevitably we end our careers with the knowledge that our bodies are older and more worn than those of people of the same age who have not been subjected to the same routine of training and collisions and stresses. The high-intensity matches we play are only part of the story. Training does it equally: the constant pounding of running gets you sore down deep in your bones. You spend so much time on your feet, training and running and propping and stopping.

What those not at training or in the rehab rooms at clubs don't realise is just how much the physical players like Shane Webcke go through in getting their bodies right to do battle each week as the residual pain of injuries over the years builds up.

Michael Hagan

Training for rugby league today is almost unrecognisable from what it was when I started serious footy back in the '90s. I suppose it's fair to say that a lot of the basic stuff is the same, but the blokes running it these days have just got a whole lot sharper about what works and what doesn't. No longer is training just an exercise to make you work hard and sweat – today it's all game-related, all about things that assist what you actually do in matches. Training has become so much more scientific, with the realisation that the preparation should mimic what you set out to do on the playing field. If you don't train properly, you don't play properly. There have been a few notable exceptions to that over the years, and Allan Langer was one of them. But as a general rule, if you practise anything badly you'll carry it out badly.

My view is that within football even today there is still not enough emphasis on training, especially in the minds of many players, for whom the dominant thinking is all about 'play'. If footballers don't put training first, it's a case of the cart before the horse. If blokes think they can play well without training well, they're kidding themselves. Training is everything. The best piece of advice I can pass on to any kid who wants to play rugby league (or any game!) is that if you want to be a good player, you must train well, and with 100 per cent effort every time.

Training today is about training smart. The old practices, such as road runs, that were once the staples of preparation for football are gone. Occasionally at the Broncos we do something called 'Camp Harden Up', a special training camp designed to take us out of our comfort zone and make us tougher. Even weight training has changed. Now a lot of it is really specific stuff carried out in a flowing motion designed to match what happens on the playing field, and geared to aid the speed component of the game. And it is position-specific, with programs designed by a specialist weight-coach for the specific position you happen to play. Back when I started we had one trainer who handled the whole lot, but today there are experts to cover just about all areas of what we do.

Another example of the way preparing for football matches has changed is the amount of wrestling we do today. You never saw that in a training session until the last couple of years; now teaching footballers how to operate more effectively on the ground is a huge part of the training.

The gear has got better too. Billy Johnstone, a renowned fitness trainer, was a boxer as well as a footballer, and used to run on the road for miles and miles in basic tennis shoes with no give in them and therefore all the force running up from the heel to the hip. Now both his hips are buggered. He is one of many. Today, considerable care is taken with players' footwear because no shoe can withstand for long what we do to them. We wear out shoes quickly, and get new ones. The fact is, if you've got bad feet and you can't run then you can't play.

There is no doubt training has become harder. But making it harder has also made it easier for footballers. That sounds strange, but it's true. Training quantity is down on what it once was, but the intensity is higher and it's harder.

The visual review of matches is another area of vast change. With the computer systems that exist these days you can sit there in front of the screen and pull up every single thing you do in a match. And you can look at everyone else in the competition and pull up vital stuff on them too. The amount of information that exists, in visual form and in statistics, is amazing. There are stats for just about everything that can happen on a football field. Back not so many seasons ago no one gave a shit about the stats.

But statistics can never represent the full story of a football match. The human factor and the element of the unexpected are always right there in the mix. Statistics can never measure such qualities as spirit, determination and absolute will to win, or the luck that is part of so many games. Those are the things that make league the game it is and decide results match after match, week after week, season after season. It's the beauty of the game that 17 ordinary blokes in the midst of an ordinary season can decide on one day, 'We're going to be the better side today. We're going to win this.' There are no figures or statistics that can explain the magic of those days. It is why any team game is potentially wonderful.

When it comes to the mind games that underpin any football match, I think we have all become much better educated. It has been said that the game's greatest improvement in future years will be in the territory of the mind, and that may well be so. I know that a greater understanding of how the mind works has set a lot of us free – me included. Successful players these days come to understand that like an arm or a leg, the mind is just one more bit of equipment you take into a match. Your mind is the controlling factor of what you will do in that match – and once you understand that, it can be a great weapon. There is an old adage: your body will go where your mind takes it. It's true – and you can make yourself do things that you never thought possible.

The mind is truly amazing. I mentioned earlier the phenomenon of not being aware of any sort of fatigue in the grand final that I played with a broken arm (2000) – because I was so focused on the arm. At the end of that game I said to Wayne, 'I could have played three games today!' The world is full of stories of people who survived amazing ordeals not because of their physical attributes, but because of mind-power. I think the brain is like everything else in our lives: it has to be trained if it is to work to anywhere near full effect.

Some blokes are luckier than others in getting through the hard journey of a football career, and (touch wood) I put myself somewhere in that category. I'm going to have some health issues down the track, I know, but providing I look after myself in the post-football years I don't think they will be debilitating. I know that the issue of my weight is one thing I will have to pay close attention to. It will be very important for me not to put on weight.

To say these things about the physical realities of playing rugby league is not scaremongering or being negative. It is just the way a life in football is – and probably always has been. The other side of the coin is that there are so many compensating factors in having the chance to play the game. The financial reward, obviously, is one of them – the opportunity for young blokes to make a profession out of a game and, if they are wise and a bit lucky along the way, having then the chance to set themselves on a successful path in life. But there's a whole lot more in it than money.

In football today we are taught some very, very good life skills. Clubs today are full of experts teaching you the best ways to look after yourself. At the end of my career, if I have any advice to young players it would be this: soak up all possible opportunities to learn, take notice of what you are taught and the chance will be there for you to acquire great habits that you can carry with you for the rest of your life. We get exposed to life-learning that is probably not nearly so readily available to many people in the community – about diet and nutrition, general health and exercise and about the development of better communication skills (so important with the media these days). We get to learn in exact detail how our bodies work. After all these seasons, and all I have come to know, I understand my body very well indeed. I know what it can and can't do and I know what will put weight on me, and what won't. I'd probably sum it up this way: yes, you beat yourself up playing rugby league, but you get some pretty good rewards in the process and you are taught some handy tools that can help you deal with life beyond football.

Today's young professional footballers are lucky. It's a fact that most young people don't think much about the future – they just get on with life. My own change of attitude came about largely through a tragedy – the death of my father – which caused me to grow up and rethink my life, and what I was going to do with it. Because of the lessons learned in those struggling early years when things were so tough for Mum and Dad, when I did come into some money I was always good with it. There wasn't much around, and I was conservative with it and was always a good saver. Wayne Bennett and I have talked about that and he has said to me more than once, 'What young people don't realise is that they have time on their side.' It is so true, that message: the cumulative effect of the time/money equation being that even if you save in a pretty conservative way, without any flash investment plan, in time it will turn into heaps of money. Young players are exposed to those sort of truths now as an ongoing sideline of their careers as professional footballers.

At the Broncos we have an expert who advises players on their finances – helping with things like buying houses, setting up investment funds and the processes of normal day-to-day financial transactions. It is vital knowledge: you can't have someone holding your hand for the rest of your life on that. Yet we live in an 'instant' world in which people are always in a hurry to get somewhere as fast as possible – and that is why a lot of players still make dud investments, looking for things that pay quick dividends. To be patient and make good, solid decisions is as good a lesson as you can learn in life. My own way has always been to think more long term, rather than trying to get the 'quick hit'. I have always been happy to set up things for a bit further down the track.

For me, and therefore very likely for the other guys, there has been another very special kind of education too. The game today is a mixture of blokes of all colours and creeds. To me the experience of playing football in such a world has been one of the great educational experiences of my life. Coming from a part of the world – country Queensland – which people would probably regard as 'conservative' or maybe even 'redneck', it has been a fantastic thing to get to know blokes from other places and other cultures. For me the experience of playing with Aborigines and Pacific Islanders and all the others in the 'mix' of rugby league has pretty much killed off any deep-down beliefs and prejudices I may have harboured from earlier times. Because when you play footy with blokes, you get to know them very closely. The message is straightforward: we are all different, but all of us are no more than human beings who happen to be on a coinciding journey. Racial joking is still part of life in a football club – we might call them 'black bastards' in jest and they might call us 'white mongrels' in response – but it's done lightly and good-heartedly and in a spirit of mateship.

It has got to the stage where I virtually no longer notice colour. I don't look at a bloke and think, 'There's a black man'; I look at him and think, 'There's (whoever it happens to be).' In a football club you work in very close quarters with all your team-mates – and to me that opportunity to accept difference has been wonderful. It's a very great thing about rugby league. Many people in Australian society don't have that experience or privilege. Rugby league provides an absolutely level playing field where we are all equal . . . all just football players.

Yes, there were redneck elements of my growing-up years. I used to hear the jokes and stories and I could sense the slight fear that existed when it came to Aborigines. There was racism around, for sure – although I'm happy to say that it did not come from my parents. And if some of the black guys who were the objects of it were angry inside and struggling with their lives, well, white society over 200-odd years has definitely played its part in that. In my years with the Broncos I have been to some of the far-western communities and come to realise the truth of that . . . and come away sad at what I have seen. Maybe if I had stayed at home in Leyburn, any racism I tasted as a kid may have been built into me as an adult. Instead, I came to Brisbane, played rugby league and took a different path. I feel very fortunate. It's one of the greatest of all things about the game: no matter what your background, race, religion, social standing, you are judged only on what you can do as a sportsperson. It is exactly as it should be.

Here and there in these pages I have been critical of rugby league – but of this hugely important area I think the game can be proud.

When I think about all these things, about what being a rugby league player has meant to me, I inevitably come back to an unanswerable six-word question: 'What if I hadn't played footy'?

I shudder at the implication of those words. It is the impossible question, of course, because I *did* choose to play football in those growing-up years out west. But it is one of those life questions that fascinates me, and I think about it from time to time. More than anything else, my time in rugby league has provided me with choice. Because of the game (and what I have achieved in it, I suppose), I can pretty much do whatever I want to do in my life, and that is a wonderful thing. That is why I will stand on any mountain top you like and sing the praises of the game all day long. What the rugby league experience has done for me – being with the likes of Wayne Bennett, being at this club, being with all these wonderful players over the years – is beyond measure. Being part of all that has allowed me to grow in a way that I doubt very much I could otherwise have experienced. To have been involved in the game and had the chance to soak up the things it offers has broadened my view of the world and the way it works amazingly. I am a vastly more rounded person than I once was, with a much wider knowledge of the world. With that, I have learned to respect the differences I see in others.

I was a bank-johnny in a country town, with ambitions only to make a go of it as a farmer, which is no bad thing, of course. I'd like to think, and I take real solace from the thought, that the values that live in me and which I learned from Tom and Vicki Webcke would still be the same.

Rugby league at its highest level pays bloody good money to its players, offering the chance of material wealth. But I love the game for reasons that go far beyond that. Especially with someone like Wayne Bennett at the helm, it has the potential to teach you lessons that should provide the foundation for the rest of your life. Via the profile it creates for players, the game is an extraordinary provider of opportunity, way beyond the playing field. It connects you with business and influence and expertise at the very highest levels. It provides a chance available to very few young people. And beyond that is all the rest – the enjoyment of playing the game, the camaraderie – deep enough to be very hard to put into words – the knowledge you acquire about health, fitness, diet, lifestyle, investment, and the opportunities to travel and experience other places.

There is endless talk and speculation about the amount of

money that footballers are paid. As far as I am concerned money is no more than a by-product of what we do and in essence has nothing to do with the game of rugby league. There is not enough money in the world to pay people to do what we do – and if you were motivated purely by money, it would never be enough. I'll pose the question to readers: 'How much money is enough to go out onto a grassy field and get yourself smashed up every week?' It would be an interesting experiment: to round up a group of members of the public, bring them down to (Bronco) training on a Tuesday morning when we are doing our hardest fitness session of the week and, at the end of it, offer them $200,000 a season and ask how many of them want to take up the challenge. An overwhelming majority would say no. Because where we go physically is horrendous and frightening – and even though I've been doing it for years, I still get nervous even before we do a big fitness test, because I know the level of pain that is involved. But it *has* to be that way so that your pain threshold is increased and you can go further on the football field on match-day.

We train harder than we play, because we have to. My brother Dallas is a good example of the challenge and the reality that it is not a life for most people. As I have mentioned, he was a very good footballer and he came to trial with us and was good enough to have made it. But I can remember him saying to me one day at pre-season training in the mid-1990s: 'I don't know how you do this!' It was the first day of pre-season training and his first day tackling anything of that intensity. He knew at the end of that day that it wasn't going to be the life for him, and he accepted that and it didn't worry him. Missing the lure of football's big money didn't worry him at all either. He had put a toe in the water and decided that, for him, there would be another way.

Love of footy has to be in the mix with every bloke who plays the game. It was certainly the only emotion and motivation of my earlier years in the game. I never came to rugby league with an expectation that it was going to earn me money or take me anywhere in the world. And, you know, it hasn't changed that much. The money is a great and welcome off-shoot and it is a bloody wonderful thing that can be part of the game. It certainly makes it easier to take getting bashed up on a weekly basis. But right through my career, from first match to the last, I played rugby league because I loved the game.

Oh yes, I am a fan of what rugby league is and can be for a young bloke. And whatever flaws it may have and whatever physical price it may extract from those who play it – I will defend it until the day I die.

Chapter 19

THE ROT SETS IN

It was all too familiar. In 2001 we lost six of our last seven premiership games, then departed early from the finals. In 2002, we started the competition like an express train (unbeaten in our first nine games) then lost momentum, finally limping into the finals on a poor platform of one win in the previous five games. There, we lifted to beat Parramatta 24–14 in our last game at ANZ Stadium, inspired by big games from Gorden Tallis and Alfie Langer, who was back for a last hurrah with the Broncos in 2002. But a fortnight later the Sydney Roosters, destined to be premiers, outlasted us 16–12 in the first preliminary final and it was over. Again.

My own season was at least personally gratifying. I played 23 (of 26) club games, all three Origin matches and the winning Tests against Great Britain and New Zealand. But premiership glory was proving elusive, and what we did not fully realise at that point was that we were carving what was to become a deep and familiar groove: hopes built high early in a season and then faltering finishes which dispatched us to early springtime holidays while other teams played for the big prize.

Leaving ANZ at the end of that 2002 season was a wrench. It was the place where I had cut my teeth, a ground that held many great memories for me. It felt like home. There were periods when we were almost invincible at the ground. I always had the feeling that whenever we turned up for a game we were going to win. In that golden period during which we were drawing crowds of up to 40,000 and 50,000 it was magnificent. But it was like all big grounds: when the large crowds fall away, the ground develops a hollow, empty sort of feeling. When it happened at ANZ, something had to change – and the change for us came in the move to the new Suncorp, redeveloped at a cost of $280 million and arguably the best football ground in Australia, but one that shifted the dynamics for the Broncos. There, we were back on a level playing field. The teams that came to play us were excited and pumped up about playing on such a ground and inevitably lifted for the occasion. We struggled to win there, and hadn't thought it would be that way. Luckily, there are signs of it now changing. All teams have been to Suncorp two or three times now and the novelty factor is wearing off. These days it's down to a more normal sort of contest, and the chance is there for the Broncos to build the tradition that all teams hope for on a home ground. A succession of wins feeds on itself – and that is the plan.

In 2003 we remained trapped in what was now becoming a very worrying pattern: the graph was gradually heading steadily downwards after a season high point – the 24–0 wipeout of the Bulldogs at Telstra. The challenges were many: salary cap cuts, injuries and representative football fatigue were among them.

At the start of 2003, at 29, I signed a three-year contract with the club – the best contract I had ever had. You could say I had worked my way up the money tree and the contract they offered was some sort of reward for the time I had put in and the contribution I had made. I had reached a bloody good level of money. I remember thinking how my career path had been a fortunate one, perhaps even the ideal journey that sporting careers should take: coming into my senior years I was now on very good money, and outside football my profile and the business opportunities that existed for me had really gathered strength too. I felt great about the contract and the club and all that lay ahead. I really felt that with my football journey approaching its latter stages that I could now see the way ahead with some clarity.

I have no doubt that the majority of players who join the Broncos believe it is an honour to be at such a place. I certainly believe that. The club was born in special circumstances, with a need to be successful that was stronger than in most other clubs. The creation of the Broncos in 1988 inevitably had the effect of decimating the Brisbane competition, removing the crème-de-la-crème of Queensland players from that arena. So from the start the bar had to be set high. The Broncos didn't just chase success; they *needed* success to justify their creation. Wayne Bennett, with that 'awe' quality he brings to anything he does, has been a big part of all that has followed, but there have been many contributors through the years, many people who have worked so very hard to build what now exists. A sporting franchise of the highest quality has been constructed, plus a football club with both a tradition and an expectation of excellence. The traditions that built up over the years were no accidents. In 2003 *Rugby League Week* pinpointed various proud Bronco milestones:

- A perfect grand final record: five premierships from five visits to the grand final.
- The best win percentage in history. Coming in to 2003, Brisbane had won 67.3% of matches played. St George (58.9%) were next.

- Four 200-game players (Michael Hancock, Allan Langer, Kevin Walters and Andrew Gee). As I write these words I am proud to be a member of that club too.
- The longest serving coach in the game's history (Wayne Bennett).
- Twenty-nine internationals – double the tally of Newcastle, who entered the competition in the same year.
- Three Clive Churchill medallists.

To be the very best has always been a Broncos goal, in my experience. And if that striving was somewhat derailed in recent seasons . . . well, I never doubted it would be back.

I was pretty much a Bronco for life from the day I joined. Oh yeah, I've had the shits with them now and then, as happens in life, but I think the only thing that would have swayed me to go anywhere else would have been if Wayne had left. Even then, I suspect I always knew very deep down that I wasn't going anywhere. And when the day comes on which Wayne Bennett does decide to step away, I know that he feels enough ownership of the place to guarantee that the reins will be handed over to the right person. Post-Bennett will be a hard gig for whoever gets it. Personally, I'd love to see the (coaching) job after Wayne go to Craig Bellamy (Melbourne Storm). I rate him highly and think he would be ideally suited. He is a commonsense bloke who really has his act together as a football coach. Like Wayne, he is a man who calls a spade a spade. He wouldn't let the joint down. I feel sure about that.

I had a calf muscle problem early in 2003 and my season started slowly; so slowly, in fact, that at one stage I was quoted in the press as saying that if I'd had a rope in the first four weeks of the season, I would have hanged myself. Hmmmm. I must have been a bit low that day. But the great and reassuring thing I have found about football is that if you have a certain talent that has been proven, it doesn't go away – well, not until Father Time enters the equation anyway. That has been one of the most important lessons I have learned in football: that if there is a talent present, it remains. It never just mysteriously gets yanked away. Generally you do things to take it away from yourself. If you've hit a slump and things are not going well, if you look deeply enough you can always find a reason. Early in the year my specific problem was the injury I had and the fact that because of it I was not training well. But whatever the problem happened to be through the years, I found that the solution lay in simply getting back into a routine and doing the things that have worked in the past. That is always the pattern I have followed – to do that and wait for things to come right. And they would.

Simple truths like that in football can be a great help in getting a player through the down times. They provide sanity and clarity in a game, which is sometimes made almost mystical by people who tend to complicate it. This simple message and the things I learned from Phil Jauncey early on allowed me to really enjoy my footy. Even when things were crook I was always comforted by the certainty that if I stuck to the things that worked for me, it would turn.

It is a strengthening and reinforcing message for any young player, I think. When you have established yourself, good coaches accept that even when you're in a bad patch or have had a bad game, that is no big deal . . . it's just footy. High-standard players have something of a buffer zone with coaches. Unlike a youngster coming in, one bad game is not going to cost you. The other side of the coin in football is represented by the blokes who *can't* seem to change – players who battle weight problems or who maybe have a flighty quality about them that makes them unreliable. Rugby league is just a part of life, and people bring their individual personalities to it. Blokes with faults that they can't change, well, they're never really going to change, never going to get any better.

217

The only game we won of our last 11 in '03 came via a golden point extra-time victory over Melbourne at Olympic Park. With nine State of Origin players backing up we beat them 26–22 when Scott Minto scored a try. Wayne Bennett, on the sideline, leapt from his seat and punched the air. 'I love the golden point!' he subsequently declared. He was kidding. Wayne has made it very clear that he was firmly against the rule which (usually) contrives a result after the teams have played out a draw over 80 minutes. I feel the same way – I just don't believe in it. Its supporters trumpet how the rule is 'better for spectators' but I disagree.

A draw is a legitimate result in a rugby league match and a fairly rare event in the game. It is almost always an honourable result, too, after the teams have battled it out to the last breath over 80 minutes – the designated length of a match. In my view the argument about fans 'wanting a result' is bullshit. I'm all for the game giving fans what they want. But the drive for the 'golden point' did not come from the fans. It was some sort of tricked-up initiative, perhaps TV-inspired, to 'add extra excitement'. It was unnecessary, and it tampered with the tradition of the game. I'll concede there is some extra excitement generated in the golden-point time, but I don't think anyone would be pissed off if the golden point was pensioned off. There wouldn't be a single fan who went to the football just because there might be some golden time played. And I'll pose a question: is there really any necessity to contrive a device which is not far removed from soccer's artificial 'penalty shoot-out'? I don't believe so. Rugby league in the 21st century should learn to live with the fact that on occasional match-days we are going to get a draw . . . as we have for almost 100 years.

I suspect all losing fans would go home disappointed at seeing their team beaten via a dinky field goal three minutes into extra time after they had battled bravely for 80 minutes for a thoroughly deserved competition point. The 80 minutes of the battle is wiped off the slate and the match becomes a completely different game in those extra minutes. The golden point is probably here to stay, though, because the blokes running the game seem to be true believers. I just can't bring myself to share their enthusiasm.

It was in 2003 – now the third successive year we had petered out at the end (winning only two of our last 12 games) that I captained the Broncos for the first time. Lockey was out for a month and Gordie for five weeks with injuries – and so I got my chance. And in that period we didn't win a single thing.

On the scoreboard it was an ugly sequence: 20–26 v Manly; 10–20 v Cronulla; 6–13 v Penrith; 10–12 v Wests Tigers. Three of the four matches were played at home. Four close games . . . four losses. The experience damaged me to an extent that took quite some time to recover from. I don't think I have ever tried harder on a football field than I did that month.

It got so bad that I got to thinking the reason we couldn't win was that the other blokes didn't want to play for me. It was probably ridiculous, but it was how I felt. I was a shattered man. I just tried and tried and tried. I played my arse out because that's what I felt you had to do as captain. I thought to play my guts out was the best thing I could do and that would be enough. And we kept getting beaten.

It's funny how the mind works. I was never what you would call a warm and fuzzy sort of bloke at training. At times I could be fairly hard. And I started to think that maybe my attitude was coming back to bite me. The thought really played on my mind: These blokes don't want to play for me. Closer to the mark was the fact that we just weren't playing well, so we weren't winning. I was tremendously honoured to be named Broncos captain but at the same time there was a lot of nervous anticipation about the role. And when the losses kept stacking up I seriously wondered whether I was deficient in some quality; that thought knocked me around for quite a while.

Eventually Locky came back and took over the captaincy and then Gordie, who was skipper that year, and we then proceeded to lose another four games in a row, including the qualifying final against Penrith (18–28) and so departed the premiership scene. All of that at least brought some sense back into my thinking. It wasn't until 2005, when I had stepped down from rep football and led the side in the two club games we won at Origin time, that I really felt like I knew how to be a captain. I never had the ambition to be the Broncos' captain; I guess I never had confidence in my ability to lead the side, in terms of *knowing* how to be a captain. But I'm pleased I had the opportunity – and *very* pleased that we managed to win those couple of tough games in 2005 with me at the helm.

As skipper in 2003 I dabbled briefly with the fashionable tactic of questioning the ref aggressively. But I dropped that quick smart. It didn't feel right. *I'm mad doing this*, I thought the final time I argued the point. Commonsense took over. There was enough to do and I could see no value in fighting battles that couldn't be won. So if I had something to say to a referee I would say it in a normal, controlled manner. But I had seen both Gordie and Lockey really give it to a ref now and then and I felt I had to at least give it a go. Gordie in fact wouldn't go five minutes in a match without having a crack at the ref. That was Gordie. But as in life, there are many different ways of doing things in football, and when it came to captaincy, that wasn't my way. By the time I got to lead the side again in '05, I barely spoke to the ref. I had long since worked out that my energy was far better spent trying to help my fellow players than moaning on to some referee.

On captaincy generally, I think its importance is a little over-rated. Locky has been our captain in recent times, following

Gordie, and I have to say I didn't ever really think of them as captains; I just respected them and liked playing with them. The main thing a captain can do is to be like the coach and have a positive galvanising effect on the team. The skipper needs to play well, sure, but apart from that I just think there's a need for him to connect with the players. I felt I did that in 2005 when we won games we weren't expected to win – and I loved that. I felt the circumstances brought out the best in me as captain. I think that's the challenge for a captain – to find a way week after week to bring his team together and bring out the best in them.

What the job is *not* about is getting out onto the field and blasting blokes. Players know what they are doing; they just need a bit of encouragement and a bit of prodding. When things are looking grim and there's a bit of panic around in a game, it's amazing the effect a few calm words from someone you respect can have.

That year there were some kind words written about Gorden Tallis and me after we had backed up from a side badly beaten in Origin 2 (27–4) and done well for the Broncos a couple of days later, playing our part in the 10–8 win over the Roosters in what was a really gritty game at Suncorp at a time when they were flying high. Wayne Bennett was to comment afterwards on our performances: 'They were hurt, and when they went out there they just knew they had to dig deep and bloody well find something so that they could feel good about themselves.' Readying myself for the first hit-up that night, I dropped the ball; for the last hit-up of the match, 79 minutes later, I off-loaded to Petero Civoniceva, who scored the winning try. I felt throughout my career that I played some pretty good games after Origin matches, which Wayne Bennett has famously described as 'like playing the grand final every two weeks'. A lot of it was the mental thing – you *knew* that whatever you faced at the weekend couldn't possibly be as tough as what you had just been through. Pride is also in the mix, definitely. There is a real sense of it in playing in a big game – and then being able to back up a couple of days later. It's one of those things players talk about: 'Can he back up?' It's a quality among football players that is revered and respected.

In recent seasons I was picked in a couple of those 'best ever' dream-team exercises that occasionally take place. In 2003 John Ribot named me in his best Broncos team of the club's 15 years of life, and in 2005 I was picked in the all-time Queensland Origin team. I have to say that when things like that happen to me my overwhelming emotion is disbelief. I truly do not see myself in the same light as some of the players I find myself alongside. And that's not false modesty. I know I could play rugby league, but I honestly just don't see myself up there with those players: Meninga, Lewis, Alfie and the rest. I am honoured to be there all the same, but in no way would such recognition cause me to relax and rest on my laurels. I know that relaxing and accepting that I had 'made it' would have threatened to take away the desire I always had to try to be better. To bathe in that sort of glory, I reckon, is to put yourself on the slippery slide.

For the record, Ribot's Broncos Dream Team (1988–2003) was as follows: Darren Lockyer, Michael Hancock, Steve Renouf, Gene Miles, Wendell Sailor, Wally Lewis (C), Allan Langer, Shane Webcke, Greg Conescu, Glenn Lazarus, Gorden Tallis, Trevor Gillmeister, Darren Smith. Interchange: Kevin Walters, Chris Johns, Andrew Gee, Sam Backo.

The chosen 25 greatest Queensland State of Origin players, announced as part of Origin's Silver Jubilee in 2005, were: Arthur Beetson, Gary Belcher, Martin Bella, Kerry Boustead, Chris Close, Greg Conescu, Greg Dowling, Trevor Gillmeister, Peter Jackson, Allan Langer, Gary Larson, Wally Lewis, Bob Lindner, Darren Lockyer, Mal Meninga, Gene Miles, Rod Morris, Dale Shearer, Matt Sing, Darren Smith, Gorden Tallis, Paul Vautin, Kevin Walters, Steve Walters, Shane Webcke.

In late October 2003 I flew out of Australia with the Kangaroos, coached by Chris Anderson, for what was an overwhelmingly enjoyable and successful campaign. Early on Willie Mason summed up the carefree nature of the tour with a comment that ended up in every newspaper: 'The last couple of weeks have been mental. It's like we've been on a Contiki tour, getting on and off buses, getting pissed.'

Well, a fair bit of that went on . . .

But something bad happened, too, something that nags at me still. And while I don't plan to dwell on it, it would be remiss of me in a book that sets out to tell honestly of a life in football not to address the matter of the 'Kangaroo Tour Thief'. Anyone who followed rugby league became aware of the story – via the Internet and the general media – that our team had a thief in its ranks and that money had been stolen from players' rooms, totalling close to $6000. I will just say this about it: that the vicious whispering campaign that began, in which the name of one player (Richard Villasanti), was spread all over the Internet was a pretty ugly business. And unfair. In the end I felt bloody sorry for Richard, who proved a different sort of character on tour; a bloke who went off and did his own thing. I'd imagine no one will ever know the real story of what happened over there. But when I stepped back from it and tried to introduce a bit of reason and commonsense I came to the personal conclusion that it didn't make any sense at all that he would be doing what he was accused of. More likely that it was hotel staff, I thought – considering the way footballers on tours tend to leave doors open and money lying around. Significantly, ARL Chief Executive Geoff Carr was to announce after an official investigation: 'We have found no evidence to link a player or players with the money in question.'

The whispering campaign must have been a bloody awful thing for Richard to endure. The first time we played the Warriors in Auckland the following season, I went up to him in the dressing room after the game and said words to the effect: 'Mate, I want to clear this thing up,' and I apologised to him. Something of a herd mentality developed on tour – after all, we were understandably pissed off about losing the money. But I know we players could have done more to help Richard in the situation he was in. He was hung out to dry and I still feel some shame about that. That's all I want to say.

The unpleasantness of the stolen money aside (and I lost 500 quid!), the Kangaroo tour experience of 2003 was wonderful. The 19 players who withdrew with reasons almost exclusively to do with their health and the wear-and-tear factor, missed something very special. The Kangaroo tour traditionally used to be a massive event and I grew up soaking up the stories of those campaigns. But with international footy now, it's on every year and arguably overdone – and maybe the 'mystery' of it all has ebbed a bit and for some players the feeling of it being extra special has waned to an extent. A major factor too is the amount of footy we play in any (domestic season). The way rugby league is played now the game is tremendously competitive and tremendously demanding physically and I'm sure blokes get to the end of a season and think, 'I just can't do any more of this.' A famous old forward of past years Noel 'Ned' Kelly has written of how he would have 'crawled over broken glass' to go on a Kangaroo tour. But back then the tours used to be only every four years and the 'broken glass' analogy was a very fair and understandable one. I would have crawled over broken glass too. But when at the end of a season of the high-powered game we have today you've got a buggered knee and a buggered ankle and your back is perpetually sore and you've just played 30-odd club games and a handful of rep. matches and you've done two tours in the previous two years and you haven't really had a break, it starts to become more than a little attractive to say: 'I'm injured enough not to go.'

I can understand why some players make those decisions not

to tour, as so many of them did in 2003. The pressures on modern footballers who train full-time are very different to what they used to be. Comparisons with the past are worthless, because there are so many variables. Comparisons across eras don't work, and never will. My plan is to never allow myself to become an old player who starts out talking about: 'In our day'.

The 2003 tour experience? I loved every single second of it. Yeah, it's tough at times after a long season and there are days when you think, 'I wish I was home,' but generally I thought the experiences of that campaign and the others I was fortunate enough to be on were marvellous. Memo ARL: if they're ever looking for a manager down the track, I'll put my hand up. To be touring in countries like England, France and Spain is wonderful – like moving to a whole other world. I loved the series 'Outback House' that the ABC produced and to me going to England is like that, like stepping into a completely different world. For the seven or eight weeks of that 2003 tour, it was like being on a different planet. The first time I went to France I hated it. I thought they were a rude, arrogant mob of bastards and I never wanted to go back. But from the second time, I loved it. Now it's a country that would be high on my itinerary for any European trip.

The fact that this was the 'get-out-of-gaol' tour when we beat the Poms three straight in a fantastic series that could have gone either way, made it an even more special experience. When New Zealand beat us 30–16 at North Harbour Stadium on the eve of the departure for England, it was very good for us because it really set us up for the tour. Because of that game it was a case of: 'Okay, we're awake now!' I scored a try against the Kiwis in that match and will make the confession here that it was pure arse. Someone kicked through and it bounced off a leg and I happened to be right there at the try-line and picked it up and scored. This was not a Billy Slater-type effort, although it will get better in the telling as the years go by. Apart from a try against Russia in the 2000 World Cup, this was my only Test try. That's enough. I never pretended to be a try-scoring machine.

The three Australia–Great Britain Tests in England were brilliant value for local fans, if ultimately disappointing for them. The first game at Wigan which we won 22–18 via a very late Darren Lockyer try was famous for the first-minute send-off of Adrian Morley. I was getting myself set for my hit-up after the Poms had kicked off and all of a sudden I saw Robbie Kearns on the ground and I thought: 'Holy shit'. Morley came through at 100 kph – and he could have nearly killed him. And that's exactly what I was thinking at that time . . . how much worse it could have been if Morley had caught him just a little bit sweeter. Robbie would have had *real* big problems. He's a big, strong man, Morley, and the way he clipped him then . . . I don't want to think about it.

This was such an amazing series. In each Test we beat them in the last minute or two. With 12 men they were excellent that first night and gave a pointer of what was to come. It's funny, you know, I don't have specific memories of the games, except that they all followed the pattern, and each time when we scored our late tries I was thinking: 'How good was that!' To win the second Test (23–20) from what must have looked an inpossible 20–8 scoreline with only five minutes to play was a wonderful feeling. It meant we had won the series – and that while in no way were we going to relax, we had at least done the job we had come to do whatever happened next, and could relax and enjoy it. The pressure was off. When we came out in the third Test and did exactly the same thing, winning 18–12 after being down 12–6 at the 77th minute mark, it must have been an absolute killer to them.

Oh yes, the rugby league gods smiled on the Kangaroos that tour.

Chapter 20
ORIGIN MEMORIES

The Origin weeks of my experience (21 of them) have a sort of Groundhog Day quality in my memory. There were the same hotels and, inevitably, the same pattern of events year after year as the seasons rolled on. These weeks and these matches were a wonderful part of my career, though, and I consider myself fortunate to have had them. One unchanging certainty every season was the feeling that at all times we were under an enormous amount of pressure. That was a tribute to Origin football, to how big it had become by the time I started (1998), and how much bigger it seemed to get *every* time. For me it was always a challenge. As you may have gathered, one of the things I found difficult about football, a major hurdle to be jumped, was the question of pressure, and dealing with it. In the Origin situation you are under the microscope from the minute you are picked, living in an environment in which everyone is pumped up. The days drag on towards the big night; it is a long time to feel nervous about a game of footy – exactly the sort of thing I worked hard to *avoid* in my club duties with the Broncos. But again, I learned to live with it – and made use of the simple devices that Phil Jauncey had taught me. They were enough. And I learned to work things that I enjoyed doing into the mix. Going into an Origin camp I would always take books with me; I have always loved my reading, and books were excellent companions. I learned to try to lead as normal an existence as I could within that abnormal world and to treat it as a nice rest from the routine of the club scene.

The roommate allocation is part of the whole experience, and I was lucky to have some good ones over the years. The general rule was that they wouldn't put you with someone you knew, but would mix it up. Gary Larson from Norths, a really good fellow, was my roomie in my first year, 1998. Gary is a sensible down-to-earth sort of bloke, and for a comparative Origin new chum like me, he was quite a help. I roomed with various others over the seasons that followed, always front-rowers. There was Craig Greenhill, a different sort of character from Gary, with a wilder streak, but a good bloke too, and good fun. John Buttigieg, a country boy like me, was fine and a good roomie. Martin Lang, son of coach John, seemed a nervous bloke, who worried about his football, and was a little insecure. But Martin is a good fellow and a really brave-hearted player who would always try his guts out.

My chance to first play Origin football in '98 in a now-reunited game came via a roundabout route. I was left out of the Queensland 13 originally (picked on the bench) for Origin 1 – but with speculation from the start of the week that I may well get the call, owing to the fact that Brad Thorn was struggling with an injured foot. And that's the way it turned out, with Brad's misfortune opening the door for me. I wore No. 8, as I did in all my Origin appearances that followed, and when they kicked off at SFS on the evening of May 22, I picked the ball up and ran it back at Paul Harragon, Rodney Howe, Dean Pay and Co. I was underway . . . I was an Origin player . . . in a game which featured a Great Escape for Queensland.

That first Origin experience of 1998 contained remnants of the 'old days'. We did a fair bit of 'bonding' (if you will) at the start. I found that strange and struggled with it a little – blokes shaping up for one of the biggest events of their football lives and being out on the town and 'blind' for the first two or three nights. I came to accept that that was just the way it was, and it didn't particularly worry me. But it did seem out of whack with the way professional football was heading. I will say that once those early 'bonding' days were gone, we would settle down and get into the work pretty well. Before too long the old days were exactly that – and teams no longer started their preparation with sessions on the booze.

Wayne Bennett was coach and lived with the tradition for a while, even though it was not in line with his own lifestyle. He is a teetotaller but he doesn't constrain those who are not, unless he thinks what is going on is to the detriment of the football team. I think in that series it was right on the edge, and he oversaw the change that followed to a different kind of preparation. I have to say I enjoyed the later rep team preparations more than I enjoyed the earlier ones, although I got to the point where I got a bit sick of being in hotels and being in camp situations. But I enjoyed it more with the progression to a more full-on professional approach – because while it might have been fun getting on the grog, geez it made it hard backing up and trying to train effectively. The old way was fun, though, and I was part of it. As I got older I enjoyed the more sensible approach. I think the evolution of the game demanded a different approach whatever the other reasons for change may have been. The game got stronger and faster year by year and the preparation had to be in tune with that.

That first Origin game in Sydney, in May 1998, was a pretty remarkable experience. For posterity, the teams were as follows:

Queensland: Lockyer, Sailor, Renouf, Darren Smith, Sing, Kevin Walters, Allan Langer (C), Webcke, Hetherington, Larson, Bartrim, Jason Smith, Ryan. Interchange: Price, Lang, Ikin, Carroll. Coach: Wayne Bennett.

New South Wales: Brasher, Wishart, Ettingshausen, Hill, MacDougall; Daley (C), Andrew Johns, Howe, Toovey, Harragon, Pay, Kosef, Fittler. Interchange: Barnhill, Menzies, Matthew Johns, Ken McGuinness (not used). Coach: Tom Raudonikis.

The match was probably one of the most desperately fought in Origin history, with the lead changing five times. When Steve Menzies scored for NSW with six minutes to go it took the Blues out to 23–18. But Andrew Johns missed the conversion – and we were still 'alive', with a minute to play, and NSW had us trapped deep in our own territory. It looked a 100:1 chance. But Kevvie Walters daringly kicked for open space near halfway and replacement back Ben Ikin raced through on fresh legs to regain possession. Two plays later after slick interplay between the Smith brothers, Kevvie sent Tonie Carroll racing over the NSW line. With time gone, the game hung in the balance – and it was all down to our goal kicker, Darren Lockyer, who to that point had landed three out of three. Under enormous pressure, Lockey stepped up and booted the conversion and we had won the first 'united' Origin game since 1996, 24–23. Amazing! The critics assessed my game kindly and *Rugby League Week* gave me an '8' rating (out of 10). Allan Langer and Brad Fittler both got '9s' – a reflection of the quality of the game.

The euphoria of stealing that game away from the Blues didn't last too long. In Game 2 at Suncorp, Andrew Johns and Laurie Daley were in peak form – and NSW beat us 26–10. Some mention was made of a big hit I managed to put on Paul Harragon early in that game, and I admit it felt good. 'Of course something like that feels good, because the game is all about getting over the top of your opponent,' I told the media. 'But I can't afford to crow about one good hit, because there will be plenty of them coming my way in the years to come.'

And there were.

After Game 3 1998 (Queensland 19–4), Peter Ryan came to me and said, 'I don't think I've ever seen you play that well.' He was a bloke I respected a lot, so it meant something to me. To hear it from him, one of the players who had been at the Broncos when I first came in, meant as much to me as winning that night in Sydney my first (and only, as it turned out) Man of the Match Award. It was one of those matches in which I ran the ball well and did my defensive stuff effectively. When I off-loaded, they were good off-loads. In summary, it was a night when everything clicked. The big award was a handshake or two and nothing else. But just to win it was more than enough.

I have absolutely no intention here of taking you ball-by-ball through the 21 Origin games which featured the name S. Webcke in the Queensland team line-up. Frankly, much of it is no more than a blur of maroon and blue in my head. But of course there are incidents and characters that are sharply remembered, and what follows here is a taste of some of the stuff that shines brightest in my Origin memory through the seasons 1998–2004. It's something of a mixture: the good, the bad and the ugly.

1999 Series

Wayne Bennett had stepped away, and Mark Murray was the coach. When my brother Dallas and I had gone down to Easts to trial some years before, he had been the coach. I hadn't seen him or spoken to him since then, so it was like a reunion. We went out for a beer the first night and Mark and I sat and talked about what a funny game football is. I had been to that trial long ago and had hurt my knee. It was hard to believe we were together now, sharing the experience of Origin football. For me the Easts disappointment had reinforced my belief at that time: I can't do this . . . this is not for me. Nine years later I was sitting chatting with the Queensland coach, as part of the team. It wasn't wasted on him either.

Hooker Jason Hetherington was Man of the Match in Game 1. He was a bloke I loved playing with – a real country fella, hard as nails and with a really dry sense of humour. In camp he would tell these yarns and blokes would be killing themselves laughing. He was a pleasure to play with. After Game 2, the press made mention of a 'savage double tackle' by 'Dalton' (Hetherington) and me on Mark Carroll. I'm not sure how much of it was done by him and how much by me, but at the end of the day, gee it *was* a good tackle. He was a funny bloke, Mark Carroll, with all his carry-on; when he went out to play he looked like he was chewing barbed-wire. But he was a tremendous fella and I always enjoyed playing against him. Back in '96, in one of my early first-grade games, against Manly, I hit a ball up off the kickoff, went straight at Mark and right over the top of him. And I shit myself. I couldn't believe I'd just done what I'd done. He was a big-name player, and I was never a cocky young player; I was just dumb. I had just gone at him as hard as I could, and to my *great* surprise had kept going. He'd never know this, but he set me up to have a pretty decent game that day because that one moment gave me a tremendous amount of confidence. So I'm very grateful to him.

Bill Harrigan was in the spotlight as Origin referee at that time. I know Gordie had his run-ins with Harrigan at times, but I'm still not quite sure how how real that was. Bill had a reputation of being a bit of a media tart, and Gordie's not frightened of a bit of publicity either. I used to wonder whether they both just enjoyed the fact that they could do it, knowing it would start a melee in the media. I never had any problem with Harrigan at all. I could be out there and say, 'Bill, for fuck's sake!' and he'd just laugh and we'd get on with it. I always thought he was a pretty good guy. My cousin was in the Tactical Response

Group with Bill and I remember that in the middle of one intense Origin match we were coming off at half-time and he turned to me and said: 'Dicky's out the back and he said to say g'day.' And I said:

'What the hell are you talking about, Bill?'

'Dicky!' he said, 'Warren Dick' (my cousin). Then I put it all together, and laughed. It was funny; chit-chat in the heat of the battle.

I think Bill was a good referee; he made his fair share of mistakes, but they all do. I always enjoyed playing under him – he was professional and cool-headed. You never felt like things were getting out of control with Harrigan. And I didn't mind the bit of flashiness and Hollywood about the bloke. At least he had some character about him, and that's good for the game. If he'd been a shit referee it would have been different. But he wasn't – he was good. I always respected him.

2000 Series

In Game 1, 2000, Bill Harrigan sent Gorden Tallis off for dissent. Gordie called the ref a 'f——— cheat' I think. I can't really remember the incident, but what I can remember (and Gordie will hate me for saying this!) is thinking that Gordie went over the top and that Harrigan did the right thing. Now that's going to be seen as disloyal, but the fact was that Gordie was right in the ref's face that night. I think Bill would have copped the last blast if it hadn't come on the end of such a long-sustained interlude between them. If it had been a one-off, Bill would have said, 'Shut up, mate . . . just go away.' But Gordie was at him and at him. Referees are out there to control the game, and you can't really expect them to just sit there forever and cop it. The send-off didn't help our cause (we lost the game 20–16), but I had no great drama with it. And at the end of the day it goes down in league folklore as one of those Origin 'moments'. I was pleased I was there to see it – those moments are part of the theatre of the game, after all. And in the years since, I think the pair of them (Harrigan and Tallis) have extracted a fair bit of mileage out of what happened that night.

In the third game NSW beat us 56–16, and this was a real flogging. It also probably kicked off my dislike for the theatrics that came into the game at that time, centred around the scoring of tries. At about the 50-point mark that night, NSW staged a 'mock' event in which they all stood around in a group and Brian Fletcher (I think it was) mimicked throwing a grenade and they all fell down. I really hated that. It was bullshit. Yeah, they were giving us a touch-up on the scoreboard. They were very much superior to us that night, and they played very, very well, and I'm not going to whinge about any of that. That's football. But what the NSW team did with their little bullshit act was not in the nature or the spirit of our game. Yes it was probably clever and a bit funny. But things like that go right against the grain . . . and against the spirit of the game, I believe. The game deserves better than that. NSW should have stood on the quality of their victory that night; they had no need to dress it up with bullshit. Leave that stuff to the pro wrestlers.

A loss like that (56–16) is no great tragedy – even though the margin of victory was extraordinary for Origin football. It was no big deal. Matches like that happen occasionally. The next year, Queensland won the series. I'd suggest that it was the carry-on by the Blues that night rather than the football match that made it 'ordinary'. But thankfully the aspect of the game on display that night seems to have died down.

As it turned out, that match was a watershed. Wayne (Bennett) would have watched that game . . . and he wouldn't have been happy with it. He wouldn't have been able to stomach at all the thought that such a result might even have been the start of a pattern which would have been bad enough to threaten

Origin football. So in 2001 he stepped back in. The result in Sydney signalled the certain end of Mark Murray, and was the motivation for Wayne to return. Whether Muppet (Murray) did a good job or a bad job, I don't really know. I don't think he was the greatest Origin coach I had, but he wasn't a bad coach either. It was just that Queensland needed a shakeup at that time, a monumental change, and that sort of thing could only be presided over by someone like Wayne. The challenge at hand – new players, new ways – was a Wayne Bennett special. The bloke has never been afraid to make big, bold decisions. That's not to say that Mark wouldn't have instigated change, but I think that what did happen had to happen.

2001 Series

Of the Origin series I played, 2001 was my favourite. We struggled in 2000, and there was a bad feeling that came out of that third game. To get back under Wayne's coaching in '01 was a fresh experience. Everything changed. It was in that year that the drinking went right out of the Origin equation; it was no longer part of the program in camp to go out and get sloshed for the first couple of nights. It was a great thing to be part of that year, to win the series so decisively . . . to have Alf Langer come back into the side and do what he did. The events and the outcome (Queensland 2–1) breathed a huge lungful of fresh air back into the Origin concept. I don't know whether Origin has ever really needed a 'shot in the arm', but this year was one of those little rites of passage when the game moved from one phase to the next.

Alfie Langer's return to Origin football for the last game was a huge story. Wayne took a few of us aside at the team hotel in the lead-up to the match and told us the news that he was going to bring Alf back. Obviously he'd organised it all well before he went public, probably as early as the day after Origin 2. He certainly didn't ask *us*, the senior guys in the group, but he did brief us. And no one in the room that day thought it was outlandish. It felt right to the coach and it felt right to us. The result spoke for itself.

In his Origin debut in Game 2, Mark O'Meley got good press when he beat an attempted tackle by me and set up a try for Brad Fittler. Ah, the missed tackle on O'Meley . . . I remember it very well . . . and have been reminded of it more than a few times. In fact it was probably all I ever got asked about when it came to that game, which NSW won 26–8. At that time I was probably at the height of my powers and I remember it so well: O'Meley a young player on the way up, putting a neat little step on me and beating me beautifully. I was probably trying to knock his head off! It's what can happen in rugby league, an example of how humbling the game can be. In our game you can be quite sure that if you ever get a bit full of yourself, something like that will happen. Chances are a young player will step up to the mark and make you look like a dill. It sure brings you back to earth. I remember it as though it was only 10 minutes ago. I think it's healthy . . . quite good for you. Yeah, I got stood up that night, but that happens in football and it didn't particularly worry me. The game is a great leveller.

2002 Series

Season 2002 brought together the mix of Wayne Bennett and Phil Gould as opposing coaches, and the guarantee was of intense rivalry and competition between the pair. Gould is an interesting character. There are days when I see him on TV and I think, 'Gee, you speak a lot of sense.' Then there are days when he's completely the other way and I can't believe what I'm hearing. He's a bloke I can't pick. My opinion is that he's a man who *could* be so good for our game, because he definitely knows rugby league. He's smart, articulate, a wonderful orator who can get his message across. But every so often he does something way off-key and I really wonder – like the night at the end of the 2004 series when he did a dummy spit about the way the media had treated him. Fair dinkum, that was just bullshit. He's a bloke I have never spoken to; our paths just haven't crossed. I don't dislike Gould, because I don't know him, but I dislike some of the things he has done. Maybe he's the greatest bloke in the world! I've talked elsewhere in these pages about having made the mistake of pre-judging blokes on the score of 'impressions'. Until I meet him and decide otherwise I have no real issue with him.

It was in Game 2 in 2002 that young Justin Hodges made his disastrous debut for Queensland, throwing two in-goal passes that led to NSW tries and, eventually, to him being hooked from the field. I remember feeling tremendously sorry for him. Through all the problems Justin has had, he's a really, really nice bloke. And when things go as wrong as they did that night, my thought was just that there but for the grace of God goes any one of us! Such events can happen in the blink of an eye. You'd wonder how you could possibly have done what he did *twice*, but that's just human nature. At least we won the game (26–18), so that took some of the pressure off him. He didn't cost us the match. But the poor bugger: whatever else happens in his career, the certainty is that some people will always remember that night. It's the unforgiving part of the game – what you do out there on that patch of grass is what's remembered. You can't change it. But to Justin's credit, he kicked on after that. He pulled his head in – and if he stays on course for the latter part of his time in football he can have a remarkably good career.

Dane Carlaw's try salvaged an 18–all draw in Game 3 that year, and saved the series trophy for Queensland. I was very happy for Dane. He's had a funny career. He's had great days, or nights like that and he's played for Australia – and at other times he's really struggled. He's my roomie on tour and I know the bloke very, very well. What he did this night at Stadium Australia with his last-minute try was unbelievable, and something he'll always remember. But what really stays with me from this game was Lockey's 'try'. The decision to disallow it (made by video referee Chris Ward) was just bullshit. I don't know how anyone could say that was *not* a try. Wayne called it the hottest decision he'd ever seen and it was. There was no possible way in the world it wasn't a try, but I suppose you could say that things like that make our game what it is: unpredictable, challenging, controversial. And in such cases you just have to shape up, bury the disappointment and get on with it. What's more, it gives the media heaps to talk about the next day! I have to say there was a lot of bullshit talked after the game – that the (18–all) draw was an 'empty' way for Queensland to win the series etc. In fact justice was done. Had we been given the Lockyer try as we should have been, we would have had the game anyway.

Gorden Tallis is an extremely family-minded bloke and it showed out at the tail-end of that Game 3 Origin night, in 2002 when he took very visible offence at Stadium Australia at a sign held up by a couple of blokes, which carried offensive words along the lines of either 'Gordie, your mother's a pig' or 'Gordie, your mother's a rig'. There may have been an adjective or two in there as well. I was barely aware of it on the night. I knew that at full-time Gordie was down the end of the field, but I thought he was just geeing up the fans. There was some rambling on about it in the room afterwards, but I was too stuffed to take much notice. Like everyone else, I became aware of the drama via the newspapers the next day. The event showed the ugly side of some supporters. The debate raged for days about the actual wording of the sign – but whatever it was, you'd have to think the major aim of it was to be insulting to Gorden's mother. It was a case of fans going one step too far. People have no right to take their involvement in the game to those personal levels. It was disgraceful.

Players' families should never be dragged into the arena of football as happened that night. The 'fans' picked the wrong mark, too, and probably realised it when they felt the sting of Gordie's anger. The Tallis family grew up in hard circumstances and are extremely tight and close. Gordie's reaction was entirely understandable.

2003 Series

I can say now with the passing of time that the surface of the refurbished Suncorp Stadium for Game 1 was bloody terrible. Our brief before that match was not to talk it down. Suncorp was going to be our home base, after all, and we knew the blokes at the ground had been doing their utmost to have it right; they didn't need us jumping on their backs about it. It was probably two or three weeks short of the time it needed to be a decent playing surface. Thankfully the place was soon to boast a surface of the quality that such a ground deserved – and takes it place as a wonderful football stadium.

NSW won the series – with Andrew Johns especially dominant in Game 2. When it came to blokes who could dominate a football match, Johns was the best of them in my experience by a mile – a tremendously skilful player, and a very strong defender. I wasn't a great watcher of the game, so I don't remember a lot about Wally Lewis, but no doubt he had the same qualities. I'm told Sterlo (Peter Sterling) did, too. But when Andrew Johns made a decision that he was going to change a game . . . well, he'd just do it. It's a very rare quality; very few players have that sort of talent. That ability set him apart from everyone else. Off the paddock, he's a bloke whose company I have always enjoyed.

2004 Series

The Shaun Timmins Golden Point field goal at the end of Game 1 was just awful for Queensland (NSW 9–8), but what a great

Origin game! It was such a bloody tough match, it really was. From Game 2 of that series, Billy Slater's try is implanted in my memory. It was freakish stuff. I'd like to say I suggested the inspired kick he put over, and was right alongside Billy backing up. But I don't want to embarrass the kid, and actually it wasn't quite like that anyway. In fact I was back down the park, watching in awe like everyone else. It was a fine bit of refereeing and second-judgement from upstairs to give the try the green light. People can argue forever about whether or not Billy was onside when he chased Darren Lockyer's grubber kick. There was about a toenail in it. But what a tragedy it would have been if they'd said no and if that try today wasn't part of the game and part of Origin folklore. If there was a fraction of the benefit of the doubt given, well, that's terrific. It would have been different if it had been blatant, but it wasn't. It was line-ball.

I had no clue that Game 3, 2004, Wednesday night, July 7 at Telstra Stadium was to be my last Origin game – although I was starting to think around that time that I was getting close. As it turned out, things transpired later that season that brought the decision to a head. The firm realisation came months later 20,000 kilometres away and courtesy of my left knee. The Blues gave us a towelling that final night (36–14), which was bad enough. But for me the real sadness and disappointment was delayed until later, when I made the decision I had to make and retired from representative football. Origin Match No. 21 had been my last in the Queensland jumper. Add the three games I played in the split year of 1997 and that's 24.

It's funny how it all ended that night and I never got any great walk around the field or anything like that. But I don't care. I feel so privileged that I was ever part of an Origin experience; I didn't need some fairytale ending. The fairytale was just being part of it. I didn't need anything else . . . accolades or emotion. Whatever I gave to it, I took so much more out of it. I still pinch myself today when I think of my Origin time. I played 24 games for Queensland in a row and along the way won a Man of the Match award and a Maroons' Player of the Series award. Those things mean the world to me and are filed among my special memories. To me they are priceless, and I can only think how lucky I am to have so many great memories of the Origin experience.

So my disappointment at ending before I knew I was ending was tempered both by the pride and enjoyment I had taken from my Origin involvement, and by the bonus I had always considered that to be – remember, I had been a kid who had never given himself buckley's chance of playing for Queensland. Back then, the thought of playing even one game was an impossible dream. Now I had played 24 – and even if my involvement had reached a sudden full-stop a season or two before I would have wished, well, it had still been fantastic. I'm not greedy, and I have no regrets.

A piece I wrote for the *Big League* Origin 1 match program in 2005 captured how I felt about Origin football – at a time when I was coming to terms (with difficulty!) with the fact that I was no longer part of it:

As much as State of Origin is the toughest physical battle a player can go through, with the intensity and the pace for the entire 80 minutes that no other game can produce, it's just all mental. It really is. It is tough, real tough, but it is still a game of rugby league, and if you use all of your energy up worrying about this and that before the event, and reading this and that in the newspapers, and trying to work it all out in your mind – by the time you get to the game, you can't play, you're as flat as a tack.

It is perhaps the biggest danger an Origin player can face. It can really mess with your mind.

It's a long, long wait for the game of your life, and on top of that, because it's such a great concept and grabs so much of the public's imagination, the amount of media coverage is quite overwhelming. A player might say something very off-hand, then all of a sudden it's big news, and a little firestorm starts because of it.

There will be so many theories in the press, so many media games played by smart coaches, so much abstract nonsense from a journalist looking for a fresh angle. It can be quite daunting if you read it all.

Wayne Bennett had the best way of dealing with it. He always said if you want to get through the week and be OK for the game, don't read the papers.

I took Wayne's advice on board. I didn't read a word from the time I went into camp.

The result in Origin games really comes down to the team who has had the best preparation in camp and who best handles the hype, expectation and anxiety that naturally builds over the 10 and a half days between being selected and running onto the field.

I'm lucky that I'm such a big reader. I'd make sure I had stacks of novels and magazines (I always packed Queensland Country Life*) and that would help stop me thinking about what was coming.*

Think instead about the first two things you always do in a game, think about doing only them and doing them well and don't think about anything else in the match.

If they kick off I'm going to do a hit-up and make it a good one. If we kick to them I'll try to make two of the first three tackles. And that's all I thought about. It was easy.

The hardest time during the lead-up in Origin is game day. You don't kick off until 8 o'clock and it's a long day . . . And that's when you really have to distract yourself. There comes an important time after lunch when there's still four or five hours before you're on the team bus . . . it's a nightmare.

For years I'd have a brief 'kip'; they say 20 minutes to a half hour is plenty to top your energy level up.

Later in my career, I wouldn't sleep at all. I'd rather be active and go for a walk, I seem to feel sharper in games if I do that, but all players are different.

And there is no more spine-tingling moment in rugby league than running onto Suncorp Stadium with a full house, or to 80,000 at the vast Telstra Stadium, for that matter.

It's a massive, massive buzz to run out to that noise.

There is no use trying to fight it, trying to block it out. You just go with it.

That's when you start enjoying it. All the mental stuff is over then. You're on the paddock and you're about to rip in. It's footy now in its purest sense.

No more interviews, no more talking crap, no more waiting. All the build-up is over . . . and it's on. It's almost relief.

That's when the pressure valve went off for me, when you ran onto the field and sucked in that truly amazing atmosphere.

You see the floodlights in your eyes as you emerge from the tunnel and you think, 'Whatever happens is going to happen; now it's real.'

Game on.

Qld v NSW, Game 1, May 25, 2005

Origin games are, individually, the hardest of all in my assessment of the different levels of football: club, Origin, international. They are guaranteed knock-'em-down, drag-'em-out affairs for the entire 80 minutes, and they are run in that quick-fire sequence mid-season, played with tremendous intensity. In international footy, if we get a good game against the Kiwis it can be a bloody hard thing. But the reality for years (at least until the 2004 Tri-nations final) had been that the Australian teams are so good that usually we roll over international opposition, as we have done with the Poms, although their gradual narrowing of the gap has been an excellent thing for the game. Notwithstanding all that, club football remains the biggest challenge because it's week-to-week – and every week you are expected to perform.

That's the real challenge, sustaining the effort for eight months. You can win an Origin series in two games – but to win a comp you've got to win a *heap* of games in the face of continuing pressure, win them at the right time – and time the form of both the team and the individuals in it to near perfection. It is the perennial challenge for coaches, players and clubs.

The nature of Origin football has gradually changed, as everything does. The kids today won't respond to the sort of stuff that Mal (Meninga) and Co. used to respond to. That time is gone, and I hope the blokes running the show keep it in mind. I'm sure they will. The game still needs passion and plenty of it, but things have changed a lot when it comes to Origin football 27 years on. I think a great bloke like Chris 'Choppy' Close, one of the 'originals' struggled with all of that . . . struggled to come to terms with the reality that the feelings that once fuelled Origin football had changed. Blokes like him had grown up under that unfair system in which NSW had a monopoly on just about all the stars in the game, including the Queensland ones who had moved to Sydney, and held all the aces. Origin football in its earlier days was a hugely emotional thing, a breaking away from all that.

But today's players (and me too) grew up in an era when Queensland used to win quite regularly. So the pride and passion still exist, but it's different from what it was. I don't hate NSW as those earlier blokes did; I have no reason to. I have to say, though, that I hate some of the smart-arsed shit that comes out of there at times, though I accept that it's part of the 'theatre' of the whole thing. Teams won't win *just* on passion these days. They need a plan and they need to execute it extremely well. That's the modern game.

I write this piece at a time when the Queensland team was wrestling with a losing sequence and three straight series losses something of a monkey on their backs. Coming in to season

2006, the record at Sydney's Telstra Stadium was nine successive losses for the Maroons. Yeah, we've got trouble down there. And yet, you know, the record at Telstra was just one of those things and probably hasn't got anything to do with Telstra. We've just been unlucky enough to go there on X number of occasions and either not prepared quite right, or done something wrong. Whatever it's been, it's not the ground – and we (Queensland) have to get past that. It can get into the back of minds in the thought, Oh, shit, we're at Telstra, when something goes wrong in a game. That mind-set may well creep in even a little deeper with younger players. It never worried me. We could have been playing in Texas and it wouldn't have been any different to me. It was just another tough game of football. But maybe for some players it has seeped in, that little thought that winning is going to be even harder than normal because of where the match is being played. For NSW it's exactly the opposite. They probably go into any Telstra Stadium game with the thought, We get 'em here! But one year it'll turn around, no doubt and then it's gone. It only takes one game. As it turned out that game wasn't to be in 2006; the Maroons lost at Telstra but Origin history now records a magnificent Maroons bounceback – spectacular wins at Suncorp and Melbourne's Telstra Dome to take the series.

In Queensland, we are always on a hiding to nothing in that we don't always have the 'cattle' – although hopefully that will change over the years. Yet I think that's precisely what has made the series the triumph for rugby league that it has become since 1980, that ongoing Queensland struggle for the number of quality players and the depth that we need. If we were two evenly matched states the series mightn't have the appeal that it has had over the years. As it stands, NSW love to dominate – because they can – and we win when we can . . . and then talk about how we managed it as underdogs. It's a beautiful, simple formula. Origin has always been a case of expecting the unexpected – and that's been the beauty of it season after season – you never quite know. The sure thing is that matches and seasons rarely run to script! May it continue that way forever.

Chapter 21
THE GREEN AND GOLD DREAM

I put international football on a higher pedestal than many people in the game do. As far as I'm concerned it's the top of the tree. All the talk in the modern game seems to be about Origin, and how important that is in the order of things. But for me, playing for Australia is the greatest honour I have had in the game – nothing less than awesome. I rank playing for my country even higher than a grand final win. I remember as a kid living under the illusion that the Australian rugby league team represented the whole of the country and I used to think, How wonderful is that! I got to learn differently, of course, but the burning desire I have to see rugby league become a truly national game (and one day have a truly 'national' team) goes all the way back to those boyhood feelings. It can become that too – a national game – if enough time and passion and hard work are invested in making it grow in the other states.

A genuinely 'national' Australian rugby league represents a wonderful dream. As for my own career – I don't believe it's diminished in any way by the current reality, that the Test team is an eastern seaboard team. But how wonderful it will be in the future if young blokes run out knowing they are representing the *whole* of Australia? I hope I'm there cheering on the day a kid from Perth or Darwin or Adelaide runs out to play rugby league for Australia. Such an occasion would finally take us to where I believe we should go with our national team. But the movement towards that objective which began in the 1990s seems to have hit the wall – and I would remind the game's leaders of an old truth: if you stop going forward, you start going backwards.

This chapter reflects some personal memories of days and nights in the green and gold, and on tours in the great cause of playing for Australia. Every time I pulled on that jumper it meant something very special to me. In the light of my passion for international football, sitting out of the 2001 UK tour was one of the hardest things I have ever done. Most of the jerseys I did win are still with me – and safely packed away at home, including the first, from a fiery game against the Kiwis at Suncorp Stadium, in the second Test of the 1998 series.

The big Kiwi Jarrod McCracken made sure I would never forget my 'official' Test debut in what was a re-joined game in that year, 1998. (I had, of course, played a Super League 'Test' in '97.) In the match played at Suncorp in October, McCracken's knee caught me in the head at one stage, and left me with a deep cut across the cheekbone. He ripped in, in that game – a match that had more than its share of 'incidents' as the English ref, Russell Smith, struggled to keep control. McCracken played the game hard throughout his career, and that's why I found it difficult to believe the way he went on the way he did about the tackle he copped in 2000 from Stephen Kearney and Marcus Bai. That matter ended up in the headlines and in court and finished with a judgement for McCracken. Considering the way he played his football, McCracken was probably lucky he wasn't on the receiving end of something similar at some stage of his career. That night in 1998 we weathered the storm and won the Test 30–12 – and I was proud and pleased with my Test debut form, with second-rower Gorden Tallis and me being rated the best forwards on the field.

The Kiwis are always physical and tough and now they are getting even better (in the Tri-nations final, 2005, for instance). As a nation, they are a rugby league giant. They love the game – and they play it well. And the better they go in the wake of 2005, the more the game will grow over there.

Anzac Test, 1999

The Paul Brothers, Henry and Robbie, just off the plane from the UK, were very good players who brought something different into this game at Stadium Australia. I quickly came to realise that they were blokes we were going to have to watch. I remember walking onto the field that night and looking at the Kiwis and thinking, They've got a couple of Pommies playing for them. And of course the careers of the brothers were largely conducted in England, and they played their football in the English style. They even looked like little Pommies, right down to the haircuts. I suppose you get that way if you spend a few winters over there. And they could certainly play the game. It was an excellent Test which we won 20–12, with Mat Rogers the difference, kicking four goals from four attempts. A very capable player, Rogers, a bloke who got the job done.

Papua New Guinea (PNG) in Townsville, 2000

This was the only Test I played against PNG, and I remember getting smashed a few times and thinking, These blokes can play. I honestly think that PNG, with plenty of support and a properly managed competition up there, could be anything in rugby league. Maybe they lack something in size, but they are a hardy race of people. And they play in a country where rugby league is a religion. I've been up there a few times with the Broncos and I have found their love of the game and enthusiasm for it infectious. The more help Australia can provide, via money, expertise and structure, the better they will obviously become. They have what it takes to be the real international 'entertainers' of our sport. At the moment, when they play Australia they are almost in awe. They're out there suddenly matched against blokes who they have watched from home and probably regard as heroes.

We beat them 82–0 this time and I enjoyed the camaraderie and spirit of the match. They're fine people – friendly . . . and rugby league-loving, as we are. I hope they continue to grow and grow as a rugby league nation.

New Zealand, Anzac Test, 2000

When we flogged the Kiwis 52–0 at Stadium Australia in the annual Anzac Test it was a pretty horrible result for international football in the year of a World Cup, albeit a powerful performance from our blokes. The Kiwis were forced to make four changes in three days leading up to the Test. They competed for a time in the first half and then fell away, to be beaten nine tries to nil. It was a strong pointer to our World Cup chances later in the year.

World Cup 2000

By the time the 2000 World Cup came around, in late October, the arm I had busted in the NRL finals had completely recovered and I was enthusiastic about being part of it. In the main it turned out to be a great trip, my first under coach Chris Anderson. I found him to be a bloke of the old school, and we got on tremendously well.

The experience was a real enjoyment, especially as we came home with the cup. We stayed that campaign at the Queen's Hotel in Leeds, a rather old and rundown place then, but comfortable and friendly – and only played a couple of genuinely hard games – the first, straight off the plane, against England at Twickenham, and the last, the final against New Zealand at Old Trafford.

After a bruising game against the Poms, which we won 22–2 in foul weather conditions in London, we beat the Fijians 66–8 in a match in which Lote Tuqiri played fullback for them, then Russia 110–4, and Samoa 66–10 in the quarterfinal. In the semi-final against Wales at the McAlpine Stadium, Huddersfield, we were maybe a bit lax in our approach and they played well and gave us a real game. In the end we got away from them to win 46–22; the lively Welsh performance was credited with breathing some life into the tournament. The Welsh also gave us a perfectly timed wakeup call for the final.

The decider was a tough game; despite the final scoreline – 40–12 over the Kiwis. With 13 minutes to play it was only 18–12, but then a couple of quick Wendell Sailor tries pushed the button for a dazzling finish. Journalist Glenn Jackson wrote cleverly of us turning from 'battering rams to ballerinas' and how 'workmen's boots had been cast off for tap shoes' in the flying finish we turned on. Mission accomplished.

Afterwards there was media debate on the quality of that Australian side – how we stood in comparison with famous teams of the past, such as the 1982 Invincibles. Such things are never more than matters of opinion, and there were plenty of them around. But whatever your view, the 2000 Kangaroos who won the Cup would certainly rank as a hot side: Darren Lockyer, Mat Rogers, Adam MacDougall, Matt Gidley, Wendell Sailor, Brad Fittler (C), Brett Kimmorley, Shane Webcke, Andrew Johns, Robbie Kearns, Bryan Fletcher, Gorden Tallis, Scott Hill. I was proud to be part of the team, and of our achievement.

The 16-nation tournament was no great success, for the most part featuring lopsided games and matches played before sparse crowds in England and France. But to be part of the experience was something I valued – and it opened my eyes to an extent about international rugby league, in terms of its potential. The lukewarm reaction to the World Cup was probably not unexpected, but you know, the much-boomed rugby union World Cup, while bigger, is not a whole lot stronger or more competitive than what league can muster. For all the speculation and hot air that precedes a rugby World Cup, the truth is that just like the league, there are very few teams with a chance of winning it. I believe that with some hard work and smart development work in other countries our game could draw a lot closer.

The big difference lies in the marketing, and I have to say that the promotional work and the programming of the 2003 Rugby World Cup in Australia was bloody fantastic. What they did is precisely what we need in rugby league in 2008 when the Centenary World Cup comes around. But so far I see no evidence that the effort going in to the World Cup is likely to make it as special as it *must* be. The Cup is to be tagged onto the end of the premiership season – virtually 'out of season', in March, when people are restarting the year after the summer break. To make such an event the success that it could be requires energetic and creative planning from three or four years out. As I write these words I might be selling those responsible short, but gee, I see no evidence of anything special happening. What we need is what rugby union presented in 2003. But is it going to happen?

As a coach on that 2000 World Cup campaign, Chris Anderson was really good for me. I don't know whether he taught me anything dramatically new or that I came away from the World Cup experience thinking I was a better player, but what he did do was make the football a great enjoyment. I always felt he had confidence in me, that he saw me as an integral part of the side. I know that Anderson has his detractors, but I always felt he was an excellent national coach. Perhaps he has to wear some of the burden for behavioural problems that emerged at times under his stewardship, but personally I couldn't fault him, and I very much enjoyed the Test and international football I played under him. I also count him as a mate.

I found Anderson to be a man who understood football very well. He wasn't trying to reinvent the wheel or be super-smart. He just prepared us to be ourselves, and to play to our potential as an Australian team. The training component was always effective – he had a good way of pulling it all together.

Off the field the Anderson leadership style was pretty relaxed, and that worked well for me. I enjoy that style of approach and I suppose I am a bloke who is fairly keen on doing the right thing, even if the reins are pretty loose. His system was good for me. For the blokes who needed a tighter rein, and there were only a few of them, the Anderson approach was not so effective.

Yeah, I have good feelings towards Chris Anderson. His record was excellent, and if I was able to build a good and successful international career – and I'd like to think I did – he was a strong part of it, and for that I am grateful.

I'd rate him a great coach. But if you asked him why he turned out to be good at the coaching caper, he probably couldn't tell you. He just has the knack. Sometimes that is enough. I'm told he was an instinctive type of player and I think he coaches that way too, with a really good feel for the game. With any Australian side, the coach has players guaranteed to be able to do the job at hand. To coach with a fairly light touch and just hold things together is an entirely reasonable approach.

Stretching over more than a month and to the edge of the English winter, this was a tour of the old style, with the weather sleety and cold much of the time. It was my first big trip with an Australian side, and I loved it. The one major frustration amidst all the enjoyment I had lay in the 'hot' water system at the

Queen's Hotel. I roomed with Parramatta's Michael Vella, a different sort of character and a really good roomie. The pub was old, but generally fine – but our bloody hot water was never better than lukewarm. I reckon I was at the front desk every day for three weeks, making the point. But it was never fixed and we didn't have the luxury of a hot shower the whole time we were there. It was bloody awful. We'd get back wet, frozen and dirty from a training session, knowing for sure what awaited us.

It was the first time I had struck wintry English conditions: the heavy fields, the fog and rain and sleet, the biting cold. And when we headed out to training on those grey, damp mornings I worked out a little routine to get me through. As soon as the bus pulled up at the training ground I'd be off . . . and running. I figured that the longer I sat there in the warmth, the harder it was going to be. The sooner I was out there and falling over and getting a bit of mud on me, the better.

New Zealand in Wellington, 2001

This was my first trip to Wellington – and I thought it was a wonderful place. I know they have made bids to have a team in the NRL competition, and after seeing the stadium there and getting a sense of the place, I feel they have plenty to offer. I think there's a case for New Zealand having two teams. Obviously, to have NRL teams in places like Auckland and Wellington provides a wonderful opportunity for rugby league to lay down a pathway for young blokes into the big-time competition. In the thinking of the Shane Webcke School of Growing the Game, the idea of a team from the New Zealand capital in the NRL has merit.

This was the last game of the year, bringing a 28–10 win for Australia, and it's always a wonderful relief in those seconds when the siren sounds and you think, That's it! A break lies ahead, a chance to get on with your life for a short while and then freshen up before it all starts again.

Great Britain in Sydney, 2002

On this night, when we beat a jet-lagged Great Britain side 64–0, I played one of the best Test matches of my career. The papers made a fuss about a couple of tries I managed to set up in the second half by getting passes away. In one respect I remember the game very fondly because it was a night when things seemed to go very right for me. But 64–0? Nobody wants to see that sort of scoreline. And such a result can lead to some personal agonising, I can tell you. It's a contradiction to be wrestled with. In football can you never go out there thinking you are going to take it easy, and when you start flogging the crap out of a team, as happened that night, you don't immediately start thinking, Hang on, this isn't good for the game. The competitive drive takes over and you just put your foot down. I have always tried to put my wider love of the game first in the things I have done in rugby league. But as a footballer, whenever I play I want to win – and I want us (the team) to win as well as we can. So for me, a result like that inevitably creates mixed feelings. When we flogged them that night, I suppose the thought was at the back of all our minds that we hadn't done the game any favours. We knew that the headlines next day would not be about the way we played (very, very well) but about the sad state of international football. And they were. As a bloke who wants nothing more than to see the international game come together and be strong, I hated that. But all the same, there was also pride in my own performance and in being part of a powerful and ruthless Australian side.

Immediately after the match I was asked for my thoughts on what had happened – and I went straight on the defence for the Poms. They had travelled 19,000 km across the globe to play a one-off Test, been given only three or four days to prepare – and almost as soon as it was over they were travelling back. The program was hugely unfair to them and something of an indictment of the administrators, here and over there, who made the decision. Even more than their problems with the rushed trip, we were really battle-hardened and in intense footy mode. We had just come out of an Origin series and everyone was at peak level. For the Poms it was always going to be a huge mountain to climb. Thankfully, that game seems to have been something of a turning point, and such one-off events are now things of the past, as they should be. I think the Tri-nations concept of recent years has been wonderful – albeit a bit overdone – and it is the way for our international competition to go.

Notwithstanding, this was the best game I played for Australia, and among the top handful of games in my entire career. I remember thinking that it was a bloody shame the game ended up the way it did. But for me it was special, and I'll always remember it.

New Zealand in Sydney, 2003

The official records for the match on Friday, 25 July 2003, note that I was named Man of the Match, but you know, I can't remember a bloody thing about it! I can only presume I must have had a good one! We won the game 48–6 and I recall barely any of it. I do remember, however, saying in an interview afterwards that I felt they were disadvantaged because of the timing of the match. It was the same with that 64–10 Test against the Poms. If you're from somewhere else and you happen to play a Test at that time of the year (i.e. post Origin) you are striking Australian footballers at their hardest. If you've played Origin and survived it, you're as hard as rock and in as good form and condition as you're going to be. It's a BIG ask for any visiting side to face an Aussie team in that mood, at that time.

New Zealand, Anzac Test in Newcastle, 2004

This was Darren Lockyer's first Test as a five-eighth. Put him at front row and he'd go all right . . . he's such a great player! That was an enjoyable week. I thought it was a great move by the ARL to take the game to Newcastle. With a bumper crowd and a great atmosphere, it was a very successful experiment. It was a good pointer for the possibilities of the 2008 World Cup and the match was a good lead-up to the Tri-nations campaign that lay ahead. We won the game, 37–10.

The longer tours of my experience were something of a strain on family back home and I can only imagine what it must have been like on those early Kangaroo campaigns when teams would be away as long as seven or eight months. I found it difficult to be away from the family – and the kids would always be a little stand-offish when I finally got home, although that would only last a couple of hours, and then all would be back to the way it was. At those times, I would remember my own father being away on work assignments for stretches up to a year, which was a whole heap tougher than being away playing footy for six or seven weeks. Oh yes, I missed Ally and the kids terribly – but in the larger scheme of things it wasn't that tough.

And so it went . . . The memories here are a small taste of my green-and-gold experience. You will find others dotted through-out this book, the fact being that the thrill of playing for Australia was part of every one of my seasons from 1998 to 2004, and the records tell the story that I played 20 times for my country. A great positive of my international career was the chance to tour and play with two outstanding coaches: Chris Anderson and Wayne Bennett. When I think of them I think North Pole and South Pole. I really enjoyed playing under Chris Anderson (1999–2003). I had a great time and he was good for my footy – he let me be what I wanted to be and made me feel confident in myself. At that stage I had played under Johnny Lang in the

Super League year (1997) and then with Wayne (1998), but only in home Tests.

Until I linked up with Chris in 1999 I felt really nervous and uncomfortable playing in the Australian side. But he made me really feel that I deserved to be there and I loved playing for him. It's fair to say that the Chris Anderson tours were very, very 'loose'. He had grown up in the era of the old tours, on which blokes drank heaps of grog and played up, and on which, occasionally, trouble brewed and damage was done. Our tours under him were never the way it *had* been, I'm sure, but his attitude was that if you were doing your job for him as a footballer then he didn't really care what you did. There were no curfews, and if blokes had a beer on the night before a game and then came out and did their job on match-day – well, okay.

His coaching was a total contrast to that of the man who both preceded and succeeded him, Wayne Bennett (1998, 2004–05). They have a shared quality; both are great coaches with outstanding communication skills. I don't think Chris is a particularly great 'tactical coach'. Footy is just footy, after all. But he knows how to get players to play for him. He won me over and I enjoyed his company. He's a man I would always enjoy having a beer and a yarn with. I like the bloke.

With Wayne, I was looking forward enormously to going away on his tour (2004) because I knew we'd do some different stuff after the Anderson tours. I knew he would bring out another side of me. I was a different bloke with each of them. With Chris I felt I could get on the grog now and then, even get pissed. He didn't care, so I felt comfortable doing it. With Wayne, I wouldn't feel right about doing that. I would feel (and know) that he wouldn't respect that. He is not a wowser, but I know he would think I was letting myself down by being excessive. And that's good. That's the good influence he has had on me.

For blokes who had been with me on tour with Ando, I was probably seen as a different character on the 2004 tour. It's only that I feel differently about the two coaches – and I don't think there's anything wrong in catering to people's needs that way. So if there are things that Wayne doesn't want his footballers to do, I won't do them. Regardless of any personal thoughts a player may have, the coach is the boss on a football tour. I never had any problem playing under those rules.

The other thing is that I really enjoy Wayne's company. We are friends as well as workmates – and that's a comfortable situation even though he's been the 'boss' throughout. So in 2004, when he was heading out on a tour or to look at a castle or something historic, I'd 9 times out of 10 go along with him. Maybe you look a bit nerdy doing that. But we're good mates and we think on the same wavelength on a lot of things. With Chris there was never really a 'cultural' option. We'd go to the pub. And that would be fine. It's about flexibility, I think, about respecting the differences and the men and accepting their different ways of doing things.

With Wayne, I think some players tended to howl him down a bit about the tours and visits, but if they cared to admit it, once they went to some of the places they enjoyed it a lot. It comes largely from his understanding of what a great privilege it is to be able to travel overseas on the sort of tours the Kangaroos undertake. Make the most of it, is his philosophy on that. The message is probably roughly along these lines: while you are over here, instead of just drinking and carrying on all the time, you should take the opportunity to experience these new and different things. Because you may never come back again.

But players being players, there was certainly some resentment on the 2004 campaign. Wayne really curbed the drinking and, being human beings, we had got used to it being very different under Anderson. Numbers of players in that tour party had been in the green and gold for a few years, as I had been, and had got used to partying on. I knew what was coming under the new coach, so it didn't worry me too much. But some of the blokes really struggled with it – and I probably did too at different times. There'd be days when I would think, Loosen up a bit, mate. But even at those times I'd know deep down that Wayne was right. The bloke has never given me a bum steer in my life – and I always keep that in mind when he is telling me things.

Wayne ran a bloody good tour. And I'm sure that regardless of the constraints that the players may have felt they were under, just about all of them would say they enjoyed the experience. The US leg, for example, was pretty much down to Wayne's enthusiasm for going there; he really pushed hard for that. It was a great time. New York was just unbelievable – an incredible city. Then, after the match in Phildaelphia it was on to Los Angeles and Las Vegas. Not being a punter, I never thought that Vegas and me would be much of a match, but I had a magnificent time there.

It was a terrific adventure, really. In France, where I hobbled around on my increasingly troublesome knee, we saw the new super-jumbo in Toulouse. Bloody huge! I'm fascinated by aviation. I watched a television show later on the project – about how the plane was conceived and built and how when it first took off they had all the parachutes at the ready. Technically they knew it could fly, but that didn't mean it was going to! It's hard to get your head around the statistics – that it can carry 800 people! I'd like to travel on one, one day. But I'm going to let them fly for a year or two before I give it a go.

As a purely football operation that tour was a big success. Bringing in Craig Bellamy as assistant coach was an enormous move. I can't give him a big enough wrap. The staff was excellent – Tony Ayoub (physio), Tony Spencer (head trainer) and John 'Chow' Hayes (manager). Chow is from another era; he played with Wests back in the 1960s when the Magpies were doing battle with the legendary St George team. But he's a terrific fella and I clicked with him straight away. He's my sort of bloke, a man with plenty of spirit and a gentlemanly quality about him – but one who can also be a ratbag like the rest of us. It's the sort of mix I like. And he knows a good feed, Chow. He took us to a restaurant in the Rocks area of Sydney one day, and it was sensational.

So when it came to the tours of Chris Anderson and Wayne Bennett, it was a case of different strokes for different blokes. I consider myself fortunate to have been a member of the Australian team under both of them: two very good football coaches, but totally different in their ways. As I said, North Pole and South Pole. And in my time in the green and gold I was lucky to have had them around.

Chapter 22
2004: ME AND MY KNEE

In the first week of the 2004 finals we led Melbourne 8–0 at half-time in the qualifying final at Suncorp Stadium. But, inspired by five-eighth Scott Hill, they ran over us in the second half and won 31–14. We were pretty poor that night . . . I even felt we chucked in the towel a bit at the end. I can tell the story now: in the days before that game something went badly wrong with my left knee. When I woke up on the morning of that match I knew I was in real trouble. I went down to the Brisbane Botanical Gardens for a walk and limped around and worried like mad about whether the knee would stand up. A lump of bone was afloat and the bloody thing kept catching. I thought, God, what am I going to do here? I decided finally that I wouldn't tell anyone and I'd just hope I'd be okay in the match. I wasn't. On the paddock I was hurting badly, with the knee 'stopping' and locking up. I played most of the game, but eventually it was giving me so much trouble I had to come off. 'There's something in this knee,' I said to the doc,

Peter Myers. He checked me over. 'Yeah ... there is,' he answered.

We had come to that early finals showdown with the Storm via a powerful finish to the premiership season. We had installed ourselves in the top four early in the year and then thrown down the gauntlet as (we believed) genuine title contenders with seven wins and a draw in nine matches running up towards the finals. Then Penrith outgunned us 46–20 and now Melbourne had done the same. To add my own personal distress, I was also now in deep trouble...

Right there, around 8.45 pm on a Brisbane Saturday night, began one of the most worrying and eventful weeks of my football career. Benny came over and asked what was going on. I told him, and a plan was hatched on the spot. It was Saturday night and Peter Myers said he could operate the next morning and take the piece of bone out. 'What do you think?' said Wayne. 'Will you be able to play next week?' 'Well, I've got to be classed a doubt,' I told him, 'but I'll have a go at it.' At that point I honestly had no idea of whether I was a chance. But Wayne did some of his pumping-up stuff, which he's very good at. 'If anyone can do it, you will!' he said. The coach has always been very good at pushing the right button with me, at getting me fired up.

The following morning, as gently as he could, Peter Myers removed a piece of floating bone from my knee. I still have it at home, in a jar, along with a few other bits accumulated in the years I have had my knee problem. A spur had grown because of the absence of cartilages in that knee – and it had broken off. It's what happens when you haven't got (knee) cartilages – the body reacts by growing little bits of bone spur. The problem that existed for me after the procedure was that once you have (surgical) instruments going into your body, the area automatically swells up and won't work. On the Sunday night, at a Brisbane private hospital, I lay there and thought about the possibilities. I thought about the things I had learned about injuries and my body. And I thought about the method I had used on other injuries: to try to start treating the injured or repaired part as normal, as soon as possible. If you can convince your mind to accept that it (the injury) is normal, your body will let it work. What happens when you have a 'scope, as I did, is that all your muscles in the area shut down. They are telling you to rest it. It is the body's natural defence mechanism.

Monday was a quiet recovery day. On the Tuesday, I tried to run. It was still bloody swollen, but I knew I had to do that. It was just awful – every time I broke into a run it felt like the whole knee was going to snap in half. We didn't work all that hard, but I was sweating profusely through sheer concentration and discomfort. I won't forget that session. There were occasional moments when it wasn't too bad . . . then I'd step into a little hole or uneven piece of ground and it was as if everything switched off in the knee and I would almost fall over. On the way home from training I thought, I'm not going to be able to do this.

But there at home I sat quietly for a time and thought it through. The immediate problem that had been in the knee was gone, I knew that. 'There is no reason now why it shouldn't work,' I told myself. It's just that I had to get my mind to convince my knee of that. So on a warm early spring afternoon I went out onto the lawn on my front yard at home and started running. For an hour I ran, and jumped and jammed the sore knee, stopping and starting on the grass.

By then the match that would decide our fate in the 2004 premiership, against the Cowboys, had been switched from its planned venue to Dairy Farmers Stadium in Townsville. On one hand the decision was further evidence of my contention that the Broncos are a club very much capable of thinking wider than most – and for the greater good of the game. On the other hand, we didn't want to play the match in bloody Sydney, and we knew that at home they would be under enormous pressure, having gone this far in the competition after seasons of under-achievement. A lot of things had to happen for that game to go ahead up there – the fact that it did was a credit to everyone involved.

The week moved on, bit by bit, hour by hour. I had a little process going and gradually I felt the knee was coming good. I knew one thing for certain: no way was it going to be 100 per cent right for Saturday night in Townsville. But with all the physio and private running I was doing, I was getting there.

We trained in Brisbane on the Thursday and Wayne wanted me to run at the session, it being something of a club rule that any doubtful player has to train the last full session before being cleared to play. I knew I was getting close, but that I wasn't yet ready to run flat out. I had been out on my own that morning and run pretty well and felt like my confidence was coming back. But I was still worried about it, and the last thing I wanted to do was go out in front of the cameras and all the media and have the knee give way and have it appear that I'd done something to it and spark some sort of media frenzy. Wayne had seen me after my morning run and probably presumed I would train with the side in the afternoon. When I told him I couldn't do it yet, he started to worry. It was agreed that I would do a fitness test up there on the Saturday morning.

So it was that on the morning of the match in Townsville I put my footy boots on and was out on a nearby park doing all sorts of drills. The knee was feeling good, and for the first time in seven days I was starting to feel all right about it. I just knew I had to keep it warm. When it got cold it would start to get a bit funny. This had been a really hard week, a mentally draining week. Was I going to play, or wasn't I? Those questions had been my constant travelling companions. That morning I knew I was going to be okay. I had won my little personal battle – me against my knee.

Wayne remembered later how the physio had watched the fitness test (in which I had stumbled a couple of times early until my knee warmed up) and then turned to him when I declared I was okay and said, 'He's kidding!' I told Wayne, 'If we lose here tonight, I want to be with them (my teammates) . . . and if we win, I want to play my part. If you see me limping out there on the knee, don't take me off – it won't be because it's sore but because I'm still trying to get the muscles working properly.'

And I ran out onto Dairy Farmers that night and it was like I'd never had a problem. It was amazing. History of course records the fact that we lost the game 10–0 and so closed the shutters on 2004. But apart from the result, it was a wonderful game and a wonderful night and I felt fortunate to be part of it. Never in my life have I heard a louder crowd. When the time came late in the game that they were close to getting through to the grand final, there was just this enormous sustained roar. Twenty-five thousand people and every single one of them shouting their head off. It was very disappointing for us to lose. But my personal assessment was that I played pretty well under the circumstances – and I knew that I couldn't have done any more than I did. I was proud that I had come back to football from an arthroscopy in less than a week and played in the match.

And if you'll excuse a cliché: rugby league was the winner, and if ever defeat tasted a little bit better than it usually does, it was on that night of September 18, 2004.

But the injury came back to haunt me again, and of all the things I have been forced into doing in football, this next phase in the saga of my left knee was close to the worst. In England, on the morning of the Tri-series final in 2004, in which the Poms were given a great chance of beating us, I found myself in desperate trouble – at the breakfast table. I'd had something rolling around inside my knee, another one of those broken bone spurs, and it chose the morning of the match to put itself in the wrong place. When I went to get up from the brekkie table, I almost fell over.

I made out that I'd just tripped – because the last thing you want to do when you're in trouble is reveal it. But I told Wayne I had a problem and headed upstairs in the hotel to see the physio, Tony Ayoub. By now the knee was locking up badly. It felt as if it might have been an even bigger piece of bone than the one I had had removed before the final in September against the Cowboys. Tony started work . . . and ended up working on it all day.

At one stage, when I went back up briefly to my room, I was just sick in the guts. Late on the morning of a huge game I was sitting there on the bed on my own, just shattered. The prospect of not playing was bad enough, but I knew Wayne would want me to play, and the prospect of having to battle through with this bloody thing was even worse! After what I'd been through the week before the Cowboys game, I just didn't know if I had the energy for it again. I really didn't need the drama. Anyhow, Wayne came into the room and he said to me, 'Look, just don't worry about the fucking knee. What we'll do is when we get out to the game we'll go through the warm-up and if you can play, you'll play . . . if you can't, you can't.' They were the words I needed to hear. It took things out of my hands.

I was deadset shitting myself about the final anyway. I thought we were really going to struggle. Game 1 of the series had had a touch of déjà vu about it when we knocked them off at the death – again – via a Luke Rooney try in the last minute at Manchester Stadium, the *fourth* such event in a row. But then their win at Wigan (24–12) breathed new life into the tournament. I expect all of England held its breath, daring to think that this, at last, might be the year.

Not for a single minute that day of the final did I think I was going to be able to make it. The piece of bone felt like a big marble sitting up underneath my kneecap, and every time I moved it would grab and lock and grab and lock. All the old messages were coming from the knee – it just didn't want to work.

Down at the Elland Road ground I was afraid to run. I reckoned I knew what would happen for sure: the knee would lock and just kill me. Tony Ayoub asked me if I wanted to strap it up. 'No, don't strap the bastard. That won't do anything for it,' I told him. So I stripped for the match and got myself ready for the warm-up that I knew would make or break me. I was sick with anticipation, especially as the warm-up would be done out on the field in front of the crowd. And I got out there . . . and I ran . . . and I couldn't feel anything . . . and I ran a bit more . . . and I still couldn't feel the knee. I tried sprinting . . . and it was fine. And I thought to myself . . . This bloody knee is alright! I would play, and there would be no pain-killing needles.

It's amazing what took place that night. You know, I really think sometimes it's God's will whether something happens or doesn't happen in life. I must have done something good that year to get the reward that came my way for 41 minutes of the Tri-nations final. After falling over at the breakfast table and pretty much accepting that I wouldn't be part of the match, I got to play the full first half, and a couple of minutes more. And that Australian display at Elland Road, Leeds, on November 27, 2004, has been proposed – not unfairly – as 'probably the greatest half of rugby league ever played'. At half-time, against a strong Great Britain side with which we had been neck-and-neck through the preliminaries (12–8, 12–24), we led 38–0! Their spirit was broken and the Tri-nations trophy was in the bag.

As I ran back onto the field in the second half there was a 'click' and my knee was locked and gone. A couple of minutes later I was off; the match was over for me and so was the tour. It was just a freakish, incredible night. Before that first-half blitz of ours there was no hint at all that it was going to happen.

Sometimes you get the sense before a match that everything is as it should be; you just know the team is going to play well. Before the 1998 grand final, if I had had three wives and three houses I would have put the lot on us to win (sorry, Ally). Sometimes it works the other way too; sometimes there is a sense of foreboding . . . a sense that's it's just not going to happen today. I have to say I had that feeling before games towards the end of our fading 2005 season. It's not a tangible thing, either way, but you some- how get a sniff of it. In the lead-up to the match that would decide the Tri-nations series of 2004, there seemed to me – later, when I thought of it – no clue as to what was going to unfold. In the cramped, shitty little dressing shed with bugger-all room in it, no sign registered with me before the kick-off that this night was to be one of the special ones. Maybe I was too consumed with my own dramas.

On reflection, at best the feeling in the room was 'neutral'. And some days it's like that too. You think, Well, things seem fairly okay . . . let's hope it runs for us. The warm-up was good and sharp, but we knew we were facing a formidable opponent, and the feeling of quiet confidence wasn't there, in my estimation.

But then, when it started, on a ground more famous for the round ball game than for ours, there was magic. I can't really explain what happened; it just happened. Everything we touched turned to gold.

It's as if the 13 players out there (plus four on the bench) all just decided to have the very best game of their life on the same night. I can't remember anyone doing anything wrong. We scored early, too, and that helped boost the confidence – a Matt Sing try off Anthony Minichiello's kick – and then scored another almost straight away, when the ball passed through 10 pairs of hands before our fullback scored. If you get away to a good start, particularly in a huge game like this one, all that nervous energy and tension that is just waiting to be channelled into *something* goes into the positive. This night we all thought, How good is this! and away we went. Maybe if they'd scored first, it would have been different. We'll never know.

There is a moment that sticks in my mind from early in the game. I took off down the sideline and passed the ball inside to Lockey, not seeing this Pommy bloke coming. He hit Lockey hard and pushed the ball out the back. But it was one of our blokes who picked up the loose ball, and next thing we scored. If it had been a second or two either way one of *their* blokes could have got the loose ball and maybe they would have scored. Maybe. Football is like that. It's funny what sticks in your head from football matches. In this game that is the only thing I can really clearly picture. At that point we were flying, really flying. And when that happened, for an instant I thought, Oh shit, don't let me be the one! But the gods smiled that day, and all was well.

It was a wonderful and unique game, which we ended up winning 44–4 after a second half which faded from memory almost as soon as referee Russell Smith called a halt; it was an enormous contrast to the first 40 minutes, which will live on for those who played, and those who watched. As it turned out, it was my last game of international football. I was in the stand when we played the United States team in Pennsylvania in the final game of the tour – and in 2005 I made the decision that for me, representative football was over.

I probably should have come home straight after the 2004 final in Leeds and had my knee operated on. But I wasn't going to miss that last leg of the tour. I was excited about that. So I stayed and did the tourist bit for a couple of weeks. And I struggled. Where my piece of wandering bone had ended up in the second half of the match was in a bloody painful spot. There it stayed. And so I limped and limped my way through France and the US. And I drank some grog and flew more kilometres than was probably good for me. But I had a great time and

I don't think I did the knee any more harm. It was damaged enough.

I have many happy memories of that campaign. A small one concerns the outstanding English front-rower Stuart Fielding. Stuart is a really good fella. But he's probably another one of those blokes I wanted to dislike initially because of the impression I had of him. Then the Pommy team-liaison bloke, who I'd got to know, told me one match day that Stuart wanted to swap jerseys with me – and of course I was happy to do it. He had asked me to sign it and so I wrote a message (I can't even remember the words) – and the liaison bloke came back to me a little later and said Fielding had almost cried when he read it – because it had come from me. I was really touched by that. Fielding is a terrific player and I was wondering that day, Why does he think that about me? Why would he be 'in awe' of me when he's such a wonderful player himself? But I took it as a fine mark of respect, and I appreciated it a great deal.

I think it's fair to say that in both the French and the American games on the 2004 tour, what you might call the 'gentlemanly' side of rugby league was on display. The scorelines indicate that the Kangaroos were stretched in both games. But particularly in the French match there was an element in the Australian performance of being understanding of the situation – of respecting France's ambition to fight their way back up in rugby league. Many years ago the French produced outstanding teams, which could match or better the best of Australian and British rugby league. Now, after years in the doldrums, they are building again, on the back of a team from Perpignan, which plays in the English Super League competition. We beat the French 52–30 after leading only 34–30 with seven minutes to go, and the US Tomahawks 36–24 after trailing 24–6 at half-time! I think it's fair to say in both cases that the Australians were 'mindful' of the match they were playing. Never would an Aussie side be told to 'go easy'

– and they weren't before those games. But the players were well aware that a team like the French was never going to get to where they were heading overnight. The Kangaroos would be handing out no favours by belting the crap out of them. So they didn't – and the French took positives from the game. So too did the Americans.

Injuries in the US game, which was played on a synthetic surface over four quarters – notably to Willie Mason and Mark O'Meley – brought predictable bleating from back home along the lines that the US initiative was an indulgence and a waste of time.

The Bulldogs led the charge, and then Souths and Roosters officials joined in the whinge. It's an attitude I really can't cop. Yes, the injuries were disappointing for the players and club involved. But the game was no waste of time. Who is to say that the sport of rugby league won't one day strike a real spark in the US (and how good would that be if it happened)? We'll never know unless we give it a chance. But the prospects are surely hamstrung by the narrow-mindedness of people who care about nothing except their own tiny corner of the league world and who are not prepared to pay any price to give the game a chance of taking root in other places.

There is a perfect analogy. Twenty years ago who would have thought the AFL could possibly have constructed a stronghold in rugby league-mad Brisbane? To make it, the AFL had to be strong and do those things that give the other clubs the shits – like bringing teams to Brisbane to play promotional games, and providing special support for the fledgling (Lions) Club.

Rugby league wrestles with this all the time. In December 2005 I attended the game's end-of-year conference in Sydney and found the clubs blueing there about the Centenary World Cup, which is scheduled to be played in Australia in 2008. The whinge-ing about playing the cup as a pre-season event had started already – the moaning about what a tough year that would make for the clubs. Well, hang on a sec. Sometimes, as the AFL Brisbane example shows, small sacrifices are worthwhile. Sometimes things are greater than what you want to do for yourself. So if a club has to have a tough year because a World Cup is going to be played for the good of the game in March 2008 (which it won't be now, thanks to club pressure), well, have a tough year! Just because it doesn't suit everyone's little agenda doesn't mean it's not worth doing. That's just shit . . . and the sort of thinking that will always drag the game down.

In terms of the bigger picture, I have always believed that the game is such a good one that it deserves to be a genuinely international sport – on a much larger scale than it has managed so far. To hear about the competition running in a country such as Russia genuinely gives me a thrill. Yet nowhere near enough happens to push the game's boundaries, and the responsibility for that must weigh pretty heavily on Australia's shoulders, considering that we are world leaders in the game. With that position of strength comes the responsibility to drive and guide the game – and to vigorously work for expansion. There should be a grand plan for rugby league's (bigger) future. Is there? I doubt it. Internationally, there should be goals, a focus, something solid that everyone is committed to. I suspect there is nothing of the sort and I have to say that I get terribly frustrated by that lack of action.

I was, of course, happy and proud to finish my international career in a match such as the 2004 Tri-series final. It was extraordinary – both the game itself and the circumstances of me being part of it – and I suspect I'll remember it for as long as I am around. There was some nagging disappointment too at the realisation that it *had* to end for me. This knee of mine is just not going to let me keep doing this, I thought as early as the evening of the final in Leeds, as I hobbled around. So I was sad about that

... about what I knew I had to do – reduce my playing load – and sad too that the tour experience was coming to an end for me. I had loved the tours, loved England and the chance to travel to different countries. The brief US experience on the 2004 tour was wonderful too – and I can't wait to get back over there. Ally hasn't had the chance to do the travel thing. But for sure we will.

Chapter 23

I WON'T PLAY . . .
DON'T ASK ME

I came back home from the Tri-nations campaign on a bung knee and facing the certainty of another date with the scalpel. I was at the doctor's the day after we arrived back. 'Doc,' I said to Peter Myers, a wonderful bloke, 'don't spare the scalpel this time: get it all cleaned out!' I felt I still had plenty to give the Broncos, but, at 30, I knew the clock was ticking. I just wanted him to tidy the knee up as best he could and get me ready for a couple more seasons. In the operation that followed, in early December 2004, Dr Myers went in deep. The bits and pieces he took out are still at home, in a jar – souvenirs of a life in rugby league.

Over the years I have been very good with operations and their aftermath. It's either that I've got a very high pain threshold or I'm too stupid to feel things, but I have managed my post-operation time pretty well . . . until this one. I have never felt as much pain, or as bad as I did this time.

I remember waking up in hospital and feeling as if someone was driving a hammer and chisel into my knee. It just ached and throbbed and ached and throbbed – and that went on for days that turned into weeks. It just wouldn't come good. About the only positive was that my knee didn't 'crackle' any more, as it had for years. Now it was dead quiet, bone on bone . . . but it hurt like buggery. The occasional keyhole operations I had had over the years had never given me much pain – but, oh boy, this one did. There were days when I seriously doubted that I would ever be able to play football again. It was so bloody sore, but the doc told me it would be because this time he had gone very deep into the bone to take the roughness off.

My knee problem and the reluctant decision to step down from rep football that went with it sowed seeds of doubt in my mind at the start of 2005. For a time I honestly wondered if I'd play at all, so slow was my knee to work its way back after the operation. More subtle, but just as important, was the nagging subconscious thought that my rep decision was some sort of 'beginning of the end' in my career. I wondered whether I would now be on a slippery slope on which I might start to demand and accept a little less of myself. I was genuinely worried that I might do that – and looking back on the season, I can now see the worry as a real indication of why I *wouldn't* do it.

Four or five weeks down the track, when the time came to get back to training, the knee wasn't even near right. For the first time the thought was in my head that I might have to give the game away. That was scary. 'Never mind worrying about retiring from rep footy,' I told myself. 'You might have to retire full-stop!'

For those weeks from the middle of January to late February I limped and trained in absolute discomfort. Pain was my constant companion – and so too was the swelling that followed any training session. I had the growing feeling that even the blokes around me were starting to think I wasn't going to make it back. I couldn't keep up with fitness. I couldn't keep up with anything in training and I had always prided myself on that. I was just dragging myself around. I was in a really bad place.

It was a time in my career that really scared the shit out of me. Peter Myers put the situation this way: 'Your knee is like a tyre that is wearing out. You're down to the wire now and sometime you are probably going to get a blow-out.' It put things in context. What I had now was about as good as it was going to be. When Peter uttered those words I knew for sure that I didn't have a choice about Origin and international football. I didn't want to pull the plug, but I knew I had to. So I made my announcement.

The doc had told me right at the start that the knee would take longer to heal this time than before. 'Be patient,' he had said. But it was slow all right . . . and I think even he was getting worried. Then, one week at training, as the season neared, I turned the corner. I can't put a time on that, but suddenly I had the feeling that the knee was starting to work properly again.

By the time the premiership started I was okay, and in the team – although touching wood all the time in those early weeks of the season. I kept thinking that the problem would come back and bite me on the arse sometime. It never did, and I ended up playing all but one of our games, and won the Broncos' Player of the Year award. From the perspective of that painful February, that was a fantastic outcome.

To have a strong year and win my second Broncos' Player of the Year meant a great deal to me. To win the award once was unbelievable . . . to win it twice was beyond my comprehension. It's not something I'm going to stop and think much about right now because I need to continue to look forward before I can look back. But sometime in the future when I'm up on the farm and I can afford to have a little peek at some of the things I did as a footballer, those two club awards will sit up there as the greatest things I have. I look forward to that day, when I can sit down and think about things like that and reflect on how lucky I have been. To be named the No. 1 prop in *Rugby League Week*'s annual players' poll, with 50 votes (Petero second) was gratifying too, and a reflection of the sort of season I had had.

My knee survived the year so well that I found myself having to stoutly defend the decision I had made to pull the plug on Origin football. I guess fans were confused, and I can understand that. I made my call to quit rep football in absolute good faith, based on the fact that I had, and have, a *very* dicey right knee. I had retired from that part of my career because the knee was pretty close to stuffed. Then people saw me play strongly in the club comp, apparently unaffected. I can understand the fans wondering – especially when I won the big award at the end of the season.

I made my initial decision very reluctantly, but based on what I knew, and know. If I had played Origin I would have wanted to play Test football too, and that would have been another seven to eight-week campaign on top of the six weeks of Origin. A plan took shape firmly in my head: I would give my all to the Broncos for two more seasons, 2005 and 2006, then hang up my boots. To push the envelope in 2005 by taking on the rep football challenge again was to increase both the load and the risk. At Origin time I knew it was not just the weight of playing two games in close proximity; it was all the extra training and extra pressure too. I did my best to convince people of the very genuine reasons for my decision.

But the whole thing came to a head after two games of the State of Origin series, with the teams level at 1–all. Speculation was huge: will he or won't he? It was almost like a book was being run on whether I'd come back and play Origin 3 after Steve Price was ruled out of the game and the Maroons were in trouble. There was this huge call for me to step in – a massive amount of pressure.

I can say now that it was never going to happen. I must have been asked 300 times, but I knew I wasn't going to change my mind, and I held the line. In the end I was fed up with being asked the question. Asked yet again by the media on June 21, I responded: 'I'm not even going to say it and I'm not going to answer one more question about it because, to be fair, I've said it a thousand times.' People came up to me after it all settled down and asked me if I had felt the pressure. I told them no, I felt no pressure. In my mind there was nothing to be pressured about. I had made my decision. But I copped some flak because of it, and perhaps I was seen as being a bit disloyal to the Queensland cause. And, yes, I was officially asked to come back.

Michael Hagan, Maroons coach and a decent bloke, came and saw me on the issue at the time we were playing Newcastle. My exact words were: 'Michael, you know I can't do that and you know I won't do it. My word is my word and if I haven't got that, I haven't got anything.' 'I agree with you,' said Michael, 'but I had to ask.'

The valuable lesson I had learned back in 2001, when I didn't go on the Kangaroo tour, was that whether people agreed or disagreed with me on the decision I had made, they respected the fact that under pressure I remained true to what I said I would do. Back then I stuck to my guns because I knew that, for me, it was the right thing to do. I was out in the wilderness at that time and it would have been very easy to stop all the bullshit and speculation by saying I would go on the tour after all. But I got so much more out of it because I *didn't* do that. So it was with Origin 2005.

Honestly, with the Origin thing the easy thing would have been for me to say, 'Yeah, I'll play' and try to be some quasi-hero to the people. But that would have been bullshit.

He pulled out of Origin for all the right reasons. The process was all put in place – but then he had to think it through and sort himself out then when they lost Origin 2 and had lost Stephen Price and the pressure came on him to come back. And I know I am not kidding myself with this: there was only one guy who would have got him to play Origin – and that was me, if I went to him. I knew that and there was some pressure being put on me to do exactly that. So I walked into the gym one day and said to him, 'I think you should play Origin' and he looked at me and said, 'You're fucking kidding me, aren't you?' And I said 'No, I'm not, mate, I am serious.' 'What are you trying to do to me?' he said. 'You're trying to fuck with my head, aren't you?' 'No,' I said and then I laughed, and he said, 'Thank Christ for that!' And I told him then, 'Listen, Shane, I wouldn't do that to you, because I know the most I important thing to you is your word; you said you weren't going to play Origin again and you have been true to your word all your football career and you wouldn't be the person you want to be if you went back to play Origin now. Mate, if you did that you'd be going back on your word . . . and I know that is everything to you.' And he said to me, 'That's exactly right, and that's why I won't go back. I thought it all through and I did it for all the right reasons, and those reasons haven't changed. So I would be dishonest with myself. You know that and I know that.' Of course it would have been easier for him to say yes and agree to play. But that's not what Webcke is about.

Wayne Bennett

Not long after all the Origin drama something horrible happened. It was a truly awful moment, when young winger Jake Webster hit the ground head first at Suncorp Stadium in the Round 19 Broncos–Melbourne game on July 17, 2005.

I have always been a vocal opponent of spear tackling. I play the game and love it – and the last thing I want to ever have happen to me is for someone to flip me on my head, so that I never walk again. But what happened at Suncorp that afternoon was a lesson to me about how quickly and easily it can happen in a football match. From now on I will never *not* believe someone who says they didn't mean it to happen after a similar incident. Because I know what happened with me.

It's an accepted thing in football now that when someone is wrestling with a ball-carrier up the top, you have a couple of choices to make. You can either go in and become another wrestler, and the tackle gets not much better, or you can grab a leg and take away the centre of gravity and the bloke with the ball falls over. Option two is the preferred way to go – to get them onto the ground, slow things down, and give your team a few precious seconds to regroup in defence. That plan is in my mind in matches and I carry it out regularly.

The error I made on that day, at that moment, was just this: I saw Jake Webster's leg as Corey Parker, who is a strong bloke, 'wrestle-tackled' him – and I grabbed it to complete the tackle. Normally I would grab and push at the same time, but on this one occasion, the second I latched onto the leg, the bloke up top (Parker) threw him in the same direction as I was lifting. So strong was the momentum that I could have lifted him with my little finger. Next thing the kid's legs went straight up in the air, and in that instant I let him go. In the rush of the moment I thought to myself, He's in a bloody horrible position, this kid.

And then he hit the deck.

I was charged with a Dangerous Throw (Grade 1) and pleaded guilty. I was given 93 demerit points, but no suspension. There was every reason to suggest I should have been suspended. The only thing that saved me with the judiciary was that I let Webster's legs go as soon as I realised he was in a dangerous position. I subsequently went public, via my column in *Big League* magazine, expressing my regrets at what had happened, admitting that I had been at fault and promising that I would address my technique to make sure it never happened again. The point

I wanted to get across more than anything was that I certainly wasn't feeling smug because I had 'got away with it'. I'm not in the category of players who might argue the line that 'in a good tough game like rugby league that sort of thing will sometimes happen'. That's shit. I just wanted to get across my remorse and my determination that it wouldn't happen again.

When I escaped suspension, I copped some flak in the Sydney media. In the *Daily Telegraph*, senior journalist Ray Chesterton wrote:

> *Brisbane prop Shane Webcke should be out for at least a month for his dangerous tackle on Jake Webster. And Brisbane coach Wayne Bennett should be sitting alongside Webcke in the grandstand as a penalty for trying to defend the indefensible.*

I wasn't too worried about that view, although there were a few who were out to crucify me. I had been penalised under the terms of the judiciary system the game is played under. If I had 'driven' Webster into the ground, of course I would have been suspended. But letting him go was at least an act of acknowledgement by me that I had (accidentally) put him in a bad situation.

The moment Webster hit the ground that day was one of the uglier and more worrying ones of my career. I was just so relieved to see him moving. I remember standing there thinking, Please get up.

I couldn't live with myself if I paralysed someone on a football field, accident or not. I would blame myself for the rest of my life. I can't even think about being part of an event like that. It's a rough game we play, and sometimes things happen accidentally, and we accept that. But if you perform an illegal act or do something that exacerbates the chance of serious injury to another player . . . how could you ever live with that?

The issue surrounding that tackle was big for a while, as such incidents tend to be in rugby league. But what really started to get to me was the other side of it: of blokes saying things like, 'It's a hard body contact game. That was just a good driving tackle.' Well, what happened to Jake Webster was *not* a good driving tackle – it was a bloody dangerous tackle. I knew I hadn't meant it, but I was terribly disappointed that I had been part of an event like that, one that put a young bloke at risk.

I want to be very clear here: I consider myself fortunate not to have been suspended. The seriousness of the situation was not lost on me. If I had been suspended, I would have copped it. There would have been no appeal. I knew I had been in the wrong.

Sometime later I ran into Jake Webster's father, a fellow Queenslander. I didn't know it was him at first, but then he told me the boy in the tackle at Suncorp was his son. We talked, and I told him I couldn't be more sorry for what had happened.

It's a story that at least has a happy ending . . . and that's not always the way in life. Jake Webster wasn't injured and so could head on with his football career. And a 30-year-old prop from Brisbane had learned something else from the University of Football.

I took exception to a Sydney newspaper reference at that time to 'spinal wards' after I had been involved in the tackle on young Jake. It appeared in the week in which I explained how I accepted that my actions were wrong and declared publicly that it wouldn't happen again. In the course of my years at the Broncos I had, of course, been to spinal wards, numbers of times, and had acquired a considerable understanding of what the people there were going through. I was not ignorant of those places or of the accidents that put people there. Yes, I knew what the outcome of a spear tackle could be . . .

As footballers, we live in a great and privileged environment – and that's why it is important that we find time for people who are troubled and far worse off. And the more of it that gets done by football clubs the better. As far as I'm concerned, publicity for such visits should only happen if the recipient really wants it. I believe that a charitable act in life is made something less if you talk about it. Wayne has a good proverb for it, the exact wording of which escapes me, but which is along the lines of: 'The measure of a man is what he will do for those who can do nothing for him.' I truly believe in that. It is a philosophy I try to use in my life. True giving is in helping someone out when there is absolutely nothing in it for you.

To go and visit a sick kid is never a comfortable thing to do. I have done it many times, visiting terminally ill kids in hospital and private homes – and for the younger players in particular it is terribly difficult and very daunting. But all of it is so worthwhile when you see the happiness shining out of a kid. It is never easy, though. I mean, what can you say to a young person who is dying: 'G'day, how're you going?' Well, yes, that's *exactly* what you say, or maybe, 'What's going on today?', 'How're you battling?' or just 'How's things?' And the kids handle it beautifully. People with serious illness handle such a situation much better than a bunch of footballers. I have become better at it, just by being myself. To bring an element of normality into an abnormal situation when you are talking to a kid who is dying . . . talk a bit of footy or whatever . . . can brighten up their day for 15 minutes or so. And that's got to be good. Afterwards you walk away with goodwill in your heart. And such days never lose their meaning to the players who do it, because they can be terribly sad, too.

At Broncos training at different times we have people who come down to watch, people with disabilities or bad medical problems. The easy thing to do is to walk past them as you head back to the sheds after training. The hard thing is to stop and say 'G'day' and give them some time, which is the most valuable thing you can give to someone else. I'm pleased to say I have got better at that. There were times earlier on when I hurried past, as some other players did, times when I ducked into the sheds and then sat in there thinking, That wasn't right – I should go back outside and do the right thing. I think a player hurrying past would always be misconstrued as the player not caring, which is just not true. It is just a sign of discomfort at an awkward time. It pretty much changed for me on one day. I just made a decision that I would take the bit between my teeth, be confident and go up and say 'G'day' and have a chat. Now, I always do. And it works a treat. The experience is never anything but positive.

It's in this and many other ways that a career in football today can both broaden a player's knowledge and instil a sense of community obligation. It's not much talked about (and should never be as some sort of club-generated 'publicity' thing), but all of us do hospital and school visits and respond now and then to requests to go and see sick kids or help out with charity events. I think players generally are very aware of the fortunate position they find themselves in and are more than happy to fulfil those sorts of obligations. The visits we undertake are doubly beneficial. Hopefully they provide a lift for the kids, and certainly they increase the awareness and understanding and a sense of compassion of the players involved.

The progress of the Broncos' 2005 season was pretty much the same story as the year before. After Round 13 of the competition, when we led, we were 3:1 favourites to take the title. We headed the competition for 16 weeks, won five out of six games around Origin time – and then faded. This was déjà vu for sure, this now heavily instilled pattern of dropping off at the end of the season. The temptation was always there through these (now five!) seasons to justify the things we had been doing on the basis that we were still comfortably making the finals. But in view of what happened – again – in 2005, it became apparent that whatever the deficiency had been, it remained, disguised, and accepted to some extent, because we would invariably do enough to get into the finals. Once again, it had gone unchecked.

It was like reading an old familiar book. After losing two of our first four games, we then won 12 of the next 13. But at the end the ink was all red: eight losses in our last nine games and, once more, farewell to all that when it came to premiership dreams.

Very early in the year, in Round 3, we hit one of those days which can provide a reality check for any team in the helter-skelter atmosphere of modern football. A week after beating the Sydney Roosters 40–22 on their home turf, we travelled to Melbourne – and lost 50–4! People asked me how that could possibly happen to a team like Brisbane.

Well, in a way it's like falling into quicksand. The more you struggle on such days, the quicker you sink. These were days when we were a little bit 'off', and they were way 'on'. When that situation occurs, one team inevitably gets stronger and stronger and the other gets weaker and weaker. It's a phenomenon of the modern game that you can run into a game like that and then the next week have maybe a 90–100 point turnaround. We did exactly that in 2005 when Melbourne beat us 50–4: the next week we beat Parramatta 54–14.

At a glance, you would think it only possible, for example, for a terrible team to get beaten 44–10, as we did by the Knights in 2002. In the modern game, with its four-point tries and accurate goal-kickers and the importance of 'momentum', all you need is this: for your team to turn up on a given day 20–25 per cent down across the board and the other mob turn up in exactly the right frame of mind and with everyone 95 per cent plus. On those days it can certainly happen. If the other side starts well and confidence builds, they'll quickly be edging up towards the magical 100 per cent . . . meanwhile, you'll be losing percentage points by the minute. If they're hot and they're rolling, you just can't pull them back. I've been involved in a few of these games over the seasons, and it's the most helpless situation. And the strange thing is that all of it seems to move quicker than you think possible. It can be six points . . . 12 . . . 18 . . . 24, and little time seems to have passed.

On the days when you're on the other side of the coin, well, it's beautiful. The final of the Tri-series, 2004, is a classic example. It didn't matter what we tried in that first half against the Poms, it worked. From the moment we got out there it just all came together for us.

There are occasional days like that in football, days when, for whatever reason, you are completely in the 'zone' – and everything goes perfectly. I remember one against Melbourne where I was just on fire right through the second half and could do no wrong. And I had a couple of Test matches like that – especially the one against the Poms in 2002, when we won by 54 points (64–10) in a game in which the Australian side was just unbelievable. That night I played probably the best game of footy of my life, with off-loads, and play-the-balls that led to tries – things were happening that usually would not happen for me. Certainly not in those numbers, anyway. Those are great occasions for footballers. You don't prepare differently – any better or any worse – you just go out and somehow it all falls into place. There are a few of those scattered through the seasons I played, and I suspect all players are the same.

On the other side of the coin, I can't remember ever having what you would call a *horrible* game, one in which I was responsible for two or three tries to the other mob, or dropping a heap of ball. I've had my moments, though – notably an early-season trial game a few years back that remains in my mind, in which I spilled some balls and threw some dumb passes. But I can't ever really remember being absolutely shattered after a game and thinking, God, almighty – how badly did I play today! Touch wood. Wayne

Bennett, of course, might have a different perspective on that. I think it's unusual for a front-rower to have a really shocking day: what we do is *hard* in terms of physical prowess, but not so much is required of us skills-wise, or in the big scheme of things in a match. Fullbacks are the blokes who are most of all on a hiding to nothing – as Darren Lockyer learned in that first Test match of 1998. They are so exposed: they can look fantastic, but if things happen not to go well . . . they are all out there on their own.

Two matches out from the 2005 finals, I suffered medial ligament damage to my left knee (the 'good' knee!) in the match against the Panthers. It was a grade 3 or worse tear – my leg was promptly placed in a brace, and the doc was talking a three- to six-week break from football. But I desperately wanted to be in the finals, so I put into practise all my old theories about getting right in as short a time as possible. I was especially keen to be there because we had been going poorly, bogged down in a losing sequence – yet, I felt, there was still some real hope that we could smash through that and be a big chance for the title. The first part of it worked out okay – I got back to football in time for the first qualifier against Melbourne at Suncorp.

The rest of the plan didn't quite work out. Melbourne beat us 24–18 in a tight game at Suncorp and then we faced the Wests Tigers, eventual premiers in this unpredictable year. This was a match which pretty much summed up how things were going for us generally. In the end we got beaten 34–6, and that looks like a hammering in anyone's language. But in the first half we made four or five clean breaks – even *I* made one! However, we didn't capitalise on a single one of them. It showed how we were going. Had we got through that Tigers game it might just have kick-started something for us. But the match was entirely indicative of at least the latter part of the season: we just weren't supporting each other. We had arrived at a place where we weren't prepared to follow each other. In the end it was a blowout. The Tigers gained confidence as they went along and we just headed on to inevitability. The match showed the fragile state we were in. For the fifth year in a row we had trekked to the finals, hoping to find the answers we needed. For the fifth year in a row we were packing our bags early. How would we stop the rot?

Looking back on the year, my feelings were mixed. To win Broncos Player of the Year in 2005 (for the second time) was one of the crowning achievements of my time in football and I felt really good about that. I have always been paranoid about the ending of my career, about the period which would take me up to the day I played my last game. Throughout my career I have felt sorry for blokes who fumbled the ending and just hung on and hung on. With some I have even thought, Let it go – just get out of the game. By staying too long, some players damage the aura and reputation they have worked so hard to build. I don't think there is anything at all dignified about limping out of a sport, having stayed too long.

At the start of 2006 I knew that if we happened to win the competition that year, that would be proof that I had worked hard enough to be a good player and that I could still do it. I decided a long while ago that that's what would decide whether I kept playing or got out. I was determined to do everything to ensure that I wasn't a player who stayed too long. I know it's one of the toughest decisions any player ever has to make – me included. But I think that if your dignity and self-respect prevails and you are honest with yourself throughout your career and continue to be that way until the end, you'll know when it's time to go.

And the way I look at it is there is such a big wide world of opportunity out there that you shouldn't risk it by putting a blemish on the achievements of a football career by overstaying your welcome.

Chapter 24

THE DRUG MENACE WITHIN

One of the greatest threats facing rugby league today is that of players using illegal drugs. Anyone who tries to tell you differently is either a liar or misguided. It has been my observation in these recent seasons that some high-profile players in our game have been close to the edge when it comes to recreational drugs. They are not 'addicts', but without doubt they are playing with fire. Imagine what it would mean to rugby league if that came out publicly, say, a revelation on a leading, much-admired player. And to be honest it's amazing that some of the stuff *hasn't* already become public knowledge. Some of the things I've become aware of seem to me the worst-kept secrets in the world. The media now and then stumbles on some of it. But there is more that isn't reported. Addictions are the dark side of this game, just waiting to trip up young players: gambling, drugs, alcohol. And generally by the time someone accepts that they have a problem, they are in deep . . .

I have no doubt that the biggest challenge facing the new

breed of young players coming into rugby league involves so-called recreational drugs. Recreational drug use is on the rise – not just in rugby league, obviously, but in society itself – and this will become a bigger and bigger issue for professional sport generally. It seems to be the accepted thing now that you can take drugs casually and they will not hurt you. We, as footballers, are not cocooned from any of it. There are drugs everywhere in society and football is part of society. There used to be a massive stigma in football attached to drug use, but recently there has been a change. It's tough stuff for a sport to address and the people running the game don't like to admit the problem – and they certainly won't like people such as me saying it. They would respond by saying that they do regular testing (and they do), but drug testers come in *after* games and no one would be stupid enough to take anything in the lead-up to a game. The blokes who take drugs are very well-educated on how it all works. They know which drugs are out of the system quickly and when they can take them . . . and when they can't. As International Olympic Committee president Jacques Rogge has said, it is possible for athletes to quickly eliminate some banned substances from their bodies. There are footballers today who take calculated risks. My view about drug testing in rugby league is that they'd be better off testing the *day* after the game.

I really worry about our younger players: what we are presiding over right now and what they will inherit from this current generation. Some young people now don't see the danger, and probably a lot of them get away with dabbling with drugs. They are young and think they are bulletproof. But the situation is fraught with danger, and the problem can become an all-consuming one for the game if it is not addressed properly. Professional footballers are prime targets, obviously: young men with money, and time on their hands . . .

All of it is very hard for me to understand. I don't have the mentality to take drugs, performance-enhancing or recreational, and I never would. It is how I was brought up, it is how I am, and it is what I believe. I don't give a shit about what (it is claimed) they do for you.

I am aware of senior clubs that have (or have had) real drug-issue problems. You won't read about them and no one (officially) will talk about it. It's a timebomb situation because there are officials at clubs who have presided over the situation that has developed without seeming to have done anything. Some of the stuff I have heard about one high-profile NRL club is stomach-turning. I am pleased to say that the Broncos these days are very much on the front foot when it comes to drugs. We have our own drug-testing unit and they'll turn up at your house, unannounced. It's zero tolerance at the Broncos. If you take drugs, you're gone, regardless of who you are. It's the right policy, the only policy.

The problem is not exclusively rugby league's, of course. As this book neared its conclusion in 2006 there were huge headlines in other codes – in rugby union and Australian football. On the morning of Sunday, May 14, 2006 my ex-teammate Wendell Sailor dominated news reports on the eastern seaboard. A rugby union Waratah and Wallaby, Sailor had been stood down from rugby after returning a positive test to a recreational drug. 'Sailor sacked over drugs' shouted one front page headline in giant type. Wendell's future playing career was in the balance. Meanwhile the hugely publicised matter of three AFL players who had twice tested positive to illicit drugs was heading to trial in the Victorian Supreme Court – for a judgement on the issue of whether the players could be named in the media.

For a bloke who loves rugby league this is a bloody difficult issue to bring into the spotlight. There are things I know that I just can't talk about here in this book . . . but if they ever saw the light of day they would turn this game on its head, considering the people involved. Gorden Tallis knows the same stuff, and that's why he's so strong on the question of drug use. The blokes involved in messing with drugs – either of the performance-enhancing or recreational type – do not seem to realise not only what they are potentially doing to themselves, but the threat they present to the game. The actions of a few in recent years could tear it apart. In his own book Gordie touched on the subject of drugs, but he faced the same dilemma that I do here. How far can you take it?

There was a tour I went on – a major tour, and I'll leave it at that – on which recreational drug-taking was apparently rife. It shows how naïve I am about the subject that I knew nothing of it at the time. From what I later learned, ecstasy was the drug in question. People perhaps see me as a bloke who it would be unwise to take drugs in front of, because they know I would be uncomfortable with it. So the thing never directly touched me. But in hindsight, when I reflected on aspects of that tour, I could better understand what had been going on. To his credit, Gordie made a lot of noise about it behind the scenes back in Australia. And there were blokes who hated him for it, seeing him as some-thing of a 'dobber'. It didn't worry him one bit, and that's the strength of his approach to life. He just believed that what had taken place on that tour was a very bad thing and he wasn't going to cover it up.

But even though I hate drugs, I can't bring myself to be too hard on the subject of those who somehow succumb and get involved. I can understand how young players can be tempted by something and fall into the trap. My personal thoughts are certainly black and white: I would never knowingly take a drug, either performance enhancing or recreational. That's fine and that's me. But some people are different, a bit more susceptible. And they need our help, not our scorn. No, I don't hate players who take drugs. They are either mistaken or misguided. It's the blokes who drag other, younger blokes into it that I think are bad people.

Performance-enhancing drugs

When Melbourne's Rodney Howe was caught out as a (performance-enhancing) drug cheat in 1998 and suspended for 22 matches, I thought he was a pretty weak bastard. I was probably even dirtier on him because he played so well via the stuff he took! Howe's suspension came in the midst of a pretty gloomy time for rugby league – in the wake of the disclosures at the Newcastle club that two players, Wayne Richards and Robbie O'Davis, had both tested positive to banned substances. The Howe issue flared again when he returned to football in 1999. Gorden Tallis sledged Howe when we played them in a match at Olympic Park in May that year – and in a subsequent interview did not back away from the things he said. 'If he's a big enough man to inject himself with steroids, he should be a big enough man to cop the flak out on the field,' said Gordie. 'Did he really think he wouldn't be sledged?' he asked. 'Did he really believe that guys like me who work their arses off in the gym to reach their physical peak, are going to welcome back to the game a bloke who has taken the easy way out. Does he think his peers will ever show him any respect again? Well, I won't. That's for sure.'

During the match Gordie called Howe 'The Chemist' and 'Stanozolol' and kept up the verbal pressure. Afterwards, Storm officials were up in arms about the 'treatment' afforded Howe. But Tallis's post-match comments reflected a wider anger in our team: 'He cheated on every guy who trains his guts out . . . he cheated on the game of rugby league that I love,' he told *Rugby League Week*'s Tony Durkin.

I roomed with Rodney Howe in an Australian side once, and

he seemed a really decent fellow. That was the way I found him – and my attitude to life has always been that I take people as I find them. My thinking on what he did in taking illegal steroids has broadened and softened in the years since and I wonder now what it was that drove him to make the decision he did. If it was a purely selfish thing – driven by ambition to be better than everyone else, and willingness to do whatever that took – well I have no time for that. But I know this: that we are all prone to weaknesses and sometimes to things that can get us when we don't want them to. I don't know the full story with Howe. Maybe he *did* have an injury he just couldn't get right and in a moment of weakness, he succumbed to the temptation of outside help.

I am not here to defend Rodney Howe. I don't know the full story. But I think that forever and a day he will be remembered much more for taking steroids than for what he achieved on the football field. That's the heavy price he has to pay – and I don't think he needs me or anyone else to ram it down his throat. It's something he will always carry with him.

The question of performance-enhancing drugs in the game was something I never dwelt on much, then or now. But when I think back to that time and of certain players – and particularly of Howe, who was as hard as a rock and a player who would never slow down in games – I recognise and understand what was going on. Adam MacDougall, suspended for 11 weeks in 1998 for using a banned substance, was another player who made an impression because he was so strong and rock-hard.

The reality of someone like Howe and the way he was physically in matches meant that whenever I came up against blokes of similar quality around that time I would always ask myself the question: is he, or isn't he (on the juice)? I could be very naïve, but I don't think it's in the game now – I just don't believe it's something players can get away with. The testing for performance enhancers is so stringent now. Unless, of course, the ways of hiding it are still a jump ahead of the testers . . .

Drug testing is certainly a routine part of life as a professional footballer these days. The tests are fairly regular – although it's the luck of the draw whether it's you or someone else. The deterrent factor is very high. In season '98 or '99 I was tested so often . . . it seemed like every second week. It's just a matter of whether your number gets pulled out. Our club does its own share of testing too, starting in the pre-season – and all of it adds up to good policy for a game that has tried, for the last 15 years or so anyway, to keep itself 'clean'.

Alcohol

Having said all that about illegal and other questionable substances, alcohol is a drug too, and I'll have a beer as quick as look at one! So which is worse? Alcohol is probably responsible for more social upheaval and unrest than any other drug in history, yet our society accepts it. My personal view, however, is that alcohol just leads to more alcohol most of the time. But with drugs, soft drugs lead to hard drugs . . . and on to harder drugs . . . and in too many cases, to death. I can't see there is responsible use of drugs, while there can be with alcohol. You can drink alcohol responsibly and never be a problem to anyone, including yourself, for your whole life. The supporters of marijuana argue for it as a 'soft' drug, but the evidence keeps coming about the possible long-term problems associated with marijuana use, and I was pleased in early 2006 to see the league take a harder line on it. To me drugs are an awful thing in society and I worry about it more now that I have kids of my own.

There is no doubt that the drug question requires ongoing vigilance by the people who run the clubs, and the game. But for all of that, alcohol remains the game's major trouble spot away from the field, probably as it always has been. Just about anything

I have ever seen go wrong in rugby league away from the playing field has been caused by alcohol. Conversely, I can't remember ever seeing a player get into trouble off the paddock when he was sober. Probably it happens, but I reckon if you guessed that 95 per cent of incidents are alcohol-related, you'd be close to the mark. And I'm no cleanskin. In the past I was probably lucky on a couple of occasions myself with confrontations that could have blown up on boozy nights out. Yes, I've done things I regret – nothing criminal or nothing that could cause damage to another person – just silly things.

I am a bloke who loves a beer. I really do. And a few years back I fought my own small battle. There was a time I felt that my drinking was starting to get out of control. I have always been sensitive to the question of alcohol because of the situation that developed in my dad's life. I did not want to ever put my own family in the situation that the Webckes had battled with earlier – and I didn't do that. But there was a period when I started to drink more and more often, to the stage where I would forget things about what had happened on a particular night. That really worried me; I am a bloke who likes to know what has gone on. I don't believe I had reached any sort of dangerous situation, but it worried me enough for me to go to Wayne Bennett one day to talk it over. 'I think I'm drinking too much,' I told him. 'Maybe I've got to cut it out.' He agreed with me.

'Yeah, I noticed you've been drinking more and more,' he said. So I went off the grog for four months . . . and it was great. And it's been good ever since. I still enjoy a beer – but everything is back in balance. That was a great little 'time-out' in my life, a chance to reassess my values and what I was doing and where I was going. Nowadays it is all positive – I just enjoy the good part of having a drink with people, the enjoyable part, the camaraderie of having a beer and a yarn. That is the sort of drinker I am, and will continue to be. To sit around with a group of blokes, or family or friends, and have a couple of beers is a really nice social thing. I don't want to be the other way – the bloke who sits at the pub until 2 o'clock in the morning, gets blind drunk and goes home and makes an idiot of himself. I won't be. I am very comfortable with where I am now.

Rugby league still has some work to do on the subject, although things are changing in a positive way. Young players these days are provided with an education on the subject of alcohol – and on drugs in general. I know that at the Broncos, our attitude to alcohol has changed immensely, and the new generation of players coming through is going to be the most alcohol-responsible group that we have had. Things are changing within the game because they have to. Professional footballers are hugely visible members of society these days and the culture of grog is changing because society won't accept the 'old ways' any more. Back in earlier days a group of footballers out on the grog in Sydney and playing up was no big deal. But the world has changed and high-profile footballers behaving badly just won't be tolerated – as some have found out to their extreme discomfort.

I am not saying these things from the perspective of any sort of 'perfect existence'. I definitely haven't led one of those. I can reveal that as a younger bloke I found myself in some precarious situations, but I had enough presence of mind to be able to extricate myself. But at the same time I can honestly say I have never been involved in some of the things that have plagued the game in recent times – and which must have the likes of the game's leaders Colin Love and David Gallop tearing their hair out. One step forward in the game is that most of us who like a drink now and then (and I'm in that category) are much more careful about where we are going to do it. If I'm going to have a really big night out – and that's happening less and less as I get older – then I'll be very careful about making sure it's in a safe environment. I am aware of my public profile, and if I want to really relax, I just pick the right moment. I don't mind being seen as a bloke who has a drink, but I don't want to be known as the bloke who gets full of piss and is the last to leave every time and becomes a real pain in the arse. Footballers are notoriously big drinkers, and no doubt have been since 1908 – and the message continues to strengthen that the stuff has to be treated with care or it can lead you down a bad path.

The question of the trend towards binge drinking in the game hit the headlines after the 2005 Kangaroo Tour of England and France. Team manager John 'Chow' Hayes mentioned it in his official report, which was leaked to the press, and fullback Anthony Minichiello was revealed to have broken a plate glass window at McDonald's in Paris. The media swooped. I have no idea of the full details of what went on, but from what I know of any Wayne Bennett-led tour, the drinking would have been far less than it was in former times – and very likely any events that happened on the 2005 tour would have been no more than a blip on the radar compared with some things that took place in the past.

As he stepped down as Australian coach at that time Wayne Bennett left no doubt as to how he felt about the ongoing problem that alcohol presented to the game. On Wednesday, December 14 the banner headline across the front page of *The Sydney Morning Herald* was this: ALCOHOL IS DESTROYING RUGBY LEAGUE – 'I'm sick of the drunks.' BENNETT'S OUTBURST. In an interview on Brisbane radio, Wayne had ripped in. 'Our game has never been in more disrepute than in the last three years because of player behaviour, and if coaches and journalists and officials think that we can continue to have a culture in our game of drinking to excess, then they live in a fairy world. I've been trying to change the culture for five years now . . . I'm sick of the drunks and I'm sick of our game being dragged through every media outlet in the country every time some guy behaves badly.' As usual, Wayne had told it straight.

And yes, binge drinking, or at least giving it a *big* whack, is a factor in rugby league today. It results from changes in the nature of the game and the way it is prepared for. The general culture now is that blokes don't drink at all mid-week, leading up to a game. As full-time professionals, the preparation for any game is intense, and grog is just not part of the equation. So when there is the occasional chance to have a crack at a big night out . . . well, the boys really go for it.

Happily, things are gradually changing. After our games it used to be a case of 'get drunk as fast as you can', but that isn't the case any more. I know I've changed – and maybe that's a bit of the age factor, and commonsense clicking in. I'll have a few beers and then arrive at a certain point where I think, That'll do me, I want to go home now. And I do. But the general trends are promising too. A lot of younger players are so much warier of alcohol today than once was the case. It makes we senior blokes feel quite proud. You think, Well, they're the next flag-bearers for the team and the game and the competition and they're going to do it well.

We have some very light drinkers at our club today – and there's no pressure on them to be any different. Years ago, for blokes playing rugby league to *not* have a drink would be looked on as very strange. But it's changed. That's not to say there still aren't some of the boys who enjoy a drink, and sometimes a big drink. But the Broncos' drinking today is certainly not done with the frequency and volume that it used to be.

Gambling

In 2005 the issue of gambling by rugby league players reared up in a big way. Cronulla's Michael Sullivan revealed publicly that a gambling addiction, which had cost him $150,000, had led to him seeking a release from the Sharks so he could play in England. Then Steve Price and ex-South's, Manly, Tigers and Newtown halfback Craig Field revealed that they too had had serious problems with gambling. Almost half of the players polled in *Rugby League Week*'s annual survey admitted knowing a player with a gambling problem. I am unsure of the depth of the problem in the game, although we had one very high profile player at the Broncos whose name was always being linked to obsessive gambling.

In him, I saw the problem at its worst. And it is bad. At its extreme levels, a gambling addiction is a disease and should be treated that way. Blokes caught up in it don't need the scorn or derision of others. They do not need to be told how hopeless they are. They need help, and in the rugby league context I hope the game's head bodies continue to provide that and continue to be vigilant – and pro-active in educating young players about the dangers. The gambling bug is a weakness, but it's a weakness because it takes over your life, and most of the various weak spots that we humans have don't necessarily do that. To gamblers caught in the trap it becomes the most important thing in their whole existence.

As to the question of how widespread the problem is in football – I honestly never know how much to believe of what I hear. But my gut feeling about it all is this: rugby league players are particularly well paid compared with the general population and there are certainly problem gamblers in the ranks – although very likely the numbers would be statistically aligned with the general community.

Rugby league players who happen to be predisposed to the lure of gambling are certainly at real risk. The footballing culture allows blokes pretty easy access to the things that attract: the poker machines and TAB outlets and casinos if they are that way inclined. The money they earn provides the wherewithal for them to get involved.

Behaviour

Professional first-grade rugby league players in the NRL competition in the 21st century live in a fishbowl. Fact. It goes with the territory now. We are heavily scrutinised: by our clubs, the media and the public. Anyone wanting to play top-level football must learn to live with that reality, whether they like it or not, and adjust their life accordingly. Among some there is resentment of the attention 'off the paddock'. But the truth of it is that whatever anyone thinks about the scrutiny that exists around high-profile sportspeople, some of the incidents that have dragged rugby league into shocking and embarrassing headlines in recent seasons do not even come close to qualifying under the heading of 'acceptable behaviour'. Apparent aspects of the Bulldogs' Coffs Harbour dramas, the Mark Gasnier obscene phone call affair on a night that other NSW Origin team members had broken camp and were seen out on the town in the early hours of the morning, Craig Gower's infamous performance at the Jack Newton Golf Tournament at Coolum, and Parramatta's Tim Smith's rise to unwanted headlines spring quickly to mind. And there are plenty of others.

The annual trip away traditionally involves a group of blokes drinking a heap of grog and having a good time, and quite often everything is fine. But in this age of intense interest in the game and media scrutiny, individuals and teams run the risk of being nailed even when they are *not* doing something wrong. Players are so recognisable through the extensive TV exposure they get that the situation is volatile at all times. As I got a bit older and got married and the family came along I had no real wish to go on the trips. But I still think they are a justifiable tradition in the game – and, properly managed, still a very valid part of a life in football. People on the outside probably think we live wonderful and glamorous lives as footballers. But it is a roller-coaster ride of peaks and troughs, and with the camaraderie built up to survive it all, it's very natural that the blokes in the team who have shared the experience want to get away and have a holiday together in a situation where nobody gives a bugger about anything, where there is no pressure and a chance to share each other's company. Those 'escapes' are about being the blokes we are, rather than being what we do. They remain a valid part of a season – but the dangers are apparent. Just check a few of the headlines of recent years . . .

The certainty is that any high-profile footballer who goes out and gets into trouble these days is going to finish up in the newspapers and on the airwaves. To me, that's a positive development, because I have become bloody sick of our game continually shooting itself in the foot via bursts of bad publicity over things that happen away from the playing field, or via administrators doing stupid things. Players are responsible for a lot of the bad stuff of recent years, but the administration has played its role too. There has been some crap from both sides – plus the occasional problem of bad crowd behaviour. League is a wonderful game, with so many good people involved, and I applaud any change in the culture that alters some of the things that have gone on.

I think the following words are the key: some of the behaviour of (a few) rugby league players in the last couple of years could not be reasonably accepted or excused at any time. Such events get more airplay today because it's us (identifiable, high-profile rugby league players). But there are times when some players need to ask themselves the deeper question: 'If I'm a decent bloke, is that really the sort of stuff I want to be doing?' All of us are representing the game we play, whether we like it or not. But even more importantly, each one of us is representing *ourselves*. How do we want to be seen? Does Craig Gower, for example, want to be remembered as a drunk, making a pest of himself at a golf tournament? That is the question.

My view is that to have any sympathy for players who step that far over the mark is ridiculous. Some of the behaviour that rugby league has endured would be wrong if you were a footballer, a carpenter, a window-dresser, or whatever! To make excuses for the players involved on the grounds that they have been nailed because they are high-profile sportsmen cannot be justified. Bad behaviour is bad behaviour. And if you happen to get away with it, that doesn't make it right either. It's my strong opinion that there should be no special rules for blokes just because they happen to be well-known footballers.

The questions of longevity and consistency represent the great ongoing challenges for anyone who wants to be good at a sport. Everyone who plays first-grade football has a good game in them here and there, but not everyone has a good game in them all the time. That *must* be the challenge for every player: to be consistently good, or even better, consistently very good. And it's bloody well not easy! To even have a chance of getting there you have to be a bit boring. You must look after yourself physically and set yourself a routine – and you've got to stick to it, regardless of how you are feeling, regardless of how things are going. In your life, and in training session after training session, you have to do the same things, the things that allow you to be the player you want to be. And not everyone can do it, because it isn't easy and very often it isn't fun. The rewards can be enormous, but the effort to get there is positively ginormous!

To understand that is to understand why some young blokes in sport fall prey to the temptations: boozing and drugs and gambling. The pressure of doing what has to be done to play a sport like rugby league weighs down all of us, and sometimes blokes cut loose. Next thing, the event is in the newspaper head-lines and rugby league has another scandal on its hands. My reaction used to be, 'Bloody silly young buggers!', but as I grew up in the game I tended to take a broader view, understanding exactly why such things happen. A player only has to have a little deficiency, a little area of weakness, and then when something goes 'snap' under the weekly pressure, suddenly he breaks out or succumbs to some temptation placed in front of him.

Changing something so deeply grounded as the grog culture in rugby league hasn't been easy. Wayne Pearce found that out when he got unlucky, as coach of the NSW Blues in 1999. Pearce, a teetotaller but not a wowser, made it clear that he thought the traditional boozy bonding sessions were not a necessary part of preparing for a big footy match. He settled instead for a preparation that included such things as horse riding and yarns around a campfire out in the bush. But when Robbie Kearns and Brad Clyde fell off horses and damaged themselves, Pearce became a figure of ridicule. It was bloody unfair; he had tried something different, an approach much more in line with the total health and fitness approach that professional footballers have to take today. The horse-riding exercise was probably never a great idea, but it was worthy, and different, and especially so coming from a bloke who had been something of a revolutionary himself in helping raise the game's image.

The Pearce experiment came not long after Brad Fittler had found himself in the newspaper headlines after getting drunk and being deposited by a cab driver outside a Sydney police station. Sections of the media which revelled in reporting that story were quick to push each other aside to make fun of Pearce when he took his team down a different path ... and things, unluckily, went wrong.

If some of the issues I have tackled in this chapter create discomfort within official circles in the game, I make no apology. As I reach the end of my career I honestly feel that I have to take a stand. There is a very real problem with drugs and the game has to face up to it. There is a lot of talk about 'loyalty' in the game and to the game. But being loyal is not pretending that everything is fine when it's not, which seems to be the approach too often in rugby league. If you want to be good at anything you have to look at the bad things and fix them. Too often it seems to me that rugby league's leaders want to look at the good things and ignore the bad. If you do that in your own life, you can be sure that something will come back very quickly and bite you on the arse. And so it is in rugby league.

Chapter 25

THE WATCHERS IN
THE STANDS

For a short period early in my career I used to read most of what the rugby league media said about me. But I quickly found that if something good had been written it had the effect of making me nervous. God, what if I don't live up to that? was the thought. So I stopped reading the football media. These days my glimpses of the passing parade of the media's coverage of rugby league are no more than occasional; I am not a big radio listener or TV watcher. The other big advantage of such a policy of detachment, of course, is that if someone writes something negative about you, you probably won't even see it and so won't have to get the shits (although if it's bad enough someone will generally hop on the phone to tell you!). The Broncos have no formal policy on that, but Wayne's advice has been not to take too much notice of what is said and written, as much of it is bullshit.

It's like most things in life – there is good and bad in it – and my perspective on the whole media business has probably changed to an extent in later years via my own involvement in some TV work and in writing a regular column for *Big League* magazine. Probably what annoys me most is that in the eyes of the modern media, the negative stuff is always better news. Put a foot wrong these days and you'll get horsewhipped. But today's players have to come to terms with that and understand the most basic truth of all: it's up to them to conduct their lives in such a way as not to provide the media with the fodder. A whole generation of new players is growing up with that understanding now. They are wary, and more media savvy.

It's sort of an uneasy situation. In the bigger picture, players do not trust the media, although they may trust certain individuals. There is a separation between the two 'sides', and in one way that's natural and healthy. We are, after all, doing vastly different jobs and that gap is important. But it's sad that the trust factor is, largely, not there. As in most things, honesty and balance are the required qualities. Any player having a poor game and then not accepting that there will be criticism – well, that's bullshit. I've got no problem with a negative story and some constructive criticism when it's warranted.

I have two observations that I think are worth making: first, in my view a lot of league journalism is trite and superficial and does not do the game justice. Perhaps it's just the journos responding to the expectations of their newspapers. Match reports are too often spoon-fed by a coach or based on a single theme. Rarely have I read anything on a match that would come under the heading of 'expert analysis'.

Sometimes in my occasional glances I read something, check the byline and think, Well, you've got *no* idea of the game if you're writing that.

Second I find some of the personal barbs and insulting stuff fired around in the media and aimed at players offensive. Making it worse is the fact that quite often it comes from ex-footballers who used to do exactly the same bloody things. There is a right way and a wrong way of delivering an opinion, and in the sports media there are those who are too quick to attack and insult. Footballers are sensitive to criticism, because what they are putting on public show every weekend is their livelihood. There is a tremendous amount of pressure that goes with that. All players take pride in what they do, and being called a 'bum' or whatever by some smart-arse commentator or journo trying to whip it along a bit is insulting.

The scribes and commentators might remind themselves of this: footballers operate in a punishing, unforgiving environment. Even when you've had a bad game, that doesn't mean you have tried any less or been free of the pain that just about every footballer carries through a season. You've been out there doing your best, and maybe it hasn't worked as well as you'd have liked, but you're going to be doing your utmost to make sure it's different the next week. The last thing you need is someone sitting behind glass up in some plush press box telling you that you're a mug.

For all that, my attitude has changed over the years. I now understand that media people work under their own pressures and that the job they do can be difficult too. It's an area where Wayne Bennett and I see things a bit differently. Once I had the complete mistrust of the media which is not unusual among today's footballers. But I feel that I handle them a lot better now and I tend to take my own line. After we got flogged by Melbourne in 2005, I was in the dressing room talking to one of the journos about what had happened that afternoon, and when the interview had finished Wayne said to me, 'I don't know how you can do that.' And I said to him, 'Wayne, it's a bit of a tonic for me – I find it helps me to articulate the disappointment and not keep it cooped up inside.' Wayne is the other way. At times like that he can't stand talking to them because he feels they are too often out to accentuate the negative rather than look more widely and objectively at what has taken place. Maybe a lot of times they are. For my own part, I have developed my own attitude and opinion concerning the media and they are certainly not as harsh as the coach's. He has obviously been burnt a number of times and is cautious now. I've watched him in action at times with the media and he can be bloody good. But he just can't suffer fools. Sometimes, some of the dickhead questions asked of him . . . they're just asking to be chopped in half! And he is a man with a cutting tongue. With blokes he likes and trusts, such as the ABC's Gerry Collins, he is terrific. Gerry knows his stuff and asks intelligent questions, not stupid, irrelevant rubbish. He is a bloke I enjoy talking to as well.

There were examples in 2005 of the media going way over the top – such as the way the NSW press crucified Brett Kimmorley, who played somewhere below his best for the Blues in the first Origin game and was unlucky enough to throw a key intercept pass. Similarly, after the third Origin game, in which the Maroons took a flogging, I went in to bat for the team. I'd been there at such times and I knew exactly what they felt. And I knew that whatever the bagging they were copping in the papers and on the airwaves, they were deep within themselves feeling a hundred times worse, a *thousand* times worse.

I hope that if I chance to head into some sort of media role when football is finished I never forget what I'm talking about here. I thoroughly enjoy media work – and would aim to be balanced (and, I hope, expert) in the things I said or wrote. I certainly don't have any thought that I come from such an exalted position that it's okay to sit in judgement on every player who comes along. But I wouldn't be a wallflower either. Rugby league is a tough game and it can comfortably carry tough opinion. But as I said, there are right and wrong ways of delivering opinions, however strong they may be. I guess what I'm saying is that it's about being gentlemanly and having some dignity and class.

To me, cricket's Richie Benaud is the model of what a sports commentator should be.

I am not necessarily a believer in the theory that a bloke has to have 'pulled on a boot' before he can become a good footy journalist. But I do think it's important that young journos get the feel of what it's really like to play this game. Maybe they need to see it up close at times, rather than from the sanitised position of a faraway press box or a TV screen.

My opinion that the game is not presented or promoted the way it could be extends to a longstanding TV fixture of league, the Thursday night *Footy Show*. As you will have gathered, there are a few areas in which I reckon the game needs to raise the bar, and I'd put *The Footy Show* into that category, even if it has pursued a somewhat straighter course in the last couple of years. I have talked to people at Channel 9 and I know the show generally rates well with a certain cross-section of fans. I accept that those people who watch it are very much part of the game, but to me the bigger question is always there: What are we missing out on by not having a more professional show? What about all those people who might watch a sensible rugby league show with no bullshit in it? I know plenty of people who like rugby league but who certainly do *not* watch *The Footy Show*. The ratings are fair now, but what would they be if the show changed its approach? I don't know the answer to that, but I suspect deep down that a lot of those who have become disenchanted could be enticed to tune in. Fundamentally, my point is in line with the way I feel league is administered – I have a sense that it deserves better than it gets.

When I look at the blokes on *The Footy Show*, I know that some of them at least are not the same people they were when they started out. When the show declined a few years back into silliness and women's clothes and all the rest, they just went with the flow. Once that had happened, it was not easy to climb back. They are obviously defensive about it now, and any mention of the 'bad old days' will bring a retort of: 'We haven't done *that* stuff for years.' But people don't forget. And that's why you have to be so careful about what you do and don't do.

Inevitably Richie Benaud comes to my mind. When I think of him there is immediate respect. I don't know him from a bar of soap (although I'd love to meet him), but I've watched him and listened to him and I know he's a gentleman. He's an expert, a lover of cricket, a bloke with a beautiful calmness about him – and yet there is a light side too, and a dry humour. Cricket is lucky to have him.

Having said all that, I really enjoy TV and I would like to pursue that option if it comes along when I finish playing.

Maybe I'm a bloke who expects too much when it comes to the coverage of rugby league; I'm just not too fussed with the way it's done now. I feel there are many decent, respectable, smart, intelligent, articulate people in and around our game who could be involved in its presentation. Over the years the Thursday night showcase has certainly given the game less than it deserves, in my view – and I'm pretty much on the same wavelength as the people who have said to me that they find much of the coverage of league (TV and radio) downright disrespectful considering what a great game we have. I'm not saying that the way the game is covered should be strait-laced all the time. No way. There is room for humour, and fun. I just think there is a happy medium.

Some of the Sydney radio I have heard (and I don't hear much) is self-indulgent and ego-driven, and just as poor as *The Footy Show* when it was at its lowest ebb. Rugby league deserves better. While it's the way it is, I won't be part of it. Yet I am deadset keen to do something in the media around this game that has been such a big part of my life. The only certainty is that I won't be selling my soul to do it.

Over the seasons, I never had any great problems with any individual in my dealings with the media. And I realise that developing a fair working relationship helped me with a lot of things. My advice to young players heading into the game is that via the media, if you are smart, you can present yourself in exactly the light you want to be presented in. That then progressively builds your public persona and can lead to all sorts of good and unexpected stuff. Staying solid on the things I have always believed in enabled me (and not in any contrived way) to build a tremendous rapport with the public. And that can ultimately lead to connections and jobs.

In that arena, I worked progressively harder over the seasons in 'getting it right' in my public appearances. I made sure I fulfilled every single obligation I had agreed to and that I never let anyone down. I made sure I was always punctual, that I dressed appropriately for the occasion and prepared thoroughly – in tune with whatever the function happened to be. Basically, I set out to do the best job I could for the people who had thought enough of me to invite me along. And at the end I would drop a note to say thanks. None of it was contrived. My aim was to be professional and courteous – two solid qualities which (I hope) have been part of my life. By doing those simple things, it was amazing to see what doors opened to me. In a TV interview with Andrew Denton in 2006, Bono uttered profound words when he declared: 'Celebrity is currency.' How deeply true that is. The message is: if you happen to have acquired some form of 'celebrity' because of what you do, use it wisely (as Bono has done). You will reap the rewards. I reckon every professional sportsperson should jot down his words.

In 2005 I started a fortnightly column with the magazine *Big League*. It was both a great enjoyment and an opportunity to offer an opinion or two on issues unfolding in the game. I find that the further I go in the game, the more frustrated I get about aspects of the way it is run. I look at this game and the wonderful things it has given me – both tangible and less tangible – and I hate to think that the same opportunity, of playing and succeeding at such a game, might not be there for others in some long-distant future. Now rugby league is not going to fade away anytime soon – hopefully never. But I don't believe the game can ever rest on its laurels. The challenge of the other codes is growing, and ever present. Neil Cadigan, then editor of *Big League*, understood that I was a bloke with some firm opinions and gave me my head to quite a degree. Even though I was writing for the 'official' magazine of the game, Caddo knew I was not there to toe the party line. If I was going to say something controversial he wouldn't talk me out of it, but he would make sure I had balance.

At the League's Annual Conference in late 2005 I got a lot out of a presentation by David Hill, who came out of Channel 9 Sydney and is something of a TV sports guru. He is now based in the US, and talked about how the NFL over there saw themselves as being in a contest every single day. That is how they approach the running of their business, and how they set out to attune their game precisely to what the public demands and wants. They view the public as their lifeblood: the people who support the game and pay the bills and attract TV interest because they go to games and build the perception and the reality of a successful sport.

I'm sure this is an important basic rule for any sport: if the public don't like it, don't do it! Simple as that. The Sunday night grand final is a good example of league *not* catering to the public. I think if you took a poll you'd find people overwhelmingly against the idea of a night grand final. It pissed me off at the 2005 conference when David Gallop got up after seeing a presentation on the Superbowl and uttered words to the effect: 'Anyone who thought night grand finals were a bad idea would change their minds after seeing that.' I think David would do well to contemplate the words of Benjamin Disraeli two centuries ago: 'I must follow the people. Am I not their leader?'

I love writing, and I hope to keep getting the chance to do more of it. The rest of my life is pretty crowded at the moment, and limits the chances I have. But I have done some work for *the Courier-Mail*, and I particularly enjoyed writing a piece for one of their summer editions, a recollection of days on the farm. It's good to get away from writing about footy now and then. But I much enjoy and value that opportunity too – to say some things that I want to stay.

Chapter 26
THIS GAME

In these early years of the new century the game of rugby league out on the paddock is in fine shape – and if anyone is interested in what an old front-rower would do to change the 'pure' football side of things, I would say very little. The game itself is okay, and record crowds in 2005 showed that. I do have some wider reservations, though, as you will discover here. And I certainly think there's a strong case for eternal vigilance and a process of review at the end of each season. Maybe it happens already to an extent, but it needs to be more than just some sort of token gesture. I'd like to see the annual review take place at a major level among the various stakeholders of the game – even bringing in the public. It should be about what's working and what's not in rugby league, and if there is something that is particularly annoying people in general, the people who pay their money through the gate – well, the question must be honestly addressed: why have it in the game?

A good example of that was the gradual pressure put on

administrators on the question of the unpopular unlimited interchange rule. It was a nice cosy rule for players and coaches (especially), because teams could keep endlessly running out fresh blokes. But in the end the pressure of public opinion became strong enough for administrators to switch to what we have today – limited interchange. People just got jack of the sporadic bloody interchange, of blokes on and off the paddock in a never-ending stream. So the decision-makers (finally) did the right thing and canned it.

Changes should always be carefully considered and conservatively made, with the thought always that league has been a tough, hard, good game ever since 1908 out here, and that its basic character must be retained. You'd never get consensus on something that was going to change the real guts of the game, anyway. But if there is something in the game that particularly irritates people – then administrators *must* listen. I think it is foolish to think that because they administer, coaches coach and we play the game, any of us knows everything about it. No one in the game has a monopoly on good ideas. And if ideas are not listened to because of their source, perhaps because they come from the public, then the blokes refusing to listen are bloody idiots. To respect all points of view is very important for Colin Love, David Gallop and Co.

This Webcke view of the game kicks off with a pet hate: I firmly believe that the mid-season trading of players permitted by the NRL is a blight on rugby league. Every single season is disrupted by the speculation on player movements for the *following* year – followed by the actual signing of players elsewhere for the next season after the 30 June 'no tampering' deadline. It is a stupid system, and is absolutely indefensible if the rule of commonsense is applied. No fan wants to learn mid-season that a star player or two from his or her club is heading elsewhere at the end of the year. Seeing that happening season after season is corrosive for the game. But it goes on, year after year, very likely steered in the main by powerful player-managers for whom life is made easier by such a process.

The most ridiculous thing I have heard about it is that this unpopular system is left in place specifically because players need time to find somewhere to live and get settled before they start with their new club. That is a load of crap. In the world we live in, you can decide one week you're moving, and be there to kick off the next week. It's just not as hard as it's made out to be, and I have no doubt that short-notice state-to-state or country-to-country relocations are a regular fact of life in the corporate world. But rugby league is prepared to undermine its own game on an ongoing basis by meekly tolerating a poor and disliked system.

We all accept the reality that players move about from time to time, and that players make decisions to change clubs for all sorts of reasons. When the deal is done mid-season it is always going to be unsettling, always going to put a 'splinter' in things. Even if it's your best mate going somewhere else, you might just start to wonder, though not necessarily in a big way: is his mind 100 per cent here or is it on his next (big money) assignment? It's just one more bit of drama that the game doesn't need. And every year it's the same, the certainty that speculation about which player is going to which club is going to dominate the news for a period of time leading to the June 30 deadline, at which point they can officially sign elsewhere. Sometimes the speculation around individual players starts as soon as the new season does. Sometimes the deals are done long, long before the official green light is given. People would be foolish to think otherwise.

If anyone can convince me how this huge mid-season diversion, which can bring into focus the fundamental question of players' loyalty to particular clubs, can possibly be good for the game . . . well, I'll be amazed. Our primary focus throughout any season should be on the game, the competition being played. But every year you get this big blur in the middle, the big balloon . . . and all the crap about who might be going where. I am in full agreement with Wayne Bennett, who has said about it: 'The other codes laugh at us – they can't believe we allow players to sign mid-season. The season is going along pretty well and then every second day we've got this "player leaving" headline.'

In my view it would be no disadvantage to players or clubs to be negotiating contracts in October, at the end of the season, if, after the grand final, that was to be the trading month. If the NRL set a date of, say, October 30, by which everyone had to be signed, it could certainly work. Most clubs start pre-season training in mid-to-late November. You can't convince me that players couldn't at least put temporary arrangements in place to be there for the start of training while they were in the process of making a geographical domestic move – if one was required. It's just not that bloody hard. You're busy when pre-season training is underway, but you've got plenty of downtime, too, to pull every-thing together if you have made a club change. And if you *have* to move house, clubs will chuck something at you to help out and you can get someone to walk into your house, pack and arrange the whole thing for you from start to stop, put it on a truck or a plane and land it at your door. All you really have to do is find a place, redirect all your mail and do all those little jobs that ordinary people do every day. It is not rocket science.

If you are a professional footballer and you take an opportu-nity which you see as a better one, you just move.

It would be good for the NRL to conduct a poll among fans on the question of mid-season signings. I think they'd be amazed at the lack of support for the system and at just how much it irri-tates the followers of the game. It is one of those mystifying things in rugby league that no more than a minority of people want . . . and yet it still exists.

It is not hard to fix. It would just be a matter of drawing a line in the sand and changing things.

The advantage of extending the ban on player trading until the end of the season would be, at the very least, threefold:

1. End-of-season signings would give clubs the chance to assess and make decisions on players' form on the basis of *whole season* performance. Did the player start the season at a peak but end it on the way down? How well did he sustain his form throughout the full campaign? Important questions.
2. A system that is vastly unpopular would be done away with.
3. There would be benefits to the game in extending the season's media coverage via the vast interest that would accompany an October 'trading month'.

I rest my case.

Salary cap

There will never be perfection in the salary cap system that now underpins the game. But I guess whatever your thoughts may be – and even if they are mixed ones – there is a strong case to suggest that if the cap was introduced to even up the competition, it has done its job. It will never be an easy subject in the game. I know, for example, that the Broncos have lost many good players over the seasons because of the cap.

But the challenge lies with the clubs. If you can build your club as a place that is about a lot more than the salary cap and money . . . into what I would call a *destination club*, then the cap starts to lose some of its importance. I would define such a club as being an outfit which is attractive to players not necessarily because they are getting the biggest dollar there, but because it is a good club. And I would rate the great ongoing challenge for football clubs and the people who run them is building a culture and a club that becomes something players want to be part of, a place which offers much broader attractions than just more and more money.

The Broncos have been very good at that. Their being a club that offers a lot of positive things has kept me there over the years, and I know it has kept a lot of other players there too – when many of us could have played elsewhere and made more money. For my own part I have never seen the point or the attraction of leaving such a wonderful organisation. I made it pretty clear publicly over the years that I was a Broncos man. And that was that.

The draft

I understand it works well in other comparable sporting areas, such as the VFL and the NFL, but I still have serious reservations about such a device, and my view remains that the salary cap alone has done such an effective job of levelling out the competition that it is enough. As a footballer, I have to say that I'd hate to be told where I was going to play because of being 'drafted'. Say as a young bloke I had always wanted to join the Broncos (which I didn't) but, via the draft, I was sent to a Sydney club. I would have been shattered. And if I didn't go and that meant I therefore couldn't play the game, I think that would be very wrong.

There are a lot of external issues that are factors when you join a football club, such as: where it is; who is coaching there; whether you want to live in that city or town. My understanding is that under a draft you can finish up somewhere you really don't want to be. I don't think that works. Not for me, anyway. And if you take players to clubs they don't want to be at, the danger is that they won't perform to their potential.

The length of the season

Is the rugby league season too long? Is the load too heavy on players? These are hardy perennials of league discussion and everyone has a view on them. My own is that the NRL should take a position that represents both a compromise and one of concern for players: drop a couple of rounds of the premiership. I'd take it back to 22 rounds (premiership) and leave it there – never change it again. With Origin, internationals and finals, that can still mean over 30 games a season for the top blokes. That's right at the top limit.

The great dilemma is that while most people would agree in principle on a shorter season, most (including Wayne Bennett) also still put great value on the rep international season. Finding the middle ground is not easy. The sure thing is that the season can't be allowed to get any longer; you can only get so much out of the human body at this level.

The difficulty concerns money – an enduring theme in the game. Clubs, assessing their marketability and their gates, don't want any *fewer* premiership home games per season. It's the reason the potential promotion of the game suffers too – the reluctance of clubs to take matches to country and interstate centres. I suggest that the NRL/ARL could easily fix that by guaranteeing a compensation amount to ensure that one promotional premiership game a week or a fortnight was played elsewhere. What a great boost that would be to the wider game. These could be billed as 'NRL Showcase' matches – and I can imagine the enthusiasm and support that would exist for such an idea in big centres in the bush, and in places like Adelaide, Perth and Darwin. I can see the posters now: 'If you've never seen an NRL game live . . . now's your chance!'

It *could* be done. Season ticket holders at the clubs would know before the year started that there would be one less home game – and it's very possible that the trek to wherever the 'Showcase' game happened to be could be a mini-break attraction to plenty of them. And if a club lost a handful of season ticket holders because there was to be one less home game a year, well, you'd have to think that those people were not fair dinkum fans anyway.

While it would take some doing logistically, it would be possible to play a promotional NRL match in some other centre every round – or at least every other round. I suspect, however, that such thinking is well and truly in the too-hard basket at the moment.

The sad thing is that I have a sense today of a rugby league hierarchy reluctant to make the big calls, specifically through fear that they will upset someone. There seems to me to be an attitude of being scared of any confrontation or bad feeling that might be stirred up by them doing something new and creative for the game. They talk about rugby league not needing 'another drama'. But what I'm talking about here is *good drama*, pushing for something that is entirely in the right direction in terms of expanding and popularising the game.

I reckon the public support for such a move would be terrific, and when the administrators work that out, perhaps they'll be more inclined to get on the front foot and develop some initiatives. But at the moment they seem to be walking on hot coals, with a philosophy of, 'Gee, let's not upset anyone.'

Things change, as they must – and you get nowhere with an attitude like that.

Rugby league is continually changing, throwing up new challenges to each new era of players. My mob, front-rowers, as much as any players in the game, have felt the sting of change. In league, everyone loves big fellas, but these days unless you're big *and* mobile, and with some skill too, no one is interested. It is no longer just enough to be a big bloke playing prop. Once you could even get away with being unfit if you were big. But no more. The game metamorphoses constantly – and maybe even the time of great and skilful players along the lines of Canberra's Jason Smith, whom I enjoyed playing with at Origin and Australian level, is coming to an end. Jason is old school, a bloke who likes a smoke and a drink. But he's a real footballer, and at 30-something his ability to slow a game to his pace and stamp his mark on it was a revelation when he came back from England to join the Raiders in 2005. It was great to see – it just goes to show that when it appears that everything is changing, there will be an exception to the rule. Blokes like Jason and Cliffy Lyons, who is still playing 'junior' football, are treasures in the game because of their difference. I hope they are not dinosaurs, destined to die out. Because rugby league must never become too homogenised or predictable. It is a game that must always have its elements of unorthodoxy, and its characters.

Character, and 'characters', have always been factors in rugby league's world. There are players with a difference littered throughout the game's past and present – I think immediately of someone like the champion Queensland centre of early Origin years, Chris 'Choppy' Close, a larger-than-life bloke who wears his heart on his sleeve. Choppy is a notable example of league's breed of characters – and a tremendous man whose company I much enjoyed through the Origin years. Some of them over the years have been blokes who just chose to be different, blokes who sported mad haircuts or conducted their lives in ways that are different from the rest of us, such as Balmain's Harley-riding Kerry 'Buckets' Hemsley, whom I mentioned earlier. I suspect there may have been more of them in the game some years back when things were a bit looser than they are today. Under the heavy media and public scrutiny which is a fact of the modern game, players tend to be more controlled, more alike, more stan-dardised in the way they conduct their lives. There is a lot of money at stake and a lot of pressure – and not as much room as there once was to be daringly different.

Mention has also been made of the fact that a sort of clichéd 'leaguespeak' has emerged in recent times, with blokes trotting out standard phrases: 'We stuck to our guns and came up trumps' and so on. Well, there's some truth in that, and the standard leaguespeak that has developed can be pretty grating. But I have to tell you, the media thing sometimes isn't easy. Seconds after you walk off a football field these days there's a fair chance you're going to have a microphone jammed in front of you. It's no automatic thing to be some sort of instant orator, especially when you're exhausted. Generally just the quickest and easiest things come out. I've certainly been guilty of dropping a cliché or two – and when it happens it's like a bomb going off in my head. I'll immediately launch into something else and try to cover the fumble.

The good thing is that blokes with a real difference still manage to find their way to the surface in rugby league. Alfie Langer was a good example of a 'character' . . . Kevvie Walters too . . . grand players who laughed and wisecracked their way through games, seasons and careers and lifted the spirits of everyone who played with them.

They are a reminder that football can be fun, even when you're playing what has been called the toughest game in the world. On a football field, I have to say that I can get as angry and as cranky as anyone around. But there are lighter times too, and shared moments, and occasionally flashes of humour. At the first scrum of the day I have no drama in saying 'G'day' to the bloke opposite me. Later, when we're all struggling, I might lighten it up a bit: 'How bloody hard is *this*?' Those sorts of moments bring a bit of comfort to everyone, I think. It's just someone (not necessarily me!) allaying the fears a bit . . . and just saying, 'Look, we're all in this together.' Rugby league is played at a massively competitive level. But that doesn't mean there can't be humanity in it to help get us through.

Blokes like Alf and Kevvie weren't stereotypical footballers. They could be as serious and wound up as anyone else, but I can remember plenty of games when we had got into 'comfortable' situations (either winning or losing) and they would be laughing and joking. They are two classic examples of modern-day football 'characters'. And I think of Johnny Plath, from the Broncos side of a few years back, who didn't fit the mould at all of a modern professional first-grade footballer (except that he was a bloody good player) – yet did it anyway. He drank, he smoked and he lived life *hard*, just at the time that sort of lifestyle was becoming unfashionable. Adam MacDougall was another of the breed – eccentric and different. There were those stories about him talking to his legs before a game and smacking them and ordering them to be good to him in the match. He qualifies.

Lighter moments at training can help lift the mood there too. I remember, for example, the day that Steve Irwin came down to a Broncos session. I admire the bloke because he's a bloody lunatic. This day there was some promotional thing on and he arrived at training and someone decided they'd set up this mock-tackle thing involving Steve and Gorden Tallis. Gordie, being Gordie – a publicity whore – was happy to be involved, and ran at Steve in a nice gentle jog. Steve tackled him and promptly Gordie fell down. And everyone was laughing.

Then they wanted to do it again, so Benny got hold of me and quietly pumped me up. 'You run at him this time,' he said. 'And don't you go light on him!' I always take note of the coach. So I just wound up full-pelt and got him with a well-timed bump, and down went Steve Irwin. He's a tough sort of character and he jumped up *fairly* quickly, but he was rattled. Again everyone laughed. Maybe not Steve. He was a good sport about it though, and I've found him a good guy in the times our paths have crossed since. And he's a passionate bloke with solid ideas. He's a conservationist and a greenie, but in a business sort of way. I don't mind that because I think there is definitely a place for a balanced view of the world. I suppose he'll always be remembered for the lunatic moment he had with his baby and the crocodile. But I suspect all of us have had an erratic minute or two in our lives.

That was a great wind-up. Steve had come down to training. He had played a bit of junior football and he wanted to have a go at tackling Gorden Tallis. So Gorden was running at about half pace, and as it turned out Steve had a pretty good technique. He wasn't doing a bad job at all. Anyway, Webcke walked past me and I said, 'Mate, he thinks he can tackle this bastard, just have a run for me, will you, and make sure he don't tackle you.' 'No problems at all,' he said. So he ran in at about half speed, Webcke, but as Steve came in, he hit him with the hip and shoulder and Irwin did about three cartwheels. He didn't know what hit him. Three cartwheels going backwards.

Wayne Bennett

Sometimes in the game it's the physical attributes of a bloke that put him into the category of 'character'. Paul Hauff, who stood 6 ft 6 in (198 cm) tall and played fullback, had it both ways. He towered over everyone on the paddock, and he was a funny bloke too, blessed with a real sense of humour. It's a human trait that characters are what inevitably emerge whenever you gather people together in groups, footballers included. Love him or loath him, Anthony Mundine was (and is) one, with his mouth and with his style on the field. Fans enjoyed Mundine's backflips – and Nathan Blacklock's too. And so what if Mundine was trying to model his persona on someone else? He was different anyway, a player who set people talking. Mark Riddell's 'Hitler Salute' when goal-kicking gets him onto the list too.

The opportunities are boundless for young players with a difference – especially if they happen to be blessed with a special talent. The Bulldogs' Sonny Bill Williams is a good example of what rugby league can do to you, though – how it can put you on a pedestal and then rip you down in almost the next instant.

At the time I write these words, the future for him is still potentially enormous. But he got a pretty stiff lesson early in what a
roller-coaster ride the game can present. He went from top of the
world (2004) to the disappearing man (2005) in the space of a
year, thanks to injury. Then a drink drive conviction in '05
jolted him a little further. But he seems to me a well-grounded
sort of young bloke from a good family – he is certainly no idiot.
And he's obviously a bloody good player, and a tough bugger.
Watching him in '04, it seemed to me that God had given him all
the things I missed out on: looks, natural talent, and abundant
skills. But he will have learned some early lessons about this game
he plays. It's part of the great wonder of the game that when
things are going well, everything seems easy. When it turns sour,
it's as if all your nightmares have been rolled up into one. That's
what makes it a real challenge.

I have had a fair bit to do with Carl Webb (Cowboys). In a way
he was like a little pet project for me at the Broncos. It was both a
personal undertaking and something I was prompted by Wayne
to help out a bit with. Carl hadn't had a particularly easy time in
his life. There were issues, things which I'm not really schooled
on . . . I just know he hadn't had a picture-perfect life. He is a
bloke with a tremendous amount of talent, but he struggled
with his fitness and his weight. I used to encourage him and help
him out as much as I could, and I hope that was useful to him.
We're poles apart as blokes, but for all that we became really
good mates. He's a great bloke, Carl, a really good fella with a
good heart, a vicious footballer when he needs to be, but generally a clean player, just one who is very aggressive. A sensational
try in Origin 1 2001 shot him into the headlines and he's been up
there as one of the high-profile figures in the game ever since.
Carl had his ups and downs with the Broncos, but I was sorry to
see him go when he left. To his credit, he turned his career
around – and no doubt if he'd been there at the end in 2005

(when the Cowboys lost the grand final to Wests Tigers), the Cowboys' hopes would have been boosted considerably. He has the potential to sustain a long career in the game, and a good one.

The game itself is a work in progress and always has been – and things fade in and out of fashion. I remember as a young bloke, at junior level, we had worked out all these elaborate tap penalty plays. And I have a memory of one (by Queensland) from an earlier Origin match which involved all sorts of angles and switches of play and which ultimately brought a try for Gary Belcher – and which was far too complicated to be able to describe in words, but beautiful and breathtaking to watch. Those sorts of plays went out of the game in recent years, and tap plays went back to being far more conservative and straight-forward.

More and more in modern rugby league the art of getting off the ground quickly has become important. At the Broncos we do a lot of work on that, with regular wrestling sessions at training – and part of that is about the bloke with the ball getting up quickly. It is the foundation for momentum, and teams can't get momentum if they slow play the balls, allowing the opposition to get their defence 'set'. But it is getting harder and harder to move, with teams working as effectively as they can on the edge of the rules to slow you down. Football teams know so much about each other these days, thanks to the galloping technology in the game and the available film on anything that moves. But *knowing* what might happen is not always a guarantee. Good players always find a way. By now everyone knows what Darren Lockyer does, but knowing it and stopping him doing it are two entirely different things.

I started my football at a time when the scrums were genuinely competitive, mini-wars at times. Today they are nothing – but to be honest, it's no great drama to me. I've heard the guys from other eras talking about the way it used to be, how fierce and competitive the scrums were, and lamenting that the League has given up on them. But the first thing to be said is that the scrum is no great spectacle. Also, I doubt there's anyone in the rugby league universe who would want to go back to the times when they were a mess, and refs would set them five or six times to try to get a result.

The way it is now, the scrum is set and dispatched – and the football goes on. Most of the time the team that didn't make the mistake that led to the scrum being set gets the ball, and that's the way it should be. I have never agreed with the principle of having the chance to win back the ball after *you* have made the mistake. Believing that, I can't see that even making a 'contest' at that point is relevant. But despite that, scrums are a part of rugby league that we need; otherwise the game will just get too bloody fast. We need the pause, the stoppage that separates backs and forwards. Even if only briefly and rather gently these days, the scrum locks the forwards away for a short time and creates some space.

No, I don't miss the old scrums. And in the same way, when I hear blokes from other eras talk about the violence and the brawls, I'm pleased that is not in the game any more. Those old days of king-hitting and chucking elbows in blokes' jaws . . . you can kill someone like that! And it's not manly, it's not strength, it's not anything to be respected. It's cheap-shot crap and I'm pleased it's gone with the wind. To king-hit someone, on or off the football field, is to behave in a cowardly way. There were blokes, I know, from earlier eras who were masters of that stuff and are more or less revered for it. They are no heroes in my eyes. I admire a different kind of toughness. To me toughness is about pushing yourself when you are dead tired, about doing things you don't want to do, about sacrificing. *That's* what makes hard men hard, not some illegal physical bullshit. And I see toughness in different things. I see toughness in some decent bloke who goes to a dead-end job every year of his working life just so he can provide for his family. I've always reckoned toughness is a bit of a myth in terms of actual physical prowess. It's much tougher to do many other things in this world.

The unlimited interchange rule (1996–2000) and its retention way past its use-by date was a powerful example of 'coach power' in the modern game. Getting the right bench, and using it the right way, is now a real skill for a coach. For coaches, the unlimited interchange was so much easier, and so some of them were very vocal supporters and lobbyists for the rule. If someone was getting tired – easy! – just rip him off the field. Nowadays there are just 12 changes to be made, and they have to be made with skill, care and timing. Tougher for coaches . . . better for the game. I hated playing under unlimited interchange. Your job as a footballer under that rule was to go out there and play as flat-out as you could – and if you were buggered after five minutes, well, you came off. That wasn't uncommon. There was no real challenge in it for players reared on much hardier fare – and it was in my view in no way fulfilling, or enjoyable. I think it was always a basic element in the game of rugby league to challenge yourself for as long as you could, go as long as you could, and maintain the quality of what you were doing. That is a very real and important part of the fabric of our game.

Peter Sterling, a powerful and persistent opponent of the unlimited interchange rule, summed it up well at the time: 'The gladiatorial aspect – the very essence of the game – has been lost,' he said. 'The fatigue factor is now not as evident in matches. In essence it (the rule) is rewarding mediocrity by keeping weaker teams in the contest longer.' I could only agree with Sterlo.

The old ability to 'stay the journey' in a game is still not available to (most) players, but what we have now (12 replacements and perhaps to be reduced further) is much better than what we had. In 2006 there were signs that that would be re-visited too, and the number perhaps reduced. It's a genuine 17-man game these days, and almost always the coach's call as to who goes off and who stays on. Players can make the request, but it happens very rarely, and generally only when something is wrong. A coach such as Wayne goes into a game with a certain plan in mind and we understand what that is in terms of when he might make the interchange. When it comes, we're ready for it.

I started my football career as an 80-minute player, as, basic-ally, we all were then. The football days of my late career have been of somewhere between 55 and 65 minutes in game time. All is linked to the increased speed of the play. I hear some older players muttering about how it used to be an 80-minute game, and there was pride in playing the 80 minutes and so on. Well, we could all play 80 minutes today, but the game would slow down. What we have now is no better and no worse than the way it was. For today's players it is just a case of what rugby league has become in the course of its evolution. We just follow that.

Expansion

I think that some of the decisions about the direction the game is heading are wrong. I have strong thoughts on the question of the expansion of the game. And I feel very, very strongly about the continuing need to support country rugby league, par-ticularly in those areas that are isolated. I don't believe they get anywhere near enough support. The funds from Origin series, TV rights and so on should be more generously spread to redress that imbalance.

The problem with rugby league, in my view, is that we have too many tiers of administration, too many chiefs. It is a bloody great game, but sometimes it deserves far better than it gets from the blokes running it. I think that ideally the game should be run by a single head body, with some off-shoots to get the nuts and bolts work done. But the decision-making and direction should come from one place – and all of it should be geared at all times to just one thing: what is to be done in the best interests of the game. Only then, when all the 'RLs' that exist are brought under the one central body, will we get true unity. And it's essential to have the right people doing the right jobs. For example, I think NRL CEO David Gallop does a good job. But I honestly wonder whether he's got the quality of support he needs. It's my view that the QRL up here is terribly run, and that the treatment of junior rugby league is abysmal. Honestly, if the officials were subjected to the same scrutiny that the players get . . .

More positive is the work of FOGS (Former Origin Greats). I am aware of the really good things they do. For example, I remember spending some time out at Kilcoy, a little town in the Brisbane Valley that was were struggling with its footy side – we put together a sponsorship for them. I have told Gene Miles, the CEO of FOGS, 'Anything like that, I'll always put my hand up.'

The ideal thing for any sport is to have someone at the top who is willing to get in and make decisions totally in the best interests of the game, free of agendas and pressures from other people and other places. The ideal arrangement would be to have someone at the top who was independently wealthy and who had no need to dish out favours or bend to the requests of others . . . someone who loved the sport, whatever it was, and wanted to see it do well – and so was free to make decisions strictly in the interests of that sport. Such a person is not easy to find!

Changing the way of things in rugby league is not easy. The game's ingrained problem is that for there to be dramatic change in the way it is administered, numbers of old entrenched officials virtually have to vote themselves out of office. I don't think we should hold our breaths on that.

The bush

My pet hate in the game, one of my real bugbears, is neglect of junior associations and junior footy, and particularly in the country. It is almost as if you are automatically maligned these days if you come from the country – and I think that is a bloody disgrace. The nation was built on primary production, though I know the emphasis has changed and maybe the rural sector isn't as important as it once was. This is a complex and involved issue and its wider implications certainly take in a game like rugby league, and sport in general. In rugby league, country areas are simply not well enough supported. It is as though they are not important. Yet, think about the traffic of players from the bush year after year . . . think about what a wonderful production line the country has been for the game of rugby league . . . a foundation stone for the game for much of its life.

This has been the situation through the years of my involvement in the game. In my playing days out there in the bush, survival was only guaranteed because of the commitment of parents and volunteers. In this time-short world we live in, people have to really struggle to make that commitment today – and some increased funding from the game's big end of town would be a huge help. I am building my own commitment to the bush; steps I am taking will come to light in the next 12 months. I really want to help with country league and I have already begun that project. I feel very strongly about it. After all, I grew up in a country district which was by no means remote – but it might as well have been, considering the (lack of) help that came from the QRL.

Shane does his best to keep private the things he does. He has already put a fair bit of money into junior clubs in the country. I don't think he has kept any of the money he has earned from his State of Origin or Australian appearances over the years. He has siphoned that off

*into different avenues to help the game. Sometimes it can be difficult
– like when these people from a country junior club into which he'd
put some money finished up tracking me down because they wanted
to make some sort of presentation to him. He didn't want that . . .
and doesn't want it – any sort of public recognition for those things
he does. He is determined to keep a private life within the public
profile he has.*

Vicki Webcke

There are too many sad stories of country clubs that have
died. I am well aware that there are factors away from rugby
league that affect that, such as the loss of jobs in country districts
as industries and services fold and the move of young people to
the cities. These things are way beyond football's control, and
sometimes the drift of players and the closing of clubs is
unavoidable. But I know of clubs battling on against the odds
and just able to survive – and all they need is a helping hand.
I'm not only talking money either, but administrative support,
promotional help, advice in how best to handle the money they
do generate.

But there are welcome signs of improvement and change. In
early 2006, players from 13 of the 15 NRL clubs headed out into
country areas in Queensland, NSW and Victoria in a 'Community Carnival' designed to promote both the upcoming
premiership competition and the game itself. The sweep covered
40 country destinations and thousands of kilometres, with the
players from some clubs dropping in on five or six different towns
to do skills clinics. The initiative was brief, but welcome. At the
Broncos we were pencilled in for Bundaberg, Childers and
Maryborough. There is, also another initiative, the Telstra RL
Assistance Fund, a program to help the game at grass-roots level
which makes available grants of up to $3000 out of a 'pot' of
$200,000. These were positive developments in the game, but

rugby league will need more of it as the forces of rugby, soccer and Aussie rules gather at the gates.

I am pleased to report that the Broncos have certainly done their bit for the cause. The club has done a massive amount of stuff over the seasons, touring country areas, helping out with local bush competitions, and helping all the way to outposts like Darwin. At the top (first-grade) level, we could probably do quite a bit more though. Generally, the only reason we'd be out in the country in a season would be if there was a pre-season trial game scheduled. The club, and some players, would probably argue against anything much more than that along these lines: 'Well, the players only get X amount of time off during the season!' But the fact is that we get *plenty* of time off. The season is hard, sure, and there are many commitments to be fulfilled. But there are opportunities to get out into that heartland and try to help out.

I have read of the campaign of the old Souths and Australian forward, the late Bernie Purcell, how he suggested sagely that 'bye' teams in the NRL should once a season use the bye week to go to a country area, to visit schools, run coaching classes, help with fundraising activities, maybe play a game of touch against the locals. It was such a good, simple idea and yet it never even got *close* to getting off the ground. Imagine the benefit of that: 15 or 16 first-grade sides systematically hitting different country areas in many weeks of every season and working for the game.

Growing up in a country rugby league environment I knew what a wonderful binding-together force the game could be in a community. My own early experience explains my passion for country football and my belief that those in charge of the bigger game must do more than is currently being done in preserving it. I hate to read stories of clubs folding, hate to think that the opportunities I had as a young bloke are not available to some of today's young fellas. I think about how good it was for Dallas and me, and how much we got from it. And I think about the pride when you happened to have some success as a team, and how the whole district would feel good about that. If I can be part of making sure that continues, I'll be happy.

Too often it seems to be too hard, or not worth doing or pursuing, and that really gives me the shits. I think people who have those sort of attitudes should be gone from the game. We need fresh, innovative leaders who are determined to *make* things happen. Maybe we're all a bit apathetic. I mean, I've got all these views about how I think league could be a bigger, stronger game, but what do I do about it? . . . or what *can* I do about it?

These things represent my gut feelings. I am reluctant to hop into the various blokes at the top too much because I am not a fly on the wall at meetings and I don't know all that goes on. I have two contradictory thoughts: (a) that it is a really, really hard thing to administer a game like rugby league in this age of television and big business involvement, in which there are so many pressures and agendas, and (b) it isn't quite as hard as it seems, but we just happen to have a crop of officials who don't have the strength or the expertise to take the game anywhere near as far as it could go. I don't know the full answer to that, so I am not going to really rip in. Only a fool does that without knowing the full story. My suspicion, though, is that it's the second option more than the first. In the fair dinkum department, I suspect that some of the current crop have just got to go. Until they do, rugby league will continue to be what it is now: a fine game, but less than it could be. With them there, it will be no better, and will not take those great leaps forward that I believe are possible. Survival of the game is never in question, though, when you consider some of the huge hurdles it has confronted in its recent history and somehow managed to overcome.

Maybe the problem is that the game, at its administrative level, is still too top-heavy with 'mates' and blokes who 'pulled on a boot' – and who remember nostalgically what it was like all those years ago – and whose thinking remains locked in the past. Many of them are wonderful people who have been great servants of rugby league and who will always be part of it. But their days have come and gone, and the game cries out for totally fresh thinking. Things get bogged down in bullshit committees comprised of blokes with different agendas, and inevitably any progress is slow. Maybe rugby league needs a benevolent dictator – as long as it's someone on the right track – someone with absolute power who runs the game with an open and innovative mind and sails high above the old thinking.

Perhaps it's changing. Within the clubs, a bloke like Bruno Cullen (CEO at the Broncos) would seem to be an example of the 'right stuff' for the game's future; I hope there are a few of his kind around. He came in and trimmed our club and put it on the path to making $1 million or so in season 2005. He turned the place around – and did it with a mix of bloody good business acumen plus a love and understanding of the game. Bruno is a professional who sticks to his strengths, who is prepared to make the hard calls and who set out to cut out any of the excesses or ridiculous things that were going on. His management style is based on commonsense – and he's a bloke with enough backbone to carry through what he knows needs to be done, the sort of bloke who can get a yes out of you even when you want to say no. At times he's made hard calls with Wayne – and that's as good an example as there is of a bloke showing some strength. Rugby league should hope for more of his kind. . . solid blokes steeped in the sport and unafraid of making the tough decisions that must, now and then, be made.

Chapter 27

THE LAST ROUND-UP

Whatever different views people may have had on the shakeup that followed the Broncos' fadeout 2005 season – headlined by the controversial exit of coaching staff members Kevin Walters (assistant coach), Gary Belcher (performance director) and Glenn Lazarus (Colts coach) – the certainty was that the club was crying out for a comprehensive change in the way we were doing things. The wholesale clean-out at the club was labelled by one sportswriter as 'the most drastic internal measure undertaken by the Broncos in their 18 seasons'. That may have been so. But in the wake of all the changes, and once the storm of controversy had abated, everything old was suddenly new again and there was a fine fresh breeze blowing through the place. All of us accepted that only time would tell whether the new direction would stop the rot and end the late season fade that had become a habit of the worst kind. But the feeling was good.

I like to think that if I had ever happened to reach a similar situation with the club I would have known . . . and I would have gone. Part of being loyal to a joint you love is knowing when to go. When you become a burden, how does that help the club that has been part of your life? At such a time, you've just got to make the hard call. I hope, very deep down, that if I ever reach that stage, I'll make my decision, and do it well. The last thing I'd want to do would be to carry on like Lance Thompson did at St George in late 2005, when he nearly had to be carried out, kicking and screaming.

The thing I know about what happened with the Broncos is that what Wayne did in the off-season of 2005 was in no way *personal*. The people who set up such a howl in the wake of what took place are bloody crazy. Do they think Wayne enjoyed sacking Kevin Walters or Gary Belcher, two players who he had coached and been very close to over a long period? No way would Wayne Bennett have sacked Kevvie Walters if he had truly believed it wasn't the best thing for the club. He *loves* Kevvie. But he made the tough choice and sacked a bloody close friend – and he did it for our club. He certainly wasn't sacking blokes or seeking their resignations because all of a sudden he had decided he didn't like them. I know how much time he would have spent thinking about it and looking into the situation. Only after a great deal of deliberation and some agonising would he have come to his decision, and it would have been based on just one thing: that he believed the step to be taken was in the best interests of the club. I know him well enough to speculate that his thinking would have been, We cannot keep doing what we're doing – and from there he would have made a decision on the things he would change.

The steps Wayne took after the 2005 season showed the personal strength of the bloke. As you will have gathered, it's one of the reasons I admire him. The majority of people couldn't make a call like that. Thinking about it at the time, I was not at all sure that I could have done it. But *he* did, knowing what the fallout would be, because he had come to realise that we just weren't going to move forward as a football team the way things were. He put the club first.

There was never a suggestion that Badge Belcher wasn't a good conditioner or Kevvie wasn't a good coach. If they go somewhere else, their careers will very likely flourish. But the decision made was that whatever they had been doing had stopped working for the club. Change was needed – and that was no reflection on the ability of individuals. Just like players, football club staff sometimes outgrow or outlive their value to a club. It's probably always been that way in football – right through the years, blokes have had to learn to accept that if their value to a club has waned, for whatever reason, they shouldn't be there.

There was a lot of emotion around when it happened. And there was an awful lot of bullshit trotted out – much of it from the usual suspects, ex-players leaping into the headlines to comment on things they knew very little about. There were a lot of dumb things said. And there was some more reasoned comment from the likes of Steve Renouf, who considered the controversy and suggested, in *The Australian*, that Wayne would face 'the greatest scrutiny of his illustrious career' in the 2006 season. 'He has certainly put himself in the position of being a real target next year if things don't improve,' said Renouf. That was fair comment.

Many changes, larger and smaller, came in the wake of the shakeup. Important among them was the arrival of the new performance co-coordinator, Dean Benton, who immediately put us to work.

The new pre-season training campaign was gruelling and hugely demanding, but as I told the media around Christmas time 2005 (when we had the luxury of three days off!), it was also bloody wonderful. My view was that the regime established under Dean Benton was smashing any softness out of the club. It all began in November and settled into a tough six-days-a-week program, which trimmed weight off me and a few others. The feeling was that we were all sick and tired of end-of-season flops and were happy to be trying something new to snap us out of it – no matter how tough and intense that might be. The plan was to progress from the level we had been at to the level we *should* be at. From the start, Benton seemed to me a bloke who understood what it takes to be successful in sport and was unfazed by the sacrifices that needed to be made. There was no cutting of corners; it was all hard business. It was also very refreshing.

Blokes like him are such important people at any professional sporting club these days. All the teams are right into the technology now – and the quest is always to find an 'edge' wherever you can. I was impressed with Benton, although I had some reservations too, as I mentioned back at the kickoff of this book. He arrived with fresh and good ideas and an obvious ability to think outside the box.

It was a time, I suspect, when every single Bronco reflected on the pattern of the seasons 2001–05, our fading years, and wondered about answers.

Part of it, I believe, was that we tried so hard to minimise our problems around the Origin and post-Origin period every year. We had overcome those as best we could – the overload on players, the wear and tear and the injuries – by striving to get out of the blocks really hard in a season and build a successful base because of what we knew lay ahead. The pattern was: we would play our best footy early, and shoot up the ladder. Other teams would meanwhile be on a more steady progression. Then we would level out and the others would slowly, slowly climb up to where we were – and then get us. By the end of the season, with other teams still improving, we'd be marking time. We had played our good footy for the year by then, and we couldn't muster it again.

It had become a recurring problem. And the question was there for us once again: how do we time it right? If we think, Oh well, bugger the start of the season; we'll ease into it, then other obvious problems emerge. You can't do that now; you can't think that you'll take it easy early on and that automatically means you'll be playing well at the end of the season. It's not an option – so we just continued to play flat out from the opening week and found ourselves in a pattern of disappearing early in the finals series, without the legs to take us home. It's a problem that seemed to exist for us, but not for other teams. The positive, season after season, had been that we were still getting to the finals, while some of the other top clubs missed out: the Roosters, Bulldogs and Panthers, all recent premiers, but absent from the 2005 series. But for the Broncos, just getting to the finals would never be good enough.

The Origin problem will always be with the club to some extent, although it is not an excuse we can lean on. The basis of it all is that if you are a Queenslander it's more than likely that you will want to play for the Broncos, although the increasing success of the Cowboys may well change that, as will the arrival of the Gold Coast Titans (2007). The opportunity for the Origin load to be shared much more widely is now there.

In trying to pinpoint the reasons for what happened 2001–05, my main thought is that we became less innovators and more followers in the way we approached the game of rugby league. I honestly think that some of the good winning runs we've had during the premiership proper of recent seasons have been masking some deficiencies. I don't believe we have been as good a club as we should have been for a few years. The easy view of it is that we've just petered out and lost hard-fought finals. But it's been more than that. The reason we continued to look a pretty decent footy side, and even kept making finals, is that Wayne Bennett is a great coach and as a club we have a great attitude to the business of professional football.

But it gradually dawned on me that we had changed. We had never been a club that had run off the ideas of others. Over the seasons we had cut the cloth our own way. But in recent years ideas from other clubs started to creep into what we were doing – and in saying that, in no way am I saying that the Broncos have a monopoly on good ideas when it comes to football. It's just that we had never been a club like that; we had always done it the way *we* wanted to. An example of outside influence was our adoption of the Roosters' innovative tactic of getting off the line extra fast in defence. It was known that they were doing these 100-metre drills and we started doing them too. Maybe there was nothing wrong with that, but it was just different from the Broncos way.

Approaching the 2006 season, things were different. I didn't hear a single word about what any other club was doing. It was the first time it had been like that for several seasons. I felt good about it . . . it was a promising sign for what lay ahead, I reckoned.

The further significant point about the Broncos is that the teams of the recent seasons, while good sides, had not been as good as great Bronco teams of the past. In one way, that's just the ebb and flow of football. But the salary cap has played its part in it too. We had to let go of players such as Luke Priddis, who I thought was a wonderfully talented hooker-forward, when the club would have loved to keep him. And a handful of others have departed who would have been of tremendous benefit to the club. Without the salary cap we were always pretty well placed: we could keep the players we wanted to keep.

A second factor of changing times is that the nature of modern players, the young blokes, has altered somewhat. I talked earlier about the Broncos being a desirable place for a bloke to play his football, and that remains very true. The breed of player who will accept a bit less to stay at such a club still exists. But I think the pendulum might be slowly swinging. Young kids are different now. To go and play football somewhere else would be no worry at all to them. This is something that has really struck me – how today's youngsters are so much more confident. When I was the age of some of them, I was shit-scared of everything. But with some of the kids today, I don't think the idea of shifting to Sydney to play would worry them one iota if the money was right. Young blokes are more comfortable with themselves, more confident, and seemingly much better able to embrace the whole new group and new culture that goes with any move to a new football club. These days at the Broncos we build good teams, but under the rules now it's very hard to keep them together. Additionally, for a number of seasons we were blessed with the four or five 'marque' players we had in our ranks. Those sorts of blokes – the Langers and the Steve Renoufs – don't grow on trees.

The game is cyclical in its nature, and in saying that I'm not attempting to sweep under the rug any internal deficiencies that may have developed at the club. But even down a notch on what we were, we have continued to make the finals, year after year, and that's a bloody big achievement in itself, although it tends to get overlooked because up here we are always measured exclusively by the *winning* of premierships. To many of the people who follow the Broncos it probably doesn't mean a rat's arse that we make the finals every season. They expect more.

We came under heavy fire for what happened in 2005 (beaten 24–18 by the Storm and 34–6 by the Tigers in the finals) – and rightly so. If ever there was a year that I believed we should have won the premiership, it was 2005. I'm not a punting man, but if I had been I reckon I would have been betting my house on it halfway through the year. I had played at the club for more than a decade then, and I'd like to think I'd be able to pick it when things were feeling right. But I didn't see at all what was coming at the end of the year. It was a winnable comp, one that was there to be grabbed, but we didn't do it.

However, straight away when the dust settled on that season we were back and working on it . . .

I think when you're a senior player at a football club you have to be very careful not to become one of the stuffy brigade of 'the good old days' and 'this was the way *we* did it' blokes. Generational change is inevitable as the seasons roll on, and you have to accept the certainty that there will be change, and that you may not like all of it. But I have learned to believe that you only have two choices with change: embrace it, or stay marking time where you are. Where I was once unbending in my beliefs about football, I am now much more accepting of differences, and change. Karmichael Hunt, who came to the Broncos first grade as a teenager in 2004 on a wave of publicity that added to the pressure on him, is a fair example of the difference that a new generation brings. As a bloke, he's a world away from me. We'll never go out and have a drink together, and probably he'll never come over to my house for dinner. But we can be friends in the way it is with the different age groups that populate football clubs. And I can respect his talent and ability, which obviously I do. I am only using 'Ka' as an example. It's just that with some of the new young blokes, an age differential of 12 years can seem like a lifetime! And while there may be bits about some of them that I don't like, no doubt they could look at me and say the same thing.

With Karmichael, there is no doubt at all that talent and natural ability are there in abundance. He is just going to have to watch his application. He is doing what young men do – going out drinking, enjoying himself. We all did it. But living with that reality, a lot of young blokes in footy today arrive at a point where they can go either one way or the other. With Ka I have two thoughts: we have not seen the best of him yet, and he needs to be careful in arriving at the balance he needs in his life if his football career is to reach its full potential. It's down to him. Ka and his kind represent the future of the game.

And as for me?

Well, the enjoyment of the new way of things at the club and the beginning of the new 2006 season was paralleled by another growing feeling. To an extent, I felt 'born again' by the new approach at the Broncos. Off-season preparation had been a revelation. At sprint training in late January I ran a 40 metres time that I hadn't run for 10 years. At this late stage in my career Dean Benton had managed to extract that from me. Gee, that felt good! I relished the thought of the season ahead.

But as summer rolled into autumn and footballers replaced cricketers on the available green spaces around Brisbane, I knew something else too: this year would be my last as a rugby league player. As this book neared its completion, I arrived quietly at my decision. People kept urging me to leave my options open. But I was heading with certainty towards what I wanted to do – and in considering the future then, it didn't really matter to me what sort of season I had. If it happened I had a good one, that would make it so much better. I was in as good a physical shape as I had been for a long time and I really felt I could go out with a bang. In the bigger picture, I was readying myself to move on. But in the short term of the 2006 season I knew I would have no trouble with focus. I was as determined as I had ever been to make my last Bronco year a good one.

I am excited about what lies ahead. I love footy and I'm really passionate about helping the game go forward – and that's what I hope my ongoing involvement with rugby league will be. One dream I have is to be involved, in some capacity, in helping make the 2008 Centenary World Cup the success it can be. In my opinion, they should take the games all over the place, and work hard to make every single one of them a showcase of what rugby league has to offer. Rugby league could do a whole lot worse than use the blueprint adopted by rugby union in 2003 – they had such huge success with unlikely matches in unlikely places. Find the money from somewhere and promote, promote, promote, using gun marketing people. It would take clever planning and clever hand-picking of matches, and there would have to be certainty that NSW, Queensland and Melbourne got their share of games. But it could be done. The World Cup is a real opportunity, and potentially a great springboard for rugby league's future. I believe there is not a single game that should be regarded as a throwaway; every single game should be strategically placed to maximise its appeal and potential success. I'd love to be involved and help make it a winner. I wouldn't be looking for any money – I'd just like to think I could bring some positives and some passion and some perspective to it. This is a fantastic opportunity for the game. It will happen in the wake of the Soccer World Cup (2006) and the Rugby World Cup (2007), and my fear is that without a great deal of hard work and creative planning and marketing, it might just be some little Mickey Mouse competition that will pale in comparison with the other games.

On a personal level, I have no interest at all in reliving my own past 'glories' in the game. Like all players, I have collected many rugby league bits and pieces along the journey. But in the new house Allison and I will build at Leyburn, there will be no rooms full of footy memorabilia – maybe just one or two very special pieces that are linked to precious memories. Some of the things have already gone to the Royal Hotel, where I hope they might be of some interest and provide enjoyment for others. My own enjoyment lives inside me. My footy career is in my head, and I don't need the trappings of it to remind me. I will never be one of the blokes who can't let go.

I knew I would leave the playing field with no misgivings – and I dared to hope right through 2006 that that might be after a grand final, in October. There were no guarantees. But how could I have had any misgivings considering the time I'd had in rugby league? I consider myself blessed to have been involved in some remarkable things in the game. I have had a wonderful time. I loved and enjoyed the career I had, but sporting careers are the blink of an eye in a life, and by the early months of 2006 I found myself thinking more and more about the next stage. To be honest, I could barely wait for it to start.

Heading into this last season of my life in football I was inspired daily by the thought that on the day it all finished, a new life would begin.

SHANE WEBCKE'S COMPLETE CAREER STATISTICS

SHANE WEBCKE

Born: September 28 1974, Leyburn, QLD

CAREER OVERVIEW

	Games	Trs	Gls	F/G	Pts
CLUB CAREER *1995–2006*					
Brisbane					
Premiership Games *1995–2006*	243	17	–	–	68
Super League World Club Challenge 1997	8	4	–	–	16
World Club Challenge 2001	1	–	–	–	0
TOTAL	**252**	**21**	**–**	**–**	**84**
REPRESENTATIVE CAREER *1997–2004*					
QUEENSLAND					
Super League Tri-series *1997*	3	1	–	–	4
State of Origin *1998–2004*	21	1	–	–	4
TOTAL	**24**	**2**	**–**	**–**	**8**

AUSTRALIA

Tests *1998–2004*	19	1	–	–	4
Super League Tests *1997*	1	–	–	–	0
World Cup *2000*	6	1	–	–	4
Tour matches *2003*	2	–	–	–	0
TOTAL	**28**	**2**	–	–	**8**

GRAND TOTAL
All senior matches   **304**   **25**   –   –   **100**

First grade debut: Brisbane v Norths at North Sydney Oval, 1995 (Rd 10)

Junior club: Clifton Wattles

Other information: Joined Broncos 1995 from Brisbane Brothers
Played in Brisbane's premiership-winning teams 1997, 1998 and 2000
Played in Brisbane's Super League World Club Challenge-winning side in 1997

Awards: Dally M Prop of the Year 2000, 2001, 2002
State of Origin Man of the Match Game 3 1998

Information correct as at July 21, 2006

Source: David Middleton, League Information Services

So you want to be a rugby league player?
AN A TO Z OF HOW TO GET THERE

A. Always do your best. This is the most important aspect of the game, and not just on the field. You must always do your utmost on the training paddock as well.

B. Believe in yourself. The most important thing is to believe that you have the ability to succeed.

C. Change. You must be willing to change some old habits. Along the way you will have picked up some habits that will prevent you from achieving your goals.

D. Determination. A key ingredient of success; you will only make it if you are determined that nothing will stand in your way.

E. Encounters. As you start your career you will encounter all types of things. You must learn from every situation.

F. Fatigue. Get ready for plenty of this, and not just in your legs. There will be days when mentally it all starts to get a little hard. On these days refer to 'D'.

G. Goals. It's absolutely essential to continually set and reset achievable goals. Remember, you have to be able to measure

353

your success against these goals, so you must be specific. Goals will become the navigation system of your footy career.

H. Home life. Whether you live at home with your parents or in your own place, if you don't have a stable life away from the game you will struggle. Knowing and understanding that home is a sacred haven and treating it that way is very important.

I. Interests away from the game. To give your life balance, you must have pursuits outside of league.

J. Job. Get one for a while, even if you signed straight out of school to go to a club. The discipline that it takes to hold down a job and do well in the workplace is exactly the same as the discipline required in rugby league. If you can't do this, you will not go far in the game.

K. Knowledge. Be a sponge for all those who would impart their knowledge to you. This applies not only to rugby league but generally. Knowledge is the best weapon against all sorts of things in life and in footy.

L. Learning. As with 'K', you must be prepared to learn, and not just about footy. One of the great challenges is to learn who to listen to and learn from. You will come across many people in footy who can help you learn and grow, but there are those, as in life, who cannot help you. Knowing who to listen to is the key.

M. Mastering the game. Forget it. The day you think you know it all you and no one can teach you anything new, you will start to go backwards. Guaranteed.

N. No. Learn to say this word, particularly when you are tempted to do the wrong thing. Things like drugs, excessive drinking and other dangerous behaviour can all be turned down. No is a very short, strong word; learn to use it.

O. Originality. Be yourself at all times and know that each of us is unique. Don't be a follower; instead, be a bit original. Blaze your own trail.

P. Punctuality. Be on time, to *everything*. This is something you can teach yourself, and something that people will respect you enormously for. Being on time simply means that you respect those who are giving you their time. It's an easy thing to do. Just be organised and give yourself enough time to get to your appointments.

Q. Quality. Try always to have this. Quality in your training, playing and life in general. Quality is a practised thing, and if you always attempt to have quality in all your endeavours, it will start to come naturally.

R. Respect. Everything in rugby league is underpinned by this. Respect for your elders and betters as well as respect for the game itself should always be a priority. Learn also to respect yourself. To respect yourself, you have to exhibit qualities and behaviours that warrant self-respect. In other words, you can't respect yourself if the things you do in your life can't be respected.

S. Simplicity. Learn to keep things simple. While everything will at times seem very complicated, learn to simplify things in your own mind so that they make sense to you. The key is to break down situations into small bits that you can understand. The world will seem much clearer when you do this.

T. Thoroughness. In all your undertakings in the game you must be thorough. This applies to life in general as well. It is essential to understand that attention to detail is paramount if you want to succeed.

U. Understand. Understand that there is no such thing as perfection. You must always strive towards it, but you will make mistakes. There is nothing wrong with this unless you don't learn from those mistakes. Mistakes are valuable learning aids if you acknowledge them and make adjustments.

V. Variation. Be prepared to vary what you do. Rugby league is a game of great variation, so you can't be too predictable.

W. Work ethic. You will not succeed or survive in the game without it. It is something that can be self-taught, but it is hard going. Work ethic is simply the ability to apply yourself to 100 per cent of your ability 100 per cent of the time. This includes *everything*, from making your bed to cleaning your room. You can't pick and choose; it has to be everything.

X. X-communication. Learn to do this to so-called mates and acquaintances who will bring you down. By this, I mean that if your mates are trying to entice you to do the wrong thing, you must cut them loose. The fact is that if they were truly your friends they would not try to lead you astray.

Y. Yes. This is another word you must learn to use, particularly if you are in trouble or have done the wrong thing. You must own up to it and suffer the consequences. We all do the wrong thing from time to time; it's how we accept the responsibility for that that shapes our character.

Z. A final thought for the final letter: rugby league and your life are one and the same. Try to imagine what people who look at you in all areas of your life see. If you are happy with that, you are on the right track. If not, make some changes. Being a footy player has been one of the great experiences of my life, mainly because of what it has taught me about myself. If you are willing to learn, our game is one of the greatest teachers around.

INDEX